THE WORLD VIEW OF
CONTEMPORARY PHYSICS

THE WORLD VIEW OF CONTEMPORARY PHYSICS

Does It Need
A New Metaphysics?

Edited with an Introduction by

RICHARD F. KITCHENER

State University of New York Press

Published by
State University of New York Press, Albany

© 1988 State University of New York

For information, address State University of New York
Press, State University Plaza, Albany, N.Y., 12246

Library of Congress Cataloging-in-Publication Data

The World view of contemporary physics : does it need a new metaphysics? /
   edited with an introduction by Richard F. Kitchener.
         p.   cm.
      Papers from a conference held at Colorado State University, Sept. 15–18,
      1986.
      Includes index.
      ISBN 0–88706–741–7.   ISBN 0–88706–742–5 (pbk.)
      1. Physics—Congresses.   2. Metaphysics—Congresses.
   I. Kitchener, Richard F., 1941–
   QC1.W67 1988
   530—dc19   87–24084
                                                                    CIP

10   9   8   7   6   5   4   3   2   1

CONTENTS

Preface   1

1. Introduction: The World View of Contemporary Physics:
   Does It Need a New Metaphysics?   3
   Richard F. Kitchener

2. The Relation Between Natural Science and Metaphysics   25
   Ivor Leclerc

3. Quantum Theory and the Physicist's Conception of Nature:
   Philosophical Implications of Bell's Theorem   38
   Henry P. Stapp

4. How to Kill Schrödinger's Cat   59
   Jeffrey Bub

5. The Universal Quantum   75
   David Finkelstein

6. Do the New Concepts of Space and Time Require a New
   Metaphysics?   90
   Milič Čapek

7. Space-Time and Probability: Classical and Quantal   105
   Olivier Costa de Beauregard

8. The Rediscovery of Time   125
   Ilya Prigogine

9. The Role of Physics in the Current Change of Paradigms   144
   Fritjof Capra

10. Contemporary Physics and Dialectical Holism   156
     Errol E. Harris

Contributors   175
Index   177

PREFACE

On September 15 through 18, 1986´, a conference was held at Colorado State University on the theme "The World View of Contemporary Physics: Does It Need a New Metaphysics?" Nine internationally known scientists and philosophers presented papers at the conference, which are contained in the present volume (in their revised form). In editing these essays for publication, I have attempted to remove obvious traces of a conference setting, giving the essays a unity and coherence often lacking in conference proceedings by arranging them in a logical pattern and by editing them in the same format.

There was lively discussion between the participants and the audience, culminating in a stimulating panel discussion on the last day. Unfortunately, the speakers' comments and the panel discussion could not be published in the present volume; however, they are available on tape at Colorado State University.

This conference is the first in what we hope will be a series of conferences on the relationship between philosophy and science sponsored by the Endowment for Applied Philosophy and the Department of Philosophy of Colorado State University. The Endowment was established through the generous contribution of one individual who believes philosophy can and should be relevant to contemporary science. A series of conferences is only one of the ways in which philosophy can have some bearing on contemporary scientific theory and practice, and we are currently engaged in several other projects aimed at this end. Although he wishes to remain anonymous, all of us are grateful to him for his generosity and foresight.

This conference was made possible through the financial and personal efforts of numerous individuals and administrative units at Colorado State University. In particular, I wish to thank Pat McKee (chairman of the Department of Philosophy) who, perhaps more than anyone else, has been instrumental in establishing the Endowment for Applied Philosophy and in giving it its characteristic orientation. For his help with the conference (and with all other matters pertaining to the Endowment), I am grateful. The following individuals at Colorado State University also contributed greatly to this conference: Frank Vattano and Bob Hoffert (dean and associate dean, College of Arts, Humanities and Social Sciences), John Raich (dean, College of Natural Sciences), Judson Harper (vice president of Research), Dean Jaros (dean, Graduate School), Gwyne Haddock (Office of Conferences), Linda Price and Carol Monthei (secretaries, Department of Philosophy).

Chapter 1

INTRODUCTION: THE WORLD VIEW OF CONTEMPORARY PHYSICS: DOES IT NEED A NEW METAPHYSICS?*

Richard F. Kitchener

Introduction

As long as thinking individuals have contemplated the nature of the physical world and their place in it, they have struggled to create a world view that is both cognitively adequate and personally satisfying. One of the many notable and long lasting effects of the Scientific Revolution was to raise this question of the relationship between philosophy and science and the correlative question of the part science would play in the construction and elaboration of a philosophically comprehensive and intellectually responsible view of the world. It is now something of a platitude to point out that our world view underwent a radical change

*I wish to thank Karen Strohm Kitchener, Pat McKee, and Bernie Rollin for reading and commenting on an earlier version of this paper. I also wish to thank Randel Fujimoto, librarian assistant at the Physics Research Library, Harvard University, for his valuable bibliographical assistance.

with the rise of classical Newtonian physics, its defeat of the Aristotelian world view, and the subsequence development of the Newtonian world view into the reigning paradigm. Not only did classical physics change our views concerning the nature and structure of physical reality, replacing an Aristotelian organismic view of nature with a "mechanistic" one, it also changed the conceptual categories through which we think about the world. Even more than this, it changed our views about the nature and existence of God, of the self, and society;[1] even the historical development of modern music and art was not immune from its influence.

It has appeared to many, therefore, that science has the function of telling us what things exist in nature, how they act, and how they relate to each other. Science thus gives us the latest news about the nature of reality and, hence, provides us, in some sense, with a metaphysics. It seems clear, therefore, that the results of modern science and, in particular, those of physics will play an important role in the elaboration of an adequate twentieth-century world view. Indeed, according to many individuals, recent results are so revolutionary in their philosophical import that an entirely new world view is required, one that is as different from the Newtonian world view as it is from the Aristotelian view of the world. The conference on which the papers in this volume are based was organized to determine these revolutionary implications and their bearings on our view of the world.

This conference is not the first time individuals have argued that the results of recent physics augur a new conception of the world. For many years individuals have made the point that "scientific common sense"— the ordinary view of the practicing scientist (for example, the molecular biologist, the experimental psychologist, the solid state physicist, and so on)—seems to contain a common scientific world view, roughly a Newtonian one. Based as it is on classical physics, this widespread world view of scientific common sense is in need of substantial repair. For example, as Leclerc, Harris, Capra, Čapek, and many others have pointed out, this Newtonian world view is committed, *inter alia*, to atomism, mechanism, reductionism, absolute space and time, efficient causality, and a reliance upon ordinary common sense notions about medium-sized objects (the megacosm); these basic features are still present in scientific common sense. As many individuals have argued, such a Newtonian world view is in serious empirical and conceptual error and should be replaced by a newer world view, one based on a more adequate theory of physics, incorporating the revolutionary implications of classical field theory, relativity theory, thermodynamics, quantum theory, and so forth.[2]

Metaphysics

If the world view of contemporary physics is radically different from that of classical physics and if it needs to be reevaluated because of fundamental and radical changes in recent discoveries and theories of physics, it is on the issue of metaphysics that the discussion turns. For decades physicists and philosophers have suggested that something like a new scientific epistemology is needed largely because of the implications to be drawn from relativity theory and quantum theory. But because epistemology has traditionally been associated with logic and methodology of science and because issues of metaphysics have been suppressed by the reigning hegemony of logical empiricism, an explicit preoccupation with the metaphysics of contemporary physics was an intentional part of the conference.

It seems clear that if one is concerned with the nature of a world view, one will have to be concerned with issues of metaphysics, with questions concerning "the furniture of the world": What kinds of things exist; what is their nature; how are they related to each other; and so on. Until recently, most individuals would have agreed that science is concerned with metaphysics, with informing us about the furniture of the world. But two developments—the rise of logical empiricism and the "Copenhagen interpretation" of quantum mechanics—have made many individuals dubious about whether physics can or should make such pronouncements. As anyone familiar with the recent history of philosophy knows, the once popular view of logical empiricists that "metaphysics is meaningless" is no longer tenable; indeed, in retrospect it seems clear that the logical empiricists had a metaphysics and that what they were opposed to was a metaphysics that was *transcendent*, one that made claims about a supernatural (or "super-empirical") reality that could in no way be checked empirically (Kitchener, forthcoming a). When the contributors to this volume discuss the question of whether contemporary physics needs a new metaphysics, they do not seem to be using "metaphysics" in this sense (although D'Espagnat, 1983, apparently does).

The other movement leading to the "demise" of metaphysics in physics was the "Copenhagen interpretation" of quantum theory, a strange and perhaps incompatible mixture of the views of Niels Bohr, Werner Heisenberg, John von Neumann, and others.[3] Although a discussion of this school is far beyond the bounds of this introduction and is competently discussed by several of the contributors (for example, Stapp and Finkelstein), one can characterize this view (rather simplistically) as "what you see is what you get", or there is no reality *behind* quantum phenomena (data, observations). All that is required, according to this view, is (1) a set of correct mathematical formulae (for example, the Schrödinger equation[s]), and (2) a set of experimental data obtained in the laboratory. There is nothing more!

Although such an orthodox interpretation seems to be widespread among many practicing physicists, especially (as Hooker [1972] points out) among those who do not bother to read Bohr, it is not a view shared by most of the contributors. In contrast, their concern seems to be with the question, What must reality be like in order for quantum phenomena (for example, Bell's Theorem) to be possible? This includes the possibility that there is no reality, that the physicist "creates" the reality, that there are "many realities", that the reality is "spiritual", and so forth.[4]

A fundamental question that arises in this context, therefore, is what one means by *metaphysics*. As the reader will see, the contributors use this term in several ways: as the theory of ultimate reality, the theory of the most general features and principles of all things, or a set of basic assumptions. Historically, *"metaphysics"* has meant all of these things and more, which is part of the reason the question of "the metaphysics of physics" needs unraveling. In the received, Aristotelian tradition, it meant "after the [volume on] Physics" and this was interpreted subsequently to mean "beyond physics" or "beyond the physical." In this sense, then, metaphysics has come to mean the theory of ultimate reality, in the sense of what is beyond or behind the realm of appearances or experience. But, of course, if one doesn't believe there is anything "hidden" behind experience, one will not endorse this interpretation.[5] One could still have a metaphysics, however, if one believed it was concerned with the theory of the most general principles and features of experience. Likewise, on another interpretation of metaphysics, the "ultimate reality" in physics is just the relevant set of mathematical equations—a version of Pythagoreanism.[6] Such a version of Pythagoreanism is rejected by most of the contributors to this volume, who believe there must be something more palpable to reality than just the underlying mathematics, even if this "something more" is just the correlative set of observational data gleaned in the laboratory.

In fact, one could interpret the followers of the "Copenhagen" school as being fundamentally concerned with metaphysics in the sense of a metaphysics of experience—*experientialism*. Such a metaphysics can be found, for example, in many of the process philosophers, pragmatists, phenomenologists, ordinary language philosophers, positivists, phenomenalists, instrumentalists, contextualists, and so on, notably (in the present context) William James, A. N. Whitehead, and Henri Bergson.

In a widely held view concerning metaphysics and physics, physics gives us (or purports to give us) the correct picture of reality, where reality is something lying behind phenomena. This is the classical realism of the sixteenth and seventeenth centuries (for example, Galileo, Descartes, Locke, Boyle, and Newton), according to which there is a primary versus secondary quality distinction, a correspondence theory of truth, a representational theory of meaning, a metaphysical atomism, a "mathematization" ("geometrization") of nature, and so forth. Something like this is also present in the writings of Bertrand Russell (1948) and other modern "critical realists." To a lesser extent, it also seems to be the view of Einstein, Eddington, Jeans, Schrödinger, De Broglie, Bohm, and other physicists who could be called realists. One central metaphysical issue in contemporary physics thus continues to be realism versus experientialism or "Einstein versus Bohr."

"Realism versus experientialism" is not the only metaphysical issue underlying the papers in this volume, but it is a fundamental one. An equally important issue concerns the question, What kind of ontology is adequate for contemporary physics? In modern times (for example, Taylor, 1903), metaphysics has often been divided into ontology, cosmology, and rational psychology. *Ontology* is concerned with the theory of Being (in general), *cosmology* with the nature of (physical) nature, and *rational psychology* with the nature of life and the mind. It seems clear that the present discussion of the world view of contemporary physics has implications for all three areas. That it has much to do with the first two areas seems obvious. One of the main points to emerge clearly from the conference, for example, is that *elementarism* seems to be something squarely at odds with quantum mechanics and relativity theory, and hence needs to be replaced by some kind of *holism*. Likewise, a *substance* ontology (whether in its classical Aristotelian form or the more modern form of atomism) is clearly no longer viable; a *process* ontology involving (as the fundamental category) *events*, not substances, is more compatible with recent physics (both relativity theory and quantum theory). Such a view is championed, for example, by Capra and Stapp who follow the S–matrix ("bootstraps") approach of Geoffrey Chew (1971). According to this view, the primitives of quantum physics are events related via a network; it is from this network that things and even space-time are to be derived. On the other hand, it is equally true according to many (most notably Wigner, 1967), that recent work in physics has important implications for the nature of the mind, the relation between the mind and the body, and the place of mind in nature. This is evident especially in the essays by Capra, Costa de Beauregard, and Leclerc.

Recent Physics and its Revolutionary Implications

What are the recent developments in physics, developments that many believe augur a new metaphysics? Although certain results in the last two decades have had the most widespread publicity, revolutionary metaphysical implications have been drawn from physics as far back as Einstein's special theory of relativity (1905), his general theory of relativity (1917), and quantum mechanics (1905–1926). In fact, both philosophers and scientists were quick to see that these two new "paradigms" required radical changes in our world view, not merely abandoning the older concepts of a particular scientific theory but, more drastically, abandoning many of the concepts of "common sense" concerning the physical world.

That relativity theory has such metaphysical implications no one would doubt. Milič Čapek articulates in his contribution and elsewhere (Čapek, 1961) what these implications are, especially in regard to space and time. After surveying certain classical views about space, time, motion, and matter, he then proceeds to show how these views need to be revised in light of recent physics. In particular, he points out how our ordinary megacosmic views and concepts are at variance with the macro-cosmic and microcosmic worlds and, hence, need to be reevaluated. Čapek is also critical of those who wish to "spatialize" time and thus, in some sense, to eliminate its inherent direction. Perhaps it is as true today as it was fifty years ago, that we have yet to fully assimilate Einstein's theory into our way of thinking about the world.[7]

Costa de Beauregard, although treating themes similar to Čapek's and Prigogine's (Costa de Beauregard, 1963), comes to a different conclusion about "the arrow of time." According to him, there is no inherent irreversibility to time: Although there is "fact-like" irreversibility, there is no "law-like" irreversibility. He illustrates his claim in this volume by reference to the probability calculus and its "time-reversible" formulas. He shows how the probability calculus can be mapped onto Dirac's (1982) notation of "kets" and "bras" and then shows that quantal causality is time-reversible. Finally, he draws some important implications from this concerning psychokinesis and "backward causality."

Ilya Prigogine is also concerned with the nature of time and its metaphysical status in the natural world. Based on his work on nonequilibrium thermodynamics and dissipative structures, Prigogine has drawn far-reaching philosophical consequences concerning order, chance, the arrow of time, self-organizing systems, and so forth (Prigogine, 1980; Prigogine & Stenger, 1984). In his present contribution, Prigogine suggests that physics may be undergoing its "Darwinian revolution" in that time-dependent evolutionary patterns are being discovered among elementary particles, dissipative structures, and cosmology. (His views about cosmology represent especially provocative ideas.) In such an evolutionary world view, three elements are essential: probability, irreversibility, and coherence (structure). He, therefore, continues to stress the irreducible asymmetry of time and its power to organize and create new structures. Although order emerges out of chaos, Prigogine believes we have mistakenly identified order with equilibrium and disorder with disequilibrium. Clearly the question of whether there is an irreducible direction to time, together with a host of issues arising therefrom, requires considerably more discussion by scientists and philosophers.[8]

Although the importance of the previously mentioned developments in physics for analyzing and evaluating the world view of contemporary physics cannot be overestimated, the quantum domain has been the center of attention in recent years. Beginning in the 1930s and continuing up to the present, philosophers and scientists have endlessly debated "the philosophical implications of quantum theory." Indeed, it is on the quantum level that one can most dramatically see why a new metaphysics is needed. The reason for this comes from "the quantum paradoxes": the double-slit experiment, the Einstein-Podolsky-Rosen thought experiment, Schrödinger's cat, Bell's Theorem, Aspect's experiments, Wheeler's delayed choice experiment, and so on.[9]

Most of the paradoxical aspects of quantum mechanics can be seen in the double-slit experiment. A screen is set up with two slits in it so that light can pass through either or both slits onto, for example, a photographic plate that acts as a recording device. On the one hand, light appears to be a corpuscle—a photon—since, when it passes through a *single* slit, the photographic plate records a pattern of "hits" whose frequency is distributed (roughly) according to a symmetrical curve, with the greatest frequency in the middle. The interesting result occurs, however, when light passes through *both* slits. If light were a corpuscle, one would expect it to pass through each slit about half of the time; consequently, the pattern on the photographic plate would be a linear summation of two overlapping curves, with the greatest frequency again in the middle, but with a more gradual slope on either side. In short, one would expect a unimodal curve. What is remarkable, however, is the fact that when light passes through both slits, it does not manifest this pattern at all but rather an interference pattern with alternating light and dark bands on the photographic plate. The pattern is *bimodal;* that is, there are two distinct but partially overlapping curves. Thus, light also appears to be a wave. Moreover, whether it acts like a wave or a corpuscle depends on whether it passes through one slit or both. If it passes through one slit, it acts like a particle; if it passes through two slits, it acts like a wave. As popularizers of science sometimes put it, how does a photon (or electron) "know" whether the other slit is open or not, since it "acts" accordingly? Suppose, for example, we open both slits and proceed to emit light, but now as the photon is in transit, we shut one of the slits. The same paradoxical result occurs: one slit, particle; two slits, wave! Moreover, suppose we do not shut the slit this time but record the passage of the particle through the one slit without interfering with it. Although both slits are open, we record the slit through which the particle is passing. We might naturally expect it to behave like a wave now since both slits are open. However, instead, the particle forms a pattern appropriate for particles instead of waves; that is, there is no interference. *Thus, how an electron behaves, whether as a wave or a particle, also depends on whether we observe (record or measure) it or not.* When we do somehow record it, the wave packet (wave function ψ) "collapses" into a particular particle but when we do not record it, it continues to act like a wave. Our recording of it thus changes the future distribution pattern on the photographic plate—its frequency or probability distribution (ψ^2).[10]

Although the double slit experiment represents one of the "quantum paradoxes," there are several others equally puzzling. For example, in a much discussed paper, Einstein, Podolsky, and Rosen (EPR) (1935)[11] attempted to show, by means of a thought experiment, that the standard interpretation of quantum mechanics was incomplete. Using Bohm's (1951) formulation, a light source emits a pair of parallel polarized protons in opposite directions. Since the total spin of the pair of protons is known to be zero, they will have equal but opposite spin, for example, up-down, right-left, and so on. Suppose now that one of the particles, A, travelling in one direction goes through a magnetic field produced by a Stern-Gerlach device, while the other one, B, continues to travel in the opposite direction without passing through the magnetic field. Suppose we measure the spin of A in flight and it is up. Since the spin of B is always equal and opposite to A's spin, we know (without measuring or interfering with B) that B's spin is down. Thus, according to Einstein, Podolsky, and Rosen (1935/1983), "If, without in any way disturbing a system, we can predict with certainty . . . the value of a physical quantity, then there exists an element of physical reality corresponding to this physical quantity" (p. 138). Since by measuring particle A we have not disturbed B or in any way influenced it, the spin of B (or some physical counterpart) must, according to Einstein, Podolsky, and Rosen's definition, be physically real. Therefore, since the quantum mechanical description of nature does not allow for such a "physically real element," it is incomplete. (Needless to say, Bohr and the followers of the Copenhagen school do not agree it is incomplete.) If one thought that the measurement of A's spin somehow influenced B's spin, one would believe that an action on A influences B is a *nonlocal* way; that is, there is "action at a distance."

In the same year the EPR paper appeared, another paradox (or a version of the same paradox) was added: Schrödinger's cat (Schrödinger, 1935/1983). Suppose a cat is placed in a box which contains a device that can release a gas killing the cat. Whether the gas is released is determined randomly. Now think of the cat as the electron wave function, which consists of a superposition of two wave states corresponding to 'the cat is dead' and 'the cat is alive.' When we do not look inside the box, the cat is in this intermediate state, neither dead nor alive, but when we open the box and look, the wave function collapses (the nonactualized possibility disappears and the probability of this one wave becomes zero), and we have either a dead cat or a live cat. But all of this seems absurd since cats are either dead or alive. Hence, there must be something wrong with the standard "Copenhagen interpretation."

Although Jeffrey Bub has been concerned with the interpretation of quantum mechanics for several years (Bub, 1974), in the present context he is concerned with "killing" Schrödinger's cat. Although to the untrained reader it may not be obvious, Bub's paper is fundamentally concerned with the connection between the macrolevel (for example, the level of ordinary objects) and the microlevel (the level of quanta) and the correlative issues of reductionism and emergence. In quantum mechanics, there is no possibility of reducing the macrolevel to the microlevel because a macrosystem is not just a finite collection of microsystems; in fact for Bohr, microsystems have no properties except in the context of a larger macroenvironment. When microparts combine, a whole (the macroobject) is produced with emergent (holistic) properties. Bub suggests these emergent macroproperties are determinant properties (property states) not found at the microlevel. A quantum system (with a finite number of degrees of freedom) has statistical states but no property states, whereas a macrosystem has an infinite number of degrees of freedom and, therefore, can have both kinds of states. Bub suggests a way quantum mechanics can provide a mathematical model of how this is possible. Because we are dealing with an infinite number of degrees of freedom, the superposition principle breaks down and Schrödinger's cat as a blurred reality is thus killed. Rejecting Bohr's dualistic treatment of the relation between the macro and micro, Bub argues for a more unified and extended quantum mechanical world view, one that is also a version of realism.

Of all the discoveries in recent physics, perhaps none has the far-reaching implications as Bell's Theorem (Bell, 1964) does. Physicists had interpreted the EPR paradox as suggesting the need for "hidden variables"—variables lying "below the surface," so to speak, that would allow one to give a "realistic" and deterministic interpretation to quantum phenomena. Bell proposed a test of such a hidden variable interpretation using basically the EPR design as modified by Bohm. The crucial issue in the EPR paradox concerns the question: How can the action of the experimenter on one particle (measuring it or changing its state) influence another particle so spatially separated from the first that light has no time to travel from the first to the second. (This is called *spacelike separation.*) Clearly such an effect would involve something like "action at a distance," since the two particles are separated in space and any signal (or causal influence) from the one to the other must travel "faster than light" or "instantaneously." The two key concepts here are *locality* and *separability,* concepts that are difficult to distinguish. The principle underlying them is really a requirement that the cause of something (or a causal mediating link) be "local" in the sense of "contiguous in space and time." Nonlocality and nonseparability would be the denial of this. Clearly a hidden variable approach would seem to suppose local hidden variables. According to the EPR thought experiment: (1) if there is an objective reality (that is, a reality lying beneath the quantum phenomena), and (2) if quantum theory is complete, then (3) there should be nonlocal effects. Since they assumed there could be no nonlocal effects, Einstein, Podolsky, and Rosen concluded (assuming (1) is true) that quantum theory as incomplete and hidden variables had to be added.

Bell proposed a way of testing the claim of nonlocality by carrying out the EPR experiment. As before, two twin paired-polarized protons are sent out in opposite directions and their polarization is measured. The angle of polarization α can be changed from $0°$ to $90°$. If both angles of polarization are $0°$, then we expect a perfect correlation between the measurements of the two particles. If the angle α is $90°$, we expect a lack of correlation, and if α is somewhere in between, say, $45°$, we expect a correlation in between these two figures and, therefore, a certain amount of error $E(\alpha)$. Now suppose one rotates one polarizer $45°$ to the right and the other polarizer $45°$ to the left. What would we expect? If there are no nonlocal effects, we would expect the resulting frequency of errors $E(2\alpha)$ to be twice that of $E(\alpha)$: $2E(\alpha)$. (Since the error should actually be somewhat less than this, we can say $E(2\alpha) \leq 2E(\alpha)$.) This is called *Bell's inequality,* and the argument concerning it is called *Bell's Theorem.* When experiments are performed (for example, Freedman & Clauser, 1972/1983), however, this inequality is considerably violated and $E(\alpha) > 2E(\alpha)$. Because there is a much higher correlation between the two particles than one could reasonably expect, we conclude that locality is violated. Hence, a local hidden variable approach is disconfirmed (since one of its predictions is falsified) whereas the Copenhagen interpretation is confirmed (since they correctly predict this result). Hence, *if there is a reality independent of and underlying quantum phenomena (hidden variables), this reality must be nonlocal.*

Finally, Aspect (1976, 1982) showed that one could separate locality from separability. By changing the polarization during flight of the particles every 10 billionth of a second, he showed that if there is such an independent reality, it must exert its effects *faster than light.*

These (and other) quantum paradoxes have been the starting point for many recent discussions of "the metaphysics of quantum mechanics," and it is also the point of departure for the contributions by Henry Stapp and David Finkelstein, both of whom have written numerous articles on these problems. Stapp argues that if there is an objective reality underlying quantum phenomena, then in order to get certain predictions of quantum theory, there must be faster-than-light influences. This is what Bell's Theorem and Aspect's (1982) work show. Stapp distinguishes faster than light *signals* from faster-than-light *influences.* His claim concerns the latter. He rejects the Copenhagen interpretation—at least one version of it—and argues for an objective reality that is holistic (something compatible with Heisenberg's interpretation involving "potentia"), in which events originally outside of space and time create space-time. As Stapp points out, this has important implications for the nature of a person and one's place in nature. Hence, both the world view of physics and our *Weltanschauung* must be modified.

In David Finkelstein's contribution, there is an attempt to bridge the gap between relativity theory and quantum theory by combining important methodological aspects of both. In quantum theory, the experimenter partitions the universe into the object of study and everything else (including him or herself). Within such a partition, a set of operations are performed (ψ, ψ^*, ϕ), for example, the preparation of an experiment followed by an observation. Between these two operations there are, in turn, other operations or transitions whose probability is spelled out mathematically. This quantum model may be applied, Finkelstein suggests, on a more global level to all the work of science and in particular to the universe as a whole, but with the important realization that different scientists partition the universes differently. We can use the insights from relativity theory to map (invariant) relations between these scientists, each of which has a point of view or frame of reference. Finkelstein concludes that even if there is no single universe (as an object of study), there may be a universal quantum system containing all scientists. This may be the most we can hope for as a "world view."

Even this very brief and superficial discussion should indicate why recent developments in physics have led to a reexamination of the metaphysics of contemporary physics and to the question, What new kind of metaphysics is needed? Many of the contributors to the present volume argue that the history of twentieth century physics requires us to abandon our old metaphysics (for example, the metaphysics of "locality" and "separability"—remnants of a Newtonian atomism and particularism) and lead us to some form of holism. For example, Bell's Theorem seems to lead to the conclusion that the two particles, originating from a common cause, are not separate and distinct but rather inseparably linked (in some, hitherto unknown way). Other individuals (Feinberg, 1972) argue that developments in particle physics have "as one of its consequences the remarkable result that the behavior of a given system in quantum physics is influenced not only by its constituents and its surroundings but also by all other physical systems that can exist under some circumstance in this world, that is, by everything that is possible" (p. 39). This is holism with a vengeance! In fact, holism has been present in the orthodox interpretation of quantum mechanics since the days of Bohr (1934) and has been articulated in a much newer form by Bohm (1980). Indeed, the reader of this volume will find many of the contributors arguing for (or assuming) some version of holism (as well as a process philosophy) as the only metaphysics consistent with the "new physics."

But what holism is, both as a philosophical position in general and as an interpretation of modern physics, is a notoriously difficult question. Indeed, it is remarkable that there have been so few discussions of this important concept (see however Kitchener, forthcoming b). Fortunately, however, both Errol Harris and Fritjof Capra have given us insightful accounts concerning the nature of holism, especially as it relates to contemporary physics.

Harris argues that contemporary physics needs a metaphysics of holism and, moreover, holism of a particular kind—a dialectical holism. This holism is fundamentally that of Hegel. But Harris, in delineating the major tenets of this kind of holism, overcomes many of the difficulties traditionally encountered in understanding Hegel. Unlike most Hegelian scholars of recent times, Harris (1965) is particularly concerned with showing the relevance of this kind of holism to physics.

Since there are several kinds of holism, it is not surprising to find that Capra's version is somewhat different from Harris'. According to Capra, contemporary physics requires a version of holism he calls *systems theory*, which is basically an ecological world view. Five main features characterize such a systems approach, which involves a "paradigm switch" from (1) part to whole, (2) structure to process, (3) "objective" to epistemic science, (4) a "foundations" metaphor to a network model of knowledge, and (5) truth to "approximate truth." Capra concludes by showing the implications of such an approach for our contemporary *Weltanschauung* (Capra, 1982).

Besides these two forms of holism, there are other philosophical varieties, including those of Whitehead, Bergson, James, Bradley, Aristotle, Spinoza, Alexander, and Royce, and scientific varieties such as von Bertalanffy's Systems Theory, Hierarchy Theory, and Organismic approaches. One of the things needed is a systematic conceptual delineation of the differences between the various kinds of holism present in process philosophy, pragmatism, contextualism, hierarchy theory, or-

ganismic theory, and so on, as well as a discussion of the relations
between these and contemporary science.

Physics and Metaphysics

Although I do not have space to discuss the many ways in which
physics has led—some would say *forced*—us to reexamine our metaphysics, the quantum paradoxes provide one outstanding example. Similar
case studies have already been made of relativity theory, and it is to be
hoped other studies will be made of Prigogine's work in nonequilibrium
thermodynamics and other current scientific developments.

Such a connection raises the ever present question, however, of the
precise connection between physics and metaphysics, something that Ivor
Leclerc has been concerned with for years (see Leclerc, 1986). In his
contribution, Leclerc emphasizes the ever-present need for a critical examination of the metaphysics of science. By an examination of the historical connection between physics and metaphysics, he shows why
physicists and philosophers have the view they do concerning metaphysics and science. He argues that physicists cannot avoid doing metaphysics or making metaphysical assumptions and that this should be
explicitly recognized.

Although some physicists and philosophers may still deny that physics has or ought to have a metaphysics such a view no longer seems to be
tenable. Instead, the important questions concern the nature of metaphysics, its aims and methods, and the precise connection between physics and metaphysics. The connection between physics and metaphysics is
not a recent question, however, for earlier in this century the physicists
Sir Arthur Eddington (1939/1958) and Sir James Jeans (1942/1965)
and the philosophers Bertrand Russell (1972/1954) and Alfred North
Whitehead (1929/1978) addressed this question in considerable detail.[12]
Indeed, for those philosophers who believe science has strong metaphysical implications, the following two conclusions seem to be presupposed:

1. Science and metaphysics cannot be sharply separated from each
   other.
2. Metaphysics must, in some way, be based on the best available
   science.

Such a view has more recently been championed (in different forms) by
Karl Popper (1968), Wilfred Sellars (1963), J. I. C. Smart (1963), and
many others. According to some, if metaphysics is based on an outdated

and inadequate physics, it is inadequate whether there are any philosophical or metaphysical objections to it. In fact, some would go even farther and claim that if one's metaphysics is consistent with (or entails) an outdated physics, that is, a physics that is empirically incorrect, this is sufficient to throw the metaphysics into doubt.

For most of those thinkers who believe physics has metaphysical implications and that one's metaphysics cannot be separated from one's physics,[13] some kind of metaphysical or epistemological *realism* is often being presupposed. A characteristic example of this assumption, I have suggested, is *classical realism*. According to classical realism: (1) there is a reality independent of human ideas and theories; (2) scientific theories and the theoretical entities contained in them purport to refer to those entities, processes, or structures existing independently of the theories; (3) hence, scientific theories can be judged to be true or false in some sense larger than "they allow one to describe, predict and organize the experimental data." The latter could be called "epistemic truth" whereas the former is "ontic truth."[14] Thus conceived, classical realism seems to presuppose there is a *correspondence* between our scientific theories and an independent reality (a view one can also call *representationalism*). Although such a view is not very popular among contemporary quantum physicists and explicitly disavowed by many adherents of the "Copenhagen interpretation"—who entertain various versions of idealism, positivism, phenomenalism, instrumentalism—it is a view that continues to have an allure; in fact, some version of realism seems to lie at the basis of the belief that one should take contemporary physics to have decisive metaphysical significance. On the other hand, if the "orthodox" interpretation of quantum mechanics was adequate, then a particular metaphysical view of reality might be argued to be invulnerable to science; since (on this view) quantum physics consists only of mathematical formulas and empirical data, it concerns only how observations are correlated with other observations (Wigner, 1983). Since quantum physics makes no assertions about what is *ultimately real,* it cannot be in conflict with one's metaphysics. It seems perfectly possible, therefore, for one to accept the results of contemporary science, interpret them as the "Copenhagen school" does, and then hold any metaphysics one wishes. This is precisely why many religious philosophers (for example, Pierre Duhem), existentialists (for example, Martin Heidegger), pragmatists (for example, John Dewey), logical positivists (for example, the early Carnap) and ordinary language philosophers (for example, Gilbert Ryle) have been sympathetic (or would have been sympathetic) to the "Copenhagen interpretation," which seems to be a version of instrumentalism, phenomenalism, or positivism.

On the other hand, if one is to take the recent results of quantum physics seriously and deny the orthodox "Copenhagen interpretation," one would have to countenance a radically new kind of metaphysics, one incorporating principles such as nonseparability and nonlocality. What such an underlying metaphysical view would be remains unclear, although several of the contributors have advanced ideas about this.

Aside from this question, however, there is the further question of the relation between physics and metaphysics and how each should be pursued. Although followers of the "Copenhagen interpretation" may demur, I think that most of the contributors to this volume would agree that no sharp line can be drawn between physics and metaphysics. But what then is the precise connection between the two? Can metaphysics be pursued on its own as an independent science with its own methodology (as Leclerc seems to suggest), or are metaphysical theories constrained by scientific fact and theory? If our metaphysics conflicted with our "best science" (for example, quantum mechanics), would this show our metaphysics to be flawed? If our metaphysics agreed with our "best science," would this confirm or corroborate our metaphysics? Should metaphysics be conceived as in some way analogous to a scientific theory and, therefore, as requiring empirical validation?

If the results of metaphysics are in some way subject to scientific check, this may suggest that the relation between physics and metaphysics is unidirectional, with science "calling the shots," so to speak. Can metaphysics function in a manner critical even of our best science? For example, many scientists seem to hold what many metaphysicians would call outmoded and objectionable views about metaphysics. Thus, even though one's science is perfectly adequate, one's metaphysical interpretation of it may not be. This, many would say, was the case with Newton, who believed one needed God to explain gravity. This also seems to be the case, many metaphysicians might suggest, with those physicists who too quickly take the easy way out and claim "the human mind creates reality" or "all reality is subjective illusion." Such views, too often, are proposed without the individual first examining the meaning of these concepts, the logical consequences to which they lead, or alternative and equally plausible interpretations. This is what Leclerc sees as one of the most important methodological tools metaphysics has to offer. Furthermore, as he points out, this does not mean that only philosophers can do metaphysics but rather that doing metaphysics requires a conceptual training and methodology anyone in principle can, with suitable practice and training, master; moreover, it is the same technique that physicists (tacitly) employ when they are engaged in metaphysics. Indeed, as Finkelstein points out (in his discussion comments) many of the great scientists of the twentieth century were themselves metaphysicians, although not full-time ones.

All this shows that the connection between physics and metaphysics is a complex but rich relationship, one requiring considerable clarification and discussion and one in which both philosophers and physicists are partners. For those who have the appetite, this will be a feast; not surprisingly, for some it will be too rich a bill of fare, and they will prefer a blander diet. But for the individual who has an interest in knowing the world view of contemporary physics, I can only say *"bon appetite"*!

Notes

1. In this regard, Freudenthal (1986) has argued that the metaphysical underpinnings of Newtonian physics, with its "elementarism", strongly influenced social, economic, and political views concerning the nature of the individual and society, and one's place in society, and provided a rationale for classical liberal economic theory.

2. Although individuals have pointed out the revolutionary philosophical implications of relativity theory and quantum theory, little has been done to indicate the revolutionary metaphysical implications of nineteenth-century field theory. For a recent exception, see Berkson (1974). One of the first individuals to see the revolutionary philosophical implications arising out of classical field theory was the Gestalt theorist Wolfgang Köhler (1924), whose work is rarely read today.

3. Because it is doubtful whether the standard interpretation of the Copenhagen school is really that of Bohr (and perhaps Heisenberg), I will continue to use quotes around the term. For a discussion and explication of Bohr's views, see Hooker (1972).

4. For a discussion of these and other interpretations of quantum reality, see Herbert (1958).

5. I owe this point to my colleague Don Crosby, who argues that the standard interpretation of metaphysics is too heavily indebted to Greek philosophy.

6. Although, as my colleague Ken Freeman pointed out to me, it is difficult to find physicists who really believe this—especially when they are careful to

formulate their views—they do sometimes write in this rather loose way. In a more detailed discussion of this issue, one would have to distinguish between a truly Pythagorean view in which reality is essentially mathematical (for example, geometrical), and the Platonistic view (contained in the *Timaeus*) in which empirical data by themselves are unintelligible, with mathematics, imported from the outside, making them intelligible. In this sense, Descartes was a Platonist and Galileo a Pythagorean. This is discussed more fully in Chapter 2 of Kitchener (forthcoming b).

7. Why we have not been able to do this is an interesting question. It is not merely that scientists have not adequately educated the general public, for many scientists themselves do not conceptualize the world in this "relativistic" way. Moreover, even college students who have had a course in physics continue to think in pre-Newtonian and pre-Galilean ways about falling bodies (McCloskey, 1983). That scientific theories are analogous to intellectual states of development that have a cognitive development has been argued by Jean Piaget (Kitchener, 1986) who cites both the history of science and individual development to support this notion.

8. A conference on "Time's Arrow, Irreversibility and Self-Organizing Systems" is currently being planned, to be held at Colorado State University in 1989.

9. For the reader unfamiliar with these, I would recommend Capra (1980) or Zukav (1979), followed by Gribben (1984). If the reader knows calculus, I would recommend first Eisberg and Resnick (1986) or Liboff (1980), followed by a classic text such as Bohm (1951) or Dirac (1982).

10. The wave function, representing the state of the particle is given by Schrödinger's equation(s), which describe the behavior of the electron "wave." In one of its forms, it gives the behavior of the electron-wave as a function of time, that is, how the wave "develops." Schrödinger's equation is thus the counterpart to Newton's (or Hamilton's) equations for classical motion and Maxwell's equations for classical waves. Instead of being the representation of the probability distribution of the wave, for mathematical reasons physicists use a slightly different version. See, for example, Finkelstein's contribution to the present volume.

11. To get some idea of the volume of material this article has generated, see Lahti & Mittelstädt (1985). From their title one would suppose that "the foundations of modern physics" *are* pretty much equivalent to discussions about the Einstein-Podolsky-Rosen thought experiment.

12. See also Joad (1932/1963) and Stebbing (1937/1958) for a criticism of the work of Jeans and Eddington.

13. The view of the logical empiricists or logical positivists concerning this question is surprisingly difficult to determine. In spite of their official denunciation of metaphysics, they maintained there was another kind of metaphysics that was perfectly acceptable (Kitchener, forthcoming a). Furthermore, one would

have thought that since these positivists believed in "scientism"—the view, roughly put, that the only kind of knowledge is scientific knowledge—they would have constructed a naturalistic metaphysics. Instead, however, they advanced a view that seems to entail a sharp separation of metaphysics from science.

14. In epistemic truth, one evaluates a theory in terms of epistemic criteria (for example, pragmatic success, simplicity, coherence, degrees of evidence), whereas in ontic truth one evaluates a theory in terms of nonepistemic criteria (for example, correspondence with an independent reality).

References

Aspect, A. 1976. Proposed Experiment to Test the Nonseparability of Quantum Mechanics. *Physical Review* D14: 1944–1951. Reprinted in J. A. Wheeler and W. H. Zurek, eds. 1983. *Quantum Theory and Measurement*. Princeton: Princeton University Press.

Aspect, A., Dalibard, J., and Gerard, R. 1982. Experimental Test of Bell's Inequalities Using Time-Varying Analyzers. *Physical Review Letters* 49: 1804–1990.

Bell, J. S. 1964. On the Einstein Podolsky Rosen Paradox. *Physics* 1: 195–200. Reprinted in J. A. Wheeler and W. H. Zurek, eds. 1983. *Quantum Theory and Measurement*. Princeton: Princeton University Press.

Berkson, W. 1974. *Fields of Force: the Development of a World View from Faraday to Einstein.* New York: John Wiley & Sons.

Bohm, D. 1951. *Quantum Theory.* Englewood Cliffs, N.J.: Prentice-Hall.

Bohm, D. 1980. *Wholeness and the Implicate Order.* London: Routledge & Kegan Paul.

Bohr, N. 1934. *Atomic Theory and the Description of Nature.* Cambridge: Cambridge University Press.

Bub, J. 1974. *The Interpretation of Quantum Mechanics.* Dordrecht: D. Reidel.

Čapek, M. 1961. *The Philosophical Impact of Contemporary Physics.* New York: D. Van Nostrand.

Capra, F. 1980. *The Tao of Physics.* New York: Bantam Books.

Capra, F. 1982. *The Turning Point: Science, Society and the Rising Culture.* New York: Simon & Schuster.

Chew, G. F. 1971. The Bootstrap Idea and the Foundations of Quantum Theory. *Quantum Theory and Beyond.* Ed. T. Bastin. Cambridge: Cambridge University Press.

Costa de Beauregard, O. 1963. *Le seconde principe de la science du temps.* Paris: Euil.

D'Espagnat, B. 1983. *In Search of Reality.* New York: Springer.

Dirac, P. A. M. 1982. *The Principles of Quantum Mechanics.* 4th ed., rev. New York: Oxford University Press.

Eddington, A. 1958. *The Philosophy of Physical Science.* Ann Arbor, Mich.: University of Michigan Press. (Original work published in 1939).

Einstein, A., Podolsky, B., and Rosen, N. 1935. Can Quantum-Mechanical Description of Physical Reality be Considered Complete? *Physical Review* 47: 477–80. Reprinted in J. A. Wheeler and W. H. Zurek, eds. 1983. *Quantum Theory and Measurement.* Princeton: Princeton University Press.

Eisberg, R., and Resnick, R. 1986. *Quantum Physics.* 2d ed. New York: John Wiley & Sons.

Feinberg, G. 1972. Philosophical Implications of Contemporary Physics. *Paradigm and Paradoxes: The Philosophical Challenge of the Quantum Domain.* Ed. R. Colodny. Pittsburgh: University of Pittsburgh Press.

Freedman, S. J., and Clauser, J. F. 1972. Experimental Test of Local Hidden-Variable Theories. *Physical Review Letters* 28: 938–41. Reprinted in J. A. Wheeler and W. H. Zurek, eds 1983. *Quantum Theory and Measurement.* Princeton: Princeton University Press.

Freudenthal, G. 1986. *Atom and Individual in the Age of Newton: On the Genesis of the Mechanistic World View.* Dordrecht: D. Reidel.

Gribbin, J. 1984. *In Search of Schrödinger's Cat: Quantum Physics and Reality.* New York: Bantam Books.

Harris, E. E. 1965. *The Foundations of Metaphysics in Science.* London: Allen & Unwin.

Herbert, N. 1985. *Quantum Reality: Beyond the New Physics.* Garden City, N.Y.: Doubleday.

Hooker, C. 1972. The Nature of Quantum Mechanical Reality: Einstein versus Bohr. *Paradigm and Paradoxes: The Philosophical Challenge of the Quantum Domain.* Ed. R. Colodny. Pittsburgh: University of Pittsburgh Press.

Jeans, J. 1965. *Physics and Philosophy.* Ann Arbor, Mich.: University of Michigan Press. (Original work published in 1942.)

Joad, C. E. M. 1963. *Philosophical Aspects of Modern Science.* New York: Barnes & Noble. (Original work published in 1932.)

Kitchener, R. F. 1986. *Piaget's Theory of Knowledge: Genetic Epistemology and Scientific Reason.* New Haven, Conn.: Yale University Press.

_____. Forthcoming a. Towards a Critical Philosophy of Science.

_____. Forthcoming b. *Holism: a Philosophical and Scientific Analysis.*

Köhler, W. 1924. *Die physischen Gestalten in Ruhe und im stationäry Zustand: eine naturphilosophische Untersuchung.* Braunschweig: Vieweg.

Lahti, P., and Mittelstädt, P. 1985. *Symposium on the Foundations of Modern Physics: 50 Years of the Einstein-Podolsky-Rosen Gedankenexperiment.* Singapore: World Scientific Publishing Co.

Leclerc, I. 1986. *The Nature of Physical Existence.* Lanham, N.Y.: University Press of America.

Liboff, R. 1980. *Introductory Quantum Mechanics.* New York: Holden-Day.

McCloskey, M. 1983. Intuitive Physics. *Scientific American* 248: 122–30.

Popper, Karl. 1968. *Conjectures and Refutations.* 2d Ed. New York: Harper & Row.

Prigogine, I. 1980. *From Being to Becoming.* San Francisco: W. H. Freeman.

Prigogine, I., and Stenger, I. 1984. *Order Out of Chaos: Man's New Dialogue with Nature*. New York: Bantam Books.

Russell, B. 1948. *Human Knowledge: its Scope and Limits*. New York: Simon & Schuster.

_____. 1954. *The Analysis of Matter*. New York: Dover. (Original work published in 1927.)

Schrödinger, E. 1935. Die gegenwärtige Situation in der Quantenmechanik. *Naturwissenschaften* 23: 807–12, 823–28, 844–49. J. D. Trimmer, trans. 1983. "The Present Situation in Quantum Mechanics." *Quantum Theory and Measurement*. Ed. J. A. Wheeler and W. H. Zurek. Princeton: Princeton University Press.

Sellars, W. 1963. *Science, Perception and Reality*. London: Routledge & Kegan Paul.

Smart, J. J. C. 1963. *Philosophy and Scientific Realism*. London: Routledge & Kegan Paul.

Stebbing, L. S. 1958. *Philosophy and the Physicists*. New York: Dover. (Original work published in 1937.)

Taylor, A. E. 1903. *Elements of Metaphysics*. New York: Barnes & Noble.

Whitehead, A. N. 1978. *Process and Reality* (corrected ed. D. Griffin and D. Sherburne, eds). New York: Free Press. (Original work published in 1929.)

Wigner, E. 1967. Remarks on the Mind-Body Question. *Symmetries and Reflection*. Bloomington, Ind.: University of Indiana Press.

_____. 1983. Interpretation of Quantum Mechanics. *Quantum Theory and Measurement*. Ed. J. A. Wheeler and W. H. Zurek. Princeton: Princeton University Press.

Zukav, G. 1979. *The Dancing Wu Li Masters: An Overview of the New Physics*. New York: Bantam Books.

Chapter 2

THE RELATION BETWEEN NATURAL SCIENCE AND METAPHYSICS

Ivor Leclerc

The theme of this conference manifests a growing awareness of the profound changes in fundamental thought occurring in our time. It focuses specifically on physics, and the subtitle of the conference raises the questions, "Does physics need a new metaphysics?" This implies a singular relationship between physics and metaphysics; I shall be investigating this relationship.

An examination of the relationship between physics and metaphysics will be superficial if it does not recognize that the very conceptions of physics and metaphysics respectively are themselves involved in a process of change. To clarify this, an historical perspective is requisite. For our immediate purposes, we will begin by returning to the seventeenth century.

Philosophia Naturalis

Turning to the seventeenth century, we do not find physics and metaphysics as two separate and mutually exclusive fields, as they have been the last two hundred years. What we find is one field, inherited from the preceding epoch, called either *physiologia* (the *logos,* rational account, of *physis,* nature) or *philosophia naturalis* (the philosophy of nature). *Philosophia naturalis* involves, on the one hand, the application of pure mathematics to motion—this being mechanics—and, on the other hand, the set of philosophical issues involved in the study of nature (as elaborated by Aristotle in his *Physics*). (See also Leclerc, 1986, chapters 2, 3, 7, 8, 12–15.) These philosophical issues concern the analysis of the concept of nature (matter and form, causality, necessity), the concept of motion or *kinesis* (place, void, time, the continuum and divisibility), and the prime mover. As Aristotle made clear, these are the fundamental philosophical issues concerning nature that are completely general or universal (*katholou*), underlying all special enquiries into nature; thus, they are among "the first principles and highest causes" (Aristotle, *Metaphysics IV,* 1003a, 26–27) constituting the field of "first philosophy"—later termed "metaphysics." (See Aristotle, *Metaphysics IV,* chapter 1.)

In the seventeenth century, a new concept of nature, radically different from the Aristotelian one, had been introduced; thinkers were accordingly faced with the need to rethink the set of basic issues of first philosophy presented by Aristotle and work out new and different solutions to those metaphysical issues. All this, the applied mathematics of motion (that is, mechanics), as well as the metaphysics on which it was grounded, were included in *philosophia naturalis* in the seventeenth century.

The new conception of nature as matter began developing in the first two decades of the seventeenth century, most fully by Sebastian Basso and by the new mechanics by Galileo. Thereafter, it was Descartes who, in his *Principles of Philosophy,* first developed a fully integrated *philosophia naturalis,* in which the entire range of metaphysical issues set out by Aristotle was fundamentally rethought.[1]

A few decades later, Newton, in his *Philosophiae naturalis principia mathematica,* presented an alternative to Descartes' philosophy of nature, one based on a metaphysics of corporeal atomism. Although this work mainly concentrates on the "mathematical principles" (that is, on mechanics), as its title expressly states, it is, nevertheless, a *philosophia naturalis;* the *philosophy* appeared in the Definitions, Axioms, the Scholia—notably the General Scholium at the end of the work—and the Rules of Reasoning at the beginning of Book III. The General Scholium makes it clear that included in natural philosophy is also the issue of

God as the prime mover; God is required in this system because matter is, in itself, wholly inert, thus necessitating God's act, not only to create it but also to set it into motion. Newton's conception of *philosophia naturalis* is, therefore, fully in line with that of other seventeenth-century thinkers in that for him it was also an integration of mechanics and metaphysics. For Newton, *philosophia naturalis* was not merely a synonym for mechanics, as has been assumed by all too many writers in more recent times.

The Science of Mechanics

The Newtonian system rapidly gained ascendancy over the Cartesian system, and in the eighteenth century, Newton's mechanics increasingly became accepted as confirmed by its successful application to an ever-widening range of phenomena. Most importantly, it was seen as confirming the general conception that the physical universe is indeed a mechanical structure, exhaustively understandable in terms of the laws of motion, that is, by the science of mechanics. Further, in the eighteenth century there occurred a decline in interest in the metaphysical portion of *philosophia naturalis* in proportion to this acceptance of the science of mechanics, and in particular, the role of God in this mechanistic system was rejected as a *deus ex machina;* the science of mechanics was beginning to be regarded as an autonomous science. (Parenthetically, the word *science* here has the general meaning of a branch of systematic study.[2])

This development first occurred principally in France through the work of a number of great mathematicians who were also natural philosophers: Maupertius, d'Alembert, Lagrange, and Laplace. Their considerable developments in mathematics advanced mechanics to a new level of perfection with Laplace, who, by the early nineteenth century, became entirely convinced that the science of mechanics was the complete understanding of nature as a mechanistic system and that this rendered the hypothesis of God entirely otiose.

It was Laplace who most fully appreciated what the autonomy of the science of mechanics implied: mechanics was indeed the fundamental science in the study and understanding of nature. This meant that mechanics was in fact what the earlier thinkers had conceived *physiologia* to be, namely, the rational account of nature. This conception entailed that the science of mechanics became modern *physics,* replacing Aristotle's *Physics* as the fundamental study of nature. In other words, the science of nature, physics, is the science of mechanics.

The Development of Positivism

It was not only the seventeenth-century conception of the theological component of natural philosophy that Laplace eliminated, he also eliminated the entire metaphysical component. This was simply unnecessary in the method of the science of mechanics (as he conceived it), which Laplace proved by a reexamination of the nature, scope, and method of the enquiry into nature, that is, mechanics. This enquiry, Laplace (1902) maintained,[3] proceeds by inductive generalizations from observed facts to hypotheses or theories, which were tested by the observed conformity of the phenomena to the hypotheses. Contrary to Newton, who had insisted on the strict avoidance of hypotheses in mechanics, Laplace explicitly accepted hypotheses as a means of connecting phenomena for the discovery of general laws. But what was crucial in Laplace's position was that he insisted on the need *to avoid attributing reality* to hypotheses; this was precisely what was not done in metaphysics. Concepts such as "force," "mass," "motion," "cause," and "laws" occur in mechanics, but they are legitimate there only as quantities. What "force," "mass," "motion," "cause," and "laws" *really* are had to be entirely eliminated from consideration; mechanics is concerned with such concepts solely in a quantitative respect, as ratios, for example, which could be formalized in the equations of a calculus. It is these quantities discovered in mechanics that constitute the knowledge of and truth about nature.

Laplace's conception of the science of mechanics became accepted and established in the nineteenth century by the increasing success of the science of mechanics being extended to ever further areas of phenomena: heat, light, electricity, magnetism, and so forth. For thinkers pursuing the science of nature, this Laplacian concept of the science of mechanics as excluding metaphysics seemed confirmed further by the fact that metaphysics in the nineteenth century had taken soul or mind to be the only reality. This further increased the determination to systematize the science of mechanics by the rigorous elimination of any remnants of metaphysics implicit in concepts such as "force," "cause," "law," and so on; this was done by rigidly removing from them all presuppositions or thoughts of the "nature of" or the "sources of" forces, and so on, and also of all "intuitive" conceptions of them, admitting them only as strictly quantitative concepts. This was the program carried out by Mach, Kirchhoff, Hertz, and Poincaré, a program that became determinative of the enquiry into nature.

In the course of the nineteenth century, therefore, a complete change in the conception of the enquiry into nature had come into effect. The conception of this enquiry as *philosophia naturalis,* philosophy of nature, was gone. In its place a fully autonomous science of mechanics had been established as the science of nature. All areas and phenomena were to be understood in terms of the principles of mechanics. This had successfully been done with respect to the phenomena of heat and chemical change. Clerk Maxwell had developed a wave mechanics for the understanding of the phenomena of electricity and magnetism. Then, in the early twentieth century, after the discovery of the quantum phenomenon by Max Planck, the theory of quantum mechanics was developed, and to the present, the entire enquiry into the subatomic or microentities is being pursued as a *mechanics,* that is, the mathematical analysis of entities in motion.

It is most important to note what is entailed by this change in the conception of the enquiry into nature in which the science of mechanics had become identified with the science of nature. Since *science* means "knowledge," what is entailed is that mechanics is the true knowledge of nature; in other words, mechanics, the mathematical investigation of motion, *is* science.

This new doctrine respecting *science* is what, in the nineteenth century, came to be known as *positivism,* the doctrine that *science* is the *positive* (the term derived from Auguste Comte), that is, the true, genuine, and certain knowledge of nature. In this conception, *science* stood in contrast to and excluded philosophy and in particular metaphysics.

Further, it is this meaning of the term *science* that has since then come to be generally accepted, in English speaking countries particularly, as *the* meaning of the word "science." Moreover, this meaning of the term *science* has, in our time, come to be so fully accepted that it is regarded as indeed generic. In this meaning, the word *science* has lost its previous general connotation of a systematic enquiry, which had meant there were many sciences (besides the science of nature) according to fields of systematic enquiry, including, for example, metaphysics.

Metaphysical Presuppositions

One important consequence of this positivist doctrine, which has become subtly pervasive in the thought of most natural scientists and a great many philosophers today, is that with its hostility to metaphysics, it has militated against the recognition that the science of mechanics itself has a metaphysical basis, one that has been inherited from the seventeenth century and one that, by the nineteenth century, had continued effectively as a tacit presupposition.

Among the chief of these metaphysical presuppositions of the science of mechanics were (1) the conception of nature as matter, wholly inert and in itself changeless, with locomotion, that is, change with respect to place, the only change nature is capable of; (2) the conception of this matter as being inherently mathematical in nature and structure, that is, it is essentially quantitative, not qualitative; and (3) the conception of matter and its locomotion as being exhaustively understandable in terms of mechanics, that is, the applied mathematics of motion. As Kepler, Galileo, Descartes, Newton, and others had explicitly maintained, the physical world is a mathematical structure, which ensured that the mathematical investigation of nature furnished the full truth about nature.

The first serious blow to this conception came with the discovery, in the early nineteenth century, of non-Euclidean geometry. This raised the fundamental issue of the nature and status of mathematics, for this discovery entailed that the hitherto unquestioned metaphysical presupposition of the world as the unequivocal object of mathematics, of geometry in particular, was no longer tenable.

In 1768, in a crucial paper entitled "On the First Ground of the Distinction of Regions in Space" (Handyside, 1929), Kant had come to a significant insight into an aspect of this problem concerning the status of mathematics, an insight that was in fact determinative of his momentous turn of thought, his "critical" philosophy, initially revealed in his *Inaugural Dissertation* two years later and fully expounded in his *Critique of Pure Reason* (1781). Fundamental to his new "critical" position was his "Copernican revolution": "hitherto it has been assumed that all our knowledge must conform to objects"—that is, physical things determine whether what we think about them is "knowledge" or is "true". But, Kant maintained, the contrary had to be accepted, namely, "objects must conform to our knowledge"; our faculties of knowledge determine the truth respecting physical things (Kant, 1787/1929, p. 22). Thus, Kant put into full effect the subjectivism that Descartes felt was entailed by metaphysical dualism.

The relevance of this new Kantian position as a solution to the crisis in respect of the status of mathematics was seen by Weierstrass (the leader of the Berlin school of mathematics), who proclaimed that "Die Mathematik ist eine reine Schöpfung des menschlichen Geistes" ("Mathematics is a pure creation of the human mine"), a doctrine that was fully accepted by Einstein in this century.

Now this has profound implications for natural science, in the first instance for the epistemology and methodology of natural science, as Einstein mentioned in his Herbert Spencer Lecture (1935):

> The natural philosophers of those days were . . . most of them possessed with the idea that the fundamental concepts and postulates of physics were not in the logical sense free inventions of the human mind but could be deduced from experience by 'abstraction'—that is to say by logical means. A clear recognition of the erroneousness of this notion really came only with the general theory of relativity, . . . the fictitious character of the fundamental principles is perfectly evident from the fact that we can point to two essentially different principles, both of which refer to experience to a large extent. (pp. 135–36)

The last reference is to the Newtonian theory and his own theory of relativity. Einstein was here rejecting the concept that enquiry in natural science proceeds by logical induction from sensible particulars to general principles and laws; instead, he maintained that the "fundamental concepts," "postulates," and "fundamental principles" were *hypotheses,* arrived at by the "free creation of the human mind."

Now the fundamental metaphysical issue raised by this is how, on Einstein's evident subjectivist basis, those hypotheses, or fundamental concepts, postulates, and principles, are to be accepted as "knowledge," as being "true"? Einstein was indeed aware of the problem, but he was unable to provide an adequate resolution. He maintained that "the empirical contents and their mutual relations must find their representation in the conclusions of the theory" (Einstein, 1935, p. 134). But since for Einstein theories were "free inventions of the human intellect," on what basis is it to be accepted that they do indeed accurately, or at all, "represent" empirical facts? Faced with this, Einstein (1935) could only assert his personal conviction, "I am convinced that we can discover by means of purely mathematical constructions the concepts and laws connecting them with each other, which furnish the key to the understanding of natural phenomena" (p. 136). But this conviction can per se constitute no justification. His conviction, I would submit, is grounded in a tacit seventeenth-century presupposition of metaphysical dualism and a doctrine of the world as a mathematical structure completely knowable by mathematics. This, however, is inconsistent with Einstein's conception of mathematics as a subjective creation of the intellect. It must be recognized that there are tremendous metaphysical difficulties facing that position; involved here are profound metaphysical issues, issues concerning the nature and status of mathematics, including the relation of the mathematical to physical reality. One further aspect of the difficulty involved in Einstein's position, which is shared by natural scientists in general, is that it involves the inheritance of seventeenth-century metaphysical dualism.

In our time these metaphysical issues have become even more urgent and crucial than in Einstein's. Yet, since the end of World War II, as Gerald Holton (1984) has shown, natural scientists have ceased almost entirely to have any interest in these issues, and the lively discussions among scientists that occurred in the pre-war period concerning the philosophical issues involved in their field and methodology has also virtually ceased. Instead, as Holton (1984) has illuminated, Einstein's position, detailed above, has become the accepted methodology in contemporary research, in which hypotheses and speculative proposals are made and proceeded upon "as long as there is felt to be 'good reason,' in which 'good reason' is part of an expression of the risk-taking, 'what-if?' improvisational heuristic that allows proposals to be made without regret even when they have highly implausible aspects, or when tests are not likely to be possible in the foreseeable future" (p. 1232).

But the fundamental epistemological and methodological issues involved in these fields do not disappear or cease to exist by being ignored. They continue to be important today, indeed even more urgently. The really crucial epistemological issue is how the purely subjective, freely invented and formulated mathematical "ideas" and hypotheses can provide "knowledge," "understanding," and "truth" about "physical reality," which is, in terms of the metaphysical dualism underlying this entire position, completely separate and ontologically different from the thinking mind. The answer to this, which had been provided by Descartes, Newton, and the other thinkers of the earlier epoch, was grounded in a theory of God's activity—a theory that had justifiably been rejected as an incoherent *deus ex machina*. Today it is necessary to recognize that there is ultimately no way out of this epistemological difficulty except in terms of a new metaphysics.

Metaphysics

We have now reached a point where it is necessary to look more particularly at metaphysics, to clarify what is meant by the term. We could say, following Aristotle (*Metaphysics* IV, 1003a 26–27) that metaphysics is the science that studies the first principles and highest causes of things (*de tas archas kai tas akrotatas aitias*). However, in our present context it will be more helpful and intelligible to say that metaphysics seeks the greatest or highest generalities or universalities, those that extend beyond the generalities sought in the natural sciences (such as the laws of nature) but that are involved in the enquiry into nature whose theories and concepts presuppose, usually tacitly, these ultimate or metaphysical generalities.

It must be emphasized that metaphysics is a "science" in that it is a systematic enquiry, with its own particular methodology. As a science its methodology involves the critical examination and evaluation of all putative metaphysical generalities, both those maintained by antecedent metaphysical theories and systems and those tacitly accepted without explicit recognition in systems and schemes of thought (including those of the natural sciences and the human sciences) and in practical human activity.

In addition to the critical side of metaphysics, there is also the constructive side, that of the formulation of metaphysical theories. Methodologically the formulation of metaphysical theory is not basically different from the formulation of theories in the natural sciences; that is, the procedure is the framing of hypotheses and the systematic elaboration of the implications of these basic hypotheses (including their application), all of this constituting the metaphysical system. The difference between metaphysical hypotheses and those of the natural sciences is that in the latter the hypotheses usually originate by generalization from empirical experience in particular fields or sections of nature. In many instances metaphysical hypotheses also originate by generalization from particular spheres of experience, but the generalizations necessarily will have to transcend these fields to ensure their fully general application; it is in this respect that their validity as truly metaphysical generalities is apt to be found wanting.[4]

There is today an urgent task for metaphysics, namely, the discernment and critical evaluation of the implicit metaphysical presuppositions operative in enquiry in the natural sciences. This is important for metaphysics as an indispensable prelude to the proposal of more adequate metaphysical concepts and theories. It should be noted, however, that in this situation metaphysicians face a difficulty, persisting to the present day: Metaphysics is too deeply influenced by contemporary developments in natural science. In maintaining that *locomotion* is the fundamental kind of change in the universe,[5] Aristotle had been too strongly

influenced by the astronomical and cosmological theory of his time—
which he actively participated in as a natural scientist.

Metaphysical Issues

In conclusion I shall briefly examine some metaphysical issues that
seem to me especially pertinent to physics at the present time.

As we have seen, the metaphysical theory of material atomism became dominant after Newton. In the nineteenth century, it was very
successfully applied to chemistry by Dalton, whose joining of chemistry
and physics was seen as a strong confirmation of the theory of material
atomism. From the discovery of the electron by J. J. Thomson in the
closing years of the nineteenth century it was appreciated, however, that
what had been taken to be the ultimate atoms were in fact not so, that
these entities were indeed composite. In the next decades of the twentieth
century, an increasing number of different constituents, of what continued to be called "atoms," were found; this process of discovery has continued with increasing intensity to the present. These constituents are
generally called "particles," and referred to as "matter."

But what are the metaphysical implications involved in this? The
word *particle* means "little part," which raises the question "little part of
what?" The answer evidently is "little part of matter." The issue then is
what is meant by the term *matter*? Newton (1952) was very clear about
the term in the context of the theory of material atomism: "Matter [is
formed] in solid, massy, hard, impenetrable, movable Particles" (p. 400).
The question now is whether this classical conception of matter and of
"material particles" is still in keeping with twentieth-century developments in physics.

It seems clear that these developments have made this conception
of matter no longer tenable. The large number of microentities that
have been discovered do not behave like Newtonian material particles;
their motion is not in accord with the classical Newtonian laws, and a
new mechanics has had to be developed. Moreover, it has emerged that
these particles have a wavelike character; thus, they have been called
"wavicles." Further, in certain circumstances these entities cease altogether to have a particulate character, abruptly changing into electro-
magnetic radiation.

Involved in this is a quite fundamental metaphysical issue. In the
seventeenth century it was accepted that physical existence, physical being, was basically and essentially continuous, exemplified in Descartes'

conception of matter as one *res extensa*. Newton pluralized this into material atoms, with continuity pertaining to each atom of matter; each was self-identical, continuing unchanged in its adventures of locomotive change. In the mid-nineteenth century, with the emergence into prominence of the notions of energy and force, Clerk Maxwell introduced the field concept, and the electromagnetic field had the fundamental feature of continuity. In the early decades of this century, Einstein merged space, time, matter, and energy, and once again continuity remained fundamental.

All this was deeply affected by Planck's introduction of the quantum of energy, for this entailed discontinuity, which was confirmed by Einstein's discovery of photons in 1905. But the long tradition of the metaphysical presupposition of continuity as fundamental, nevertheless, remained dominant; the various particles of matter were conceived as maintaining a self-identical continuity of existence. And today this metaphysical presupposition of continuity as fundamental persists. But it exists uneasily, with incongruities such as the notion of "wavicle"; with the concept of "particle" applied both to electrons, photons, and so on; and with all the evidence of fundamental discontinuities, indicated, for example, by Planck's constant featuring in such a large number of equations. To the rescue in this situation Bohr introduced his "principle of complementarity." However, fundamental metaphysical issues cannot be slurred over or ignored without impunity.

The basic issue involved here regarding continuity and discontinuity is an ontological one, that is, one respecting "being." The concept of "being" as continuous, unchanging in itself, immutable, has a venerable heritage; it goes back to Parmenides in the fifth century before the Christian era and became overwhelmingly dominant in thought through Plato and then Neoplatonism, from which it passed to the seventeenth-century thinkers and to most later thinkers. Aristotle's alternative ontology, of being as necessarily involving becoming, has had comparatively scant adherence. It is perhaps no small wonder that the ontology of being as continuous persists so tenaciously today as a tacit presupposition in natural science, and that an alternative to this conception seems unthinkable or untenable.

But this presupposition is inconsistent with the present-day conception of microparticles as being "active" and as "interacting" with each other. The very notion of "active particles of matter," that is, of inert entities being active, is a plain contradiction. Further, in contrast to the concept of matter as entailing continuity, the concept of "acting entities" entails discontinuity. For acting is not a continuous process; an act occurs *now*, and as that act, it is over; it can only be superseded by other similar acts. "Acting" involves quantization. This means that the concept of a "quantum" is requisite not only with respect to energy or photons; it is no less requisite with respect to all truly elementary physical entities, those entities that are not composite of other entities.[6]

What is evidently requisite regarding physical science today is a new metaphysics to clarify these issues of acting, discontinuity, quantization and what is entailed in them; all of this involves a great deal more complexity than might immediately be apparent.

In conclusion, I would like to state that throughout the modern period, and increasingly in this century, there has been manifest a very effective and fruitful partnership between theoretical physics and experimental physics. The time has evidently arrived for a third partner to be added, namely, metaphysics.

Notes

1. Since the new conception of nature as matter entailed the exclusion of mind from nature, Descartes had to lay the metaphysical and epistemological foundations for an essentially mathematical knowledge of nature in an ontologically separate *res cogitans* before proceeding, in the last two parts of the work, to the elaboration of his mathematical cosmology. Metaphysically, matter was conceived by Descartes as one *res extensa,* infinitely diversified by vortical motion, macroscopic and microscopic, this motion being inherently capable of mathematical analysis.

2. Compare the *Shorter Oxford English Dictionary,* art. 4: "A branch of study which is concerned either with a connected body of demonstrated truths or with observed facts systematically classified and more or less colligated by being brought under laws, and which includes methods for the discovery of new truths within its own domain" (p. 1725).

3. In Laplace's words: "Induction, analogy, hypotheses founded upon facts and rectified continually by new observations, a happy tact given by nature and strengthened by numerous comparisons of its implications with experience, such are the principal means for arriving at truth" (1902, p. 176).

4. This view of the methodology of metaphysics rejects the historically dominant view that metaphysics proceeds from the perception or intuition of certain ultimate, self-evident, or incontrovertible truths; Descartes and Spinoza are characteristic exemplifications of this view. In historical perspective, their putative, ultimate metaphysical truths are recognized as having the status of hypotheses.

5. A consequence of this inheritance has been a change in the connotation of the word "motion" (*motus*), from its having been the rendering of the Aristotelian *kinesis*—which included quantitative change (e.g., of size), qualitative change (i.e., of kind or sort), as well as locomotion (i.e., change in respect of place), and even coming into being and destruction—to the restricted connotation solely of locomotion.

6. Credit for being the first to have clearly recognized the necessity of a quantization of the primary physical existents must go to A. N. Whitehead (1925, Chapters 7 and 8, 1927, 1929/1979).

References

Einstein, A. 1935. *The World as I See It*. London: John Lane.

Handyside, J. 1929. *Kant's Inaugural Dissertation and Early Writings on Space*. Chicago and London: Open Court.

Holton, G. 1984. Do Scientists Need a Philosophy? *The Times Literary Supplement*. November 2: 1231–34.

Kant, I. 1929. *Critique of Pure Reason*. 2d ed. Trans. N. Kemp Smith. New York: St. Martin's Press. (Original work published in 1787.)

Laplace, P. S. de. 1902. *A Philosophical Essay on Probabilities*. Trans. F. Truscott and F. L. Emory. New York: Dover.

Leclerc, I. 1986. *The Nature of Physical Existence*. New York and London: University Press of America.

Newton, I. 1952. *Opticks*. New York: Dover.

Whitehead, A. N. 1925. *Science and the Modern World*. New York: Free Press.

_____. 1927. Time. *Proceedings of the 6th International Congress of Philosophy: September 1926*, New York.

_____. 1979. *Process and Reality*. Corrected ed. New York: Free Press. (Original work published in 1929.)

Chapter 3

QUANTUM THEORY AND THE PHYSICIST'S CONCEPTION OF NATURE: PHILOSOPHICAL IMPLICATIONS OF BELL'S THEOREM

Henry P. Stapp

Introduction

During the eighteenth and nineteenth centuries, classical physics gave a very successful account of physical phenomena; yet it was not generally accepted by philosophers as an adequate basis for an understanding of nature fundamentally because mind and matter are not connected. In a coherent understanding of nature, all parts must stand together in a way such that none can stand alone. Yet classical physics is so internally coherent as to preclude any rationally ordained coupling between the physical reality it describes and anything else. Classical physics not only fails to demand the mental, it fails even to provide a rational place for the mental. And if the mental is introduced *ad hoc*, then it must remain totally ineffectual, in absolute contradiction to our deepest experience.

Another reason for the reluctance of philosophers to accept the ideas of classical physics as a basis for a comprehensive metaphysics is that a philosophy based on strict mathematical determinism is cut off at the start from any adequate way of dealing with moral and other human issues whose resolutions are the ultimate task of a complete philosophy.

The rise of quantum theory in the present century appeared at first to render the physicist's conception of nature even less adequate as a foundation for metaphysics. There are two reasons for this: First, a principal theme in orthodox quantum thinking is precisely the rejection of metaphysics. The orthodox attitude is to renounce the quest for an understanding of physical phenomena in terms of basic realities and to settle for some computational rules that allow scientists to form expectations pertaining to observations obtained under well-defined conditions specified in terms of classical physical ideas. This revision in the announced aim of physics signifies that the clear idea of physical reality provided by classical physics has been snatched away by quantum theory, which provides in its place only computational rules of mysterious origin. Such rules may be sufficient for scientific purposes, but they are not enough for philosophers in search of a unified understanding of all of nature.

A second reason for the apparent inadequacy of the quantum physicist's conception of nature as the foundation for a unified metaphysics is that the quantum rules effectively replace the mind-matter duality of classical physics by a quantum triality. The physical world of classical physics is subdivided into two parts: a macroscopic part described in terms of classical physics and a microscopic part described in terms of the formalism of quantum theory. Thus, a new schism is added, and there is an apparent shift away from, rather than toward, metaphysical unity.

The general reluctance of quantum physicists to embrace a metaphysics, or comprehensive ontology, stems from two considerations. The first is the possibility that two different ontological systems might lead to the same computational rules. If the predictions generated by the orthodox quantum theoretical rules completely exhaust the set of empirically testable propositions obtainable from physical theory, then any metaphysical assertion that is more than the mere assertion that these rules of calculation hold is scientifically unwarranted.

The second consideration inhibiting the embracing of a comprehensive ontology is the problem of nonlocality. Apart from the so-called many-worlds interpretation, which is objectionable on other grounds, no ontology that can account for all of the predictions of quantum theory has been proposed that does not involve faster-than-light propagation of influences. Since quantum physicists are generally reluctant to accept the idea that there are faster-than-light influences, they are left with no ontology to embrace.

Three Ontologies Proposed to Account for Quantum Phenomena

For the sake of definiteness, let me briefly describe three principal ontologies that have been proposed by quantum physicists. They are the many-worlds ontology of Everett (1957), the pilot-wave ontology of Bohm (1952; Bohm and Hiley, 1986), and the actual-event ontology of Heisenberg (1958, Chapter III).

The many-worlds ontology arises directly from the assumption that the probability amplitude of quantum theory is a real physical quantity, rather than merely a conceptual device to be used by scientists to compute the probability that a measuring device will respond in a specified way. This real physical amplitude is assumed to obey an appropriate Schroedinger equation.

This probability amplitude has (when squared, and so on) the mathematical properties appropriate to the probability density. Consequently, in a measurement situation in which there are, due to quantum uncertainties, several distinct, possible alternative outcomes of the measurement, each with a nonzero probability, the region where the probability amplitude is nonzero must split into several "branches," with each branch corresponding to one of the possible alternative results of the measurement. For example, if some measurement has two possible alternative outcomes, one corresponding to the pointer on some device moving to the right by a perceptible amount and the other corresponding to this pointer moving to the left by a perceptible amount, then in terms of the location of this pointer, the region in which the probability amplitude is nonzero will, after the measurement, consist of two separated regions: one corresponding to the pointer displaced perceptibly to the right, the other corresponding to the pointer displaced perceptibly to the left. Since this probability amplitude is now assumed to represent reality itself, rather than merely a probability for a possible reality, this separation of the probability amplitude into a set of "branches" involves a separation of reality itself into a set of branches, one corresponding to each of the possible alternative results of the measurement. Only one of these possibilities is observed empirically. This disparity between what is "real," according to this ontology, and what is observed empirically is accounted for by arguing, quite plausibly, that the separation of reality into parallel noninteracting branches will induce a corresponding separation of the mental worlds of the observers into parallel noncommunicating branches.

This many-worlds ontology might appear to make sense when one considers only idealized measurement situations, in which the regions where the probability amplitude is nonzero separate into well-defined distinct branches, corresponding to the possible alternative, distinct observations. But the idea becomes totally obscure when one considers the general situation of continuous evolution in accordance with the Schroedinger equation. In particular, there appears to be no general way within this ontology to account for the distinct character of our experiences. For the ontology has no fundamental element of discreteness, but consists basically of a superposition of a continuum of possibilities.

The second important proposed ontology is the pilot-wave model. One, again, takes the probability amplitude of quantum theory to be real and requires it always to obey the Schroedinger equation. The problem of distinctness is resolved by introducing a second component of reality, a "real world" described exactly as in classical physics. However, this real world moves not in accordance with the classical laws of inertia and acceleration but rather moves always along the flow lines defined by the quantum probability amplitude. The distinctness problem is then resolved by assuming that experience is coordinated always to this single distinct real world, rather than to the continuum of such worlds represented by the probability amplitude. However, there is then the embarrassment of the "empty branches": In an ideal measurement situation with several distinct possible results, there will be, as discussed before, one branch of the probability amplitude corresponding to each of the alternative possible results of the measurement. The "real world" of the pilot-wave model will get into one of these branches, and stay there. The equations of motion of quantum theory then entail that the other branches can have essentially no influence on the subsequent motion of this real world. Yet these other branches continue to exist as parts of "reality." This is a highly noneconomical way for nature to operate, for nature must keep on generating in *perpetuum* the evolution of these "empty branches" that can never influence the experienced real world.

The third important ontology is the one proposed by Heisenberg. According to this proposal, the probability amplitude of quantum theory corresponds to an *objective tendency* or "potentia" for the occurrence of an actual event. This event effectively selects some particular macroscopic response of the measuring device from among the possibilities that were allowed prior to this event.

Heisenberg's ideas are not out of line with, or incompatible with, the orthodox position. In fact, the orthodox position is defined jointly by the ideas of Bohr and Heisenberg. Bohr's "strict" wordings avoid Heisenberg's ontological commitments, but these wordings are certainly compatible with the idea that the responses of the devices are selected in the way suggested by Heisenberg. Thus, Heisenberg's ontology can be said to be the orthodox quantum ontology, to the extent that such an ontology exists at all. In the following sections I call Heisenberg's ontology the quantum ontology.

Mind and Matter in the Quantum Ontology

The previously mentioned problem of the connection between mind and matter takes on a completely new complexion when considered on the basis of the quantum ontology, as opposed to the ontology of classical physics. The main problem from the classical point of view is that the category of ideas used to represent physical properties is separate from the category of ideas used to represent mental properties. In the words of William James (1890): "Everyone admits the entire incommensurability of feeling as such with material motion as such. 'A motion became a feeling'—no phrase that our lips can form is so devoid of apprehensible meaning" (p. 146). In the words of Tyndall:

> We can trace the development in a nervous system and correlate it with a parallel phenomena of sensation and thought. But we soar into a vacuum the moment we seek to comprehend the connection between them—there is no fusion between the two classes of facts—no motor energy in the intellect of man to carry it without logical rupture from one to the other. (James, 1890, p. 147)

These assessments were based on the ontology of classical physics, in which the physical aspects of nature were completely represented by the motions of billions of particles (and perhaps some fields), evolving in accordance with the classical equations of motion. The quantum ontology has an analogue of this classical structure, namely, the probability amplitude. This amplitude refers to the same degrees of freedom as the corresponding classical system. And it evolves according to an equation of motion that is analogous to the classical one.

However, the quantum ontology includes something that is completely different in character. This is the actual event, which represents, in effect, a decision between various possible alternative, perceptually distinct courses of action. These actual events were discussed by Heisenberg in the context of the behavior of a quantum measuring device. But they must presumably be occurring wherever quantum processes are taking place within the context of macroscopic systems. From the point of view of the quantum ontology, the actual perceived world is constructed from myriads of these actual events, each of which actualizes in a particular way the potentialities created by the prior events and, moreover, fixes the potentialities for subsequent events.

If we take over from the case of measuring devices the idea that these events occur generally at a high level of integration and effectively decide between macroscopically distinguishable behaviors of the macroscopic system, then the quantum ontology provides the element needed to fuse the mental and physical aspects of nature. "A motion became a feeling." Now there is no problem with this idea. For physical motion is represented in quantum theory as the evolution of the probability amplitude, which represents, however, only a *potentia* for an integrative act, not the actual event or act itself. This actual event or act is effectively a decision between different possible, perceptually distinct modes of behavior of the macroscopic system. Thus, a motion "becomes," or at least provides the conditions for, an act, which decides between perceptually different modes of behavior of the macroscopic system. One can contrast here the mathematically preordained, and hence spiritless, motion of the particles, as represented by the mathematical evolution of the probability amplitude, with the nonpreordained, and hence "spirited," act that decides between the alternative possibilities. The idea that this act should be *felt* as exactly what it is from the physical point of view, namely, a spirited act of deciding between the possible alternative, integrated behavior patterns of the complete organism, requires no logical rupture. For there is no identification of a mental aspect with something wholly different. Rather a mental act is identified with a physical act, and both of these acts are the very same act, that is, the act of deciding between alternative possible modes of behavior that are, prior to this act, allowed for the macroscopic physical system. I invoke here the main conclusion from von Neumann's analysis of the process of measurement: the quantum act (the decision) can be pushed all the way to the physical phenomena associated with the psychical event. Then the physical and psychical acts become the single identical act of deciding between different macroscopic patterns of behavior.

The identification of each human mental event with the effectively identically physical one does not mean that every physical event is a human mental event. Rather, in keeping with Heisenberg's ideas, the actual physical events can be associated generally with decisions between possible alternative modes of behavior involving the collective action of large numbers of quanta acting coherently. In this way the quantum ontology, which was created solely to provide an understanding of a purely physical phenomenon, namely, the behavior of quantum measuring devices, automatically provides the basis for a natural and rational comprehension of the connection between mind and matter. The quantum ontology thus dissolves the mind-matter duality and brings the physical and mental aspects of nature together in the particular mathematical juxtaposition defined by quantum theory (Stapp, 1982).

Nonlocal Character of the Quantum Ontology

Within the quantum ontology of Heisenberg, the most striking characteristic of the quantum act or event is its nonlocal nature. Heisenberg (1930) discusses this feature in connection with a wave packet that strikes a half-silvered mirror. Such a mirror reflects half of the packet and transmits half. The two parts of the wave packet can then travel to distant regions, where they may encounter measuring devices. The probability amplitude is nonzero in both devices, and hence there exists in both devices an objective tendency, or *potentia,* for the device to respond. Heisenberg (1930) notes that

> if an experiment yields the result that the photon is, say, in the reflected part of the packet then the probability of finding the photon in the other part of the packet immediately becomes zero. The experiment at the position of the reflected packet then exerts a kind of action (reduction of the wave packet) at the distant point occupied by the transmitted packet, and one sees that this action is propagated at a velocity greater than light. However, it is obvious that this kind of action can never be used to transmit a signal, so it is not in conflict with the postulates of the theory of relativity. (p. 39)

A principal characteristic that distinguishes a "signal" from a general influence is that a signal can be controlled by human choice. In the situation just described, it is nature, not a human being, that decides whether the device in one region will respond or not. Consequently, the faster-than-light action associated with the quantum event or act cannot be used to transmit a signal.

This nonlocal feature of the Heisenberg ontology is troublesome to quantum theorists. When confronted with it, most orthodox physicists will retreat to the strict interpretation of Bohr and renounce the ontological ideas; that is, the typical orthodox quantum physicist, although initially willing to accept informally the idea that something definite actually happens at the level of the device and the idea that the selection of what actually happens is not predetermined, will not be willing to follow through the consequences of this commitment as Heisenberg did; (s)he will retreat to the position that quantum theory merely provides testable rules, not an ontology. From this pragmatic point of view, the reduction of the wave packet need not be explicitly mentioned at all, and if it is mentioned, it is regarded as simply the normal change that is naturally associated with the change in the knowledge, hence expectations, of the human observer-scientist when new information is registered in his consciousness. This instantaneous change in the knowledge of the human observer evidently does not correspond to any faster-than-light physical action. Therefore, the faster-than-light actions occurring within the Heisenberg ontology are dismissed as spurious or nonphysical.

This conclusion is reinforced by the fact that the one-quantum situation discussed by Heisenberg can be described in a completely local way within the pilot-wave model. (The evolution of the probability amplitude is determined by the local Schroedinger equation, and the motion of the "classical particle" of the pilot-wave model is then locally determined by the flow lines of the probability amplitude.) Consequently, the nonlocal character of the Heisenberg ontology appears to be a nonphysical peculiarity of this ontology, rather than a reflection of any nonlocal aspect of quantum theory itself.

The logical situation changes when two-quantum systems are considered. Then the pilot-wave model also becomes nonlocal. (The model is local in the six-dimensional space of the composite two-quantum system, but is nonlocal in physical three-dimensional space.) This nonlocal character is completely explicit: The behavior of a quantum in one space-time region is dynamically influenced by *what experimenters do* to a quantum located in a second region, which is spacelike, separated from the first.

This explicitly nonlocal character of the pilot-wave model is often cited as sufficient reason for its rejection. But if both the Bohm-type and Heisenberg-type ontologies are rejected, on the basis of their nonlocal character, then the quantum physicist is left with no coherent ontology that is compatible with the validity of the quantum theoretical predictions, even for rudimentary two-quantum systems.

Failure of EPR Locality

The considerations of the preceding section were based on specific ontologies. Hence, the conclusions that can be drawn are correspondingly limited. Einstein, Podolsky, and Rosen (1935) initiated a much more general approach, which is based not on particular ontologies but rather on general principles. These authors gave an argument for the incompleteness of the quantum-theoretical description of physical reality. Their argument was based on a locality assumption that expressed the idea that nothing in one space-time region can be disturbed or influenced by *what is done* by an experimenter in another region, which is spacelike separated from the first. Einstein (1951, p. 85) expressed a firm conviction that this locality principle must hold. However, it can now be shown, on the basis of a generalization of the work of J. S. Bell (1964), that within a very general theoretical framework, this locality principle is incompatible with the assumption that some rudimentary two-quantum predictions of quantum theory are valid.

The EPR-Bell analysis (Bell, 1964; Bohm and Aharanov, 1957; Einstein, 1951; Einstein, Podolsky, and Rosen, 1935; Stapp, 1971, 1985a, forthcoming) involves two space-time regions, R_1 and R_2, that are spacelike separated: No point in either region can be reached from any point in the other without traveling either faster than light or backward in time. In each region an experimenter is to decide between two possible alternative measurements. The chosen measurement is to be performed in that region and the result recorded there. The measurement involves a sequence of n pairs of quanta that have been prepared earlier in such a way that one quantum from each pair enters each region, where it is subjected to a measurement. The measurement on each quantum is such that it must yield one or the other of two possible alternative results, which we label as $+1$ and -1, respectively. Thus, $r_{1i} = \pm 1$ and $r_{2i} = \pm 1$ specify the possible alternative results in R_1 and R_2, respectively, of the measurement performed on the quantum from pair i.

The *correlation* between the results in the two regions is defined by

$$c = \frac{1}{n} \sum_{i=1}^{n} r_{1i} \, r_{2i} = c(r_1, r_2).$$

It lies in the closed interval between plus and minus one. In the physical situation considered by Bell, the rules of quantum theory give, for each of the four possible alternative combinations of measurements in the two regions, a corresponding value $\bar{c}$, and predict that the measured value of c will tend to $\bar{c}$ as n tends to infinity. More precisely, for any $\varepsilon > 0$ and $\delta > 0$ the probability that c lies in the region $|c - \bar{c}| > \varepsilon$ can be made less than δ by taking n sufficiently large.

To discuss the influence of the choice of measurement performed in one region on the decisions that nature can be forced to make in the other region, we introduce a conceptual framework based on two assumptions. The first assumption is that, within the specific context of the analysis of the quantum theoretical predictions for the measurements under consideration here, the choices to be made by the experimenters can be regarded as free and independent variables. This does not mean that these choices are necessarily literally free, but merely that the causal determinants of these human choices are sufficiently divorced from the quantum system under consideration as to have no bearing on the fact that measurements yield results that accord with the quantum predictions; the causal determinants of the human choices *could* be decoupled from the quantum system under study without disrupting the validity of predictions of quantum theory.

The second assumption is that for each region, and for each of the two possible alternative measurements in that region if that measurement is chosen, nature must make a definite decision between the alternative possible results of this measurement; two possible values for the outcome of a single decision are either equal or contradictory. This assumption excludes the many-worlds ontology in which all of the possible alternative results are actually realized, and hence nature makes no decision.

A necessary condition for the lack of influence, within a theoretical structure, of the choice of the value of an independent variable x upon a variable y is that, within this structure, it is possible for every choice of the independent variables other than x to find a possible value y' for the variable y such that x can be varied over its domain, with y held fixed at the value y'. For even though there can be many factors that contribute to the determination of y that are not under theoretical control, such as intrinsic random variables and unspecified causal elements, the very idea that x is a free variable and that the choice of the value of x does not influence or disturb the variable y means that variations of x cannot *force* y to change; the various factors that enter into the determination of y, whatever they may be, must at least be *permitted* by the theory to remain unchanged as the value of x is varied.

Let $x_1 = \pm 1$ and $x_2 = \pm 1$ represent the possible alternative choices of the measurements in R_1 and R_2, respectively, and let $r_1(x_1)$ and $r_2(x_2)$

represent the *variables* measured in R_1 and R_2, respectively, if the choices of the measurements in these regions are x_1 and x_2, respectively. Each *possible value* $r_1'(+1)$ of the variable $r_1(+1)$ is a sequence of n values $+1$ or -1, and so on. Thus, one of the following conditions is necessary for there to be no influence of x_1 upon $r_2(x_2)$, and no influence of x_2 upon $r_1(x_1)$:

a) If $x_2 = +1$, then there is some possible value $r_2'(+1)$ for the variable $r_2(+1)$ such that x_1 can be varied over its domain $[+1,-1]$ without $r_2'(+1)$ changing.

b) If $x_2 = -1$, then there is some possible value $r_2'(-1)$ for the variable $r_2(-1)$ such that x_1 can be varied over its domain $[+1,-1]$ without $r_2'(-1)$ changing.

c) If $x_1 = +1$, then there is some possible value $r_1'(+1)$ for the variable $r_1(+1)$ such that x_2 can be varied over its domain $[+1,-1]$ without $r_1'(+1)$ changing.

d) If $x_1 = -1$, then there is some possible value $r_1'(-1)$ for the variable $r_1(-1)$ such that x_2 can be varied over its domain $[+1,-1]$ without $r_1'(-1)$ changing.

These four conditions demand the existence of a set of four values

$$[r_1'(+1), r_1'(-1), r_2'(+1), \text{ and } r_2'(-1)]$$

and a set of eight values

$$[\bar{r}_1'(+1), \bar{r}_1'(+1), \bar{r}_1'(-1), \bar{r}_1'(-1), \bar{r}_2'(+1), \bar{r}_2'(+1), \bar{r}_2'(-1), \bar{r}_2'(-1)]$$

such that the following conditions hold:

$$(r_1'(+1), \bar{r}_2'(+1)) \text{ is poss. if } (x_1,x_2) = (+1,+1) \tag{1a}$$
$$(r_1'(+1), \bar{r}_2'(-1)) \text{ is poss. if } (x_1,x_2) = (+1,-1) \tag{1b}$$
$$(r_1'(-1), \bar{r}_2'(+1)) \text{ is poss. if } (x_1,x_2) = (-1,+1) \tag{1c}$$
$$(r_1'(-1), \bar{r}_2'(-1)) \text{ is poss. if } (x_1,x_2) = (-1,-1) \tag{1d}$$
$$(\bar{r}_1'(+1), r_2'(+1)) \text{ is poss. if } (x_1,x_2) = (+1,+1) \tag{1e}$$
$$(\bar{r}_1'(-1), r_2'(+1)) \text{ is poss. if } (x_1,x_2) = (-1,+1) \tag{1f}$$
$$(\bar{r}_1'(+1), r_2'(-1)) \text{ is poss. if } (x_1,x_2) = (+1,-1) \tag{1g}$$
$$(\bar{r}_1'(-1), r_2'(-1)) \text{ is poss. if } (x_1,x_2) = (-1,-1) \tag{1h}$$

where "is poss. if" means that the pair of possible values $(r_1'(+1)$, $\bar{r}_2'(+1))$, for example, must be compatible with the constraints imposed by quantum theory under the condition that (x_1,x_2) has the value indicated. Each possible value $r_1'(+1)$, and so forth, is some sequence of n values $+1$ or -1. The two conditions (1a) and (1b) express the condition

(c) that if $x_1 = +1$, then there is some possible value, call it $r_1'(+1)$, of the variable $r_1(+1)$ such that x_2 can, within the structure imposed by the theory, be varied over its domain, with the variable $r_1(+1)$ held fixed at the possible value $r_1'(+1)$. The remaining three pairs of equations express the remaining three conditions (a), (b), and (d).

An important distinction must be drawn at this point between satisfying the four conditions (a) through (d) disjunctively, and satisfying them conjunctively. In the disjunctive case, the possibilities used to satisfy the four conditions are contradictory possibilities, within the structure imposed by our general theoretical framework, whereas in the conjunctive case, these possibilities are noncontradictory, that is, mutually compatible within this theoretical structure. It will be argued later that the disjunctive solutions are irrelevant and may be discarded.

Consider then the two equations (1a) and (1e). These two equations represent two conditions that are to be imposed under the same condition, namely, $(x_1,x_2) = (+1,+1)$. The values $(r_1'(+1), \bar{r}_2'(+1))$ and $(\bar{r}_1'(+1), r_2'(+1))$ represent two possible values for the outcome of the decision that nature would be forced to make if $(x_1,x_2) = (+1,+1)$. The requirement that these two possibilities be noncontradictory demands that they be the same:

$$(r_1'(+1), \bar{r}_2'(+1)) = (\bar{r}_1'(+1), r_2'(+1)) \tag{2a}$$

One obtains in a similar way:

$$(r_1'(+1), \bar{r}_2'(-1)) = (\bar{r}_1'(+1), r_2'(-1)) \tag{2b}$$
$$(r_1'(-1), \bar{r}_2'(+1)) = (\bar{r}_1'(-1), r_2'(+1)) \tag{2c}$$
$$(r_1'(-1), \bar{r}_2'(-1)) = (\bar{r}_2'(-1), r_2'(-1)) \tag{2d}$$

These four equations reduce the eight equations (1) to the set of four equations:

$$(r_1'(+1), r_2'(+1)) \text{ is poss. if } (x_1,x_2) = (+1,+1) \tag{3a}$$
$$(r_1'(+1), r_2'(-1)) \text{ is poss. if } (x_1,x_2) = (+1,-1) \tag{3b}$$
$$(r_1'(-1), r_2'(+1)) \text{ is poss. if } (x_1,x_2) = (-1,+1) \tag{3c}$$
$$(r_1'(-1), r_2'(-1)) \text{ is poss. if } (x_1,x_2) = (-1,-1) \tag{3d}$$

Since quantum theory makes only statistical predictions, "everything is possible." However, for any $\delta > 0$, however small, one can make n sufficiently large so that the total probability that $|c - \bar{c}|$ is greater than 10^{-2} is smaller than δ. Thus, by ignoring a set of possibilities whose total probability can be made arbitrarily small by taking n sufficiently large, we can replace the condition "is poss." with "satisfies $|c - \bar{c}| < 10^{-2}$."

Then, the four conditions (3) on the set $(r_1{}'(+1), r_1{}'(-1), r_2{}'(+1), r_2{}'(-1))$ become the four conditions such that, for each of the four alternative possible values of (x_1, x_2),

$$|c(r_1{}'(x_1), r_2{}'(x_2)) - \bar{c}(x_1, x_2)| < 10^{-2}, \tag{4}$$

where $c(r_1, r_2)$ is the correlation function defined earlier, and $\bar{c}(x_1, x_2)$ is the predicted limiting value of $c(r_1, r_2)$ as n tends to infinity under the experimental condition (x_1, x_2). In other words, the requirement that the four conditions (a) through (d) be satisfied conjunctively, within the structure imposed by the general theoretical framework, demands the existence of at least one set of possible values $(r_1{}'(+1), r_1{}'(-1), r_2{}'(+1), r_2{}'(-1))$ such that the four equations (4) can be satisfied.

For certain arrangements of the experimental parameters, the predictions of quantum theory are as follows (Stapp, 1985a):

$$\bar{c}(+1,+1) = -1/\sqrt{2} \tag{5a}$$

$$\bar{c}(+1,-1) = -1/\sqrt{2} \tag{5b}$$

$$\bar{c}(-1,+1) = -1 \tag{5c}$$

$$\bar{c}(-1,-1) = 0 \tag{5d}$$

Thus, apart from the 1 percent deviations, the four equations (4) give

$$\frac{1}{n} \sum_{i=1}^{n} r_{1i}{}'(+1)\, r_{2i}{}'(+1) = -1/\sqrt{2} \tag{6a}$$

$$\frac{1}{n} \sum_{i=1}^{n} r_{1i}{}'(+1)\, r_{2i}{}'(-1) = -1/\sqrt{2} \tag{6b}$$

$$\frac{1}{n} \sum_{i=1}^{n} r_{1i}{}'(-1)\, r_{2i}{}'(+1) = -1 \tag{6c}$$

$$\frac{1}{n} \sum_{i=1}^{n} r_{1i}{}'(-1)\, r_{2i}{}'(-1) = 0 \tag{6d}$$

From (6c) one obtains $r_{1i}{}'(-1), = -r_{2i}{}'(+1)$, which allows (6d) to be written as

$$\frac{1}{n} \sum_{i=1}^{n} r_{2i}{}'(+1) r_{2i}{}'(-1) = 0. \tag{6e}$$

This result, combined with (6a) and (6b), and the fact that each r_{1i}' and r_{2i}' is either $+1$ or -1, allows one to write

$$\frac{1}{n} \sum_{i=1}^{n} (\sqrt{2}\, r_{1i}'(+1) + r_{2i}'(+1) + r_{2i}'(-1))^2 = 2 + 1 + 1 - 2 - 2 + 0 = 0. \quad (7)$$

But the fact that each r_{1i}' and r_{2i}' is either $+1$ or -1 also entails that

$$\frac{1}{n} \sum_{i=1}^{n} (\sqrt{2}\, r_{1i}'(+1) + r_{2i}'(+1) + r_{2i}'(-1))^2 \geq (\sqrt{2} - 2)^2. \quad (8)$$

Equations (7) and (8) are contradictory. The small 1 percent deviations are not large enough to undo this large contradiction. Thus, the four conditions (a) through (d) cannot be satisfied conjunctively.

The logical structure of the argument is this. In nature itself only one of the four values of (x_1, x_2) can be selected. However, our interest is in the structure of adequate theories and ideas about nature, not nature itself. Quantum theory provides a conjunction of predictions pertaining to possible alternative experimental situations. From the standpoint of theoretical structures, both logic and common language provide a basis for contemplating and describing connections between the situations that might prevail under related, possible alternative conditions. Classical physics is essentially a compendium of such connections.

The locality principle of Einstein, Podolsky, and Rosen is a theoretical connection of this kind. It states that essentially nothing in R_i can be disturbed or influenced by what the experimenter decides at the last minute to do in R_j ($j \neq i$). This is a conjunction of conditions, each of which is required to hold only under some condition on the choices of the experimenters. Our criterion for lack of influence converts this locality condition to the requirement that there must be at least one set of possible values for the outcomes of the various decisions that nature could be forced to make such that these possible values are both compatible with the predictions of quantum theory and unaffected by variations in the choice of the experimenter in the other region. However, it has just been demonstrated that there is no set of possible values that satisfies these two conditions.

It is worth emphasizing that the argument does not depend, either explicitly or implicitly, on the idea that the outcome of nature's decision is predetermined. The whole argument is phrased in a way that tacitly accepts the idea that the outcome of this decision is not predetermined. Nor is there any assumption that the result of any unperformed experiment is physically definite or determinate. For in the formulation of equations (1), the question is only whether there are any *possible values* for the outcomes that would allow nature's decisions in each region to remain unaltered as the variable x_j, representing the experimenter's choice in the other region, is varied. And the conditions (2) merely assert that if two of these possible values represent possible values for the outcome of the same decision, then they must, if noncontradictory, be the same. What the actual result "would be" were the experiment actually performed never enters into the argument; it is neither mentioned, nor represented, nor alluded to. Thus, the argument given here avoids the assumption of "counterfactual definiteness" upon which my 1968 and 1971 proofs were explicitly based (Stapp, 1971). The present argument also avoids the assumptions of determinism and hidden variables present in Bell's (1964) original work, the hidden-variable factorization property of Clauser and Shimony (1978), and the assumption of (microscopic) local realism on which that hidden-variable factorization property is based. Indeed, in the present approach the entire universe is treated as one giant black box with two inputs, which represent two tiny elements of freedom in the mental processes of the two experimenters, and two outputs, which represent the results appearing to the two observers; there is no separation of the world into devices and "quanta." Quanta are never mentioned; the predictions of quantum theory pertaining to what we will see at the macroscopic level are merely accepted as given numbers. Thus, there are no ontological assumptions beyond the two general assumptions: one, that the choices of the two experiments can be treated as two free and independent variables and two, that two conceivable possible values for the outcome of a single decision by nature are contradictory unless they are equal.

This brings us to the question of the disjunctive solutions of the conditions (a) through (d). These are the solutions in which one or more of the four conditions (2) fail. A failure of any one of these conditions means that the solutions to the four conditions (a) through (d) use, in some instances, contradictory possible values. The problem is to show that such solutions to the set of four conditions (a) through (d) can be ignored, and the necessary condition for noninfluence taken to be the conditions that the four conditions (a) through (d) can be satisfied conjunctively.

Let the four conditions (a) through (d) be called the four conditions C_i. Each condition C_i is a necessary condition for a corresponding property of noninfluence P_i. Each property P_i is of the form: "If the variable x_j has the value $x_j{}'$ then the choice of the value of the variable x_k ($k \neq j$)

does not influence the outcome of the decision that fixes the value of $r_i(x'j)$."

Each condition C_i is a necessary condition for the corresponding property P_i. The simple conjunction of the properties C_i is simply the conjunction of necessary conditions for the individual properties P_i to hold separately. This simple conjunction of the properties C_i allows the disjunctive solutions; there is no requirement that the possible values used to satisfy the four different conditions be noncontradictory. But one must distinguish the conjunction of the conditions C_i that the four properties P_i hold separately from the condition, C, that follows from the condition that they hold together.

This condition C can be expected to be stronger than the simple conjunction of the four properties C_i. For example, suppose P_1 were the property: a set of points S is confined to the x axis. Then P_1 would imply the condition C_1: the set S is confined to a set of dimension one. And if P_2 were the property: the set S is confined to the y axis, then P_2 would imply the condition C_2: the set S is confined to a set of dimension one. But the conjunction of P_1 and P_2 implies the condition, C, that the set S be confined to a set of dimension zero. This condition C is stronger than the conjunction of the two conditions C_1 and C_2.

In our case, the requirement that all four conditions P_i hold does not mean that, for each i, condition P_i holds while others fail. It means that within the theoretical structure under consideration, all four P_i hold conjunctively, hence without contradiction. Thus, the requirement inherent in the demand that all four conditions P_i hold conjunctively is that all four conditions be imposed together within a realm of noncontradictory possibilities. In order to show that these four conditions P_i cannot be satisfied within such a realm, it is sufficient to show that the four corresponding weaker conditions C_i cannot be satisfied within such a realm. But that is exactly what was shown when it was demonstrated that the four conditions C_i cannot be satisfied conjunctively.

This completes the proof that within the general theoretical framework established here, it is not possible to satisfy together the requirements that (1) there be no faster-than-light influences and (2) certain rudimentary two-quanta predictions of quantum theory hold. This theoretical framework is based on two assumptions. The first is that the choices of the two experimenters can, within the present, very limited context, be treated as free and independent variables. The second is that two possible values for the outcome of any decision nature can apparently be forced to make are either equal or contradictory.

The logical foundation for this EPR nonlocality property is the simple mathematical fact, which was proved above, that for the experiments under consideration here, it is impossible even to conceive or imagine any possible results for the outcomes of the four possible alternative measurements that conform to the predictions of quantum theory, but in which the possible results in each region are unaffected (that is, unaltered) by variations in *what is done* in the far-away region.

Consequences for Philosophy

The inadequacy of the concepts of classical physics as a foundation for a comprehensive metaphysics has prompted the view that physics has little to contribute to philosophy. Indeed, classical physics reduces each man to a local automaton, essentially cut off from any greater whole. This bleak isolation, compounded with inexorable predetermination, provides a basis for the most mundane philosophy. There is no possibility for a spiritual essence that man has unceasingly claimed as his birthright and no possible basis for human values other than self-interest. Moreover, the intractable irrationality of the classical mind-matter dichotomy defeats the whole enterprise of a comprehensive rational philosophy.

Today, however, the basic concepts of classical physics are known to be profoundly and fundamentally incorrect. Nature behaves in ways that are strictly incompatible with the basic idea of classical physics, namely, that the world is built up out of elementary, localizable real parts. These real parts were believed to be the atoms, or their constituents, and the local fields associated with them. But orthodox quantum theory tells us that these things can be represented only by probability amplitudes. And if one tries to find the meaning of these probability amplitudes by identifying the realities to which they refer, then these realities turn out to be the perceptible behavior of macroscopic measuring devices (Stapp, 1972). Yet these devices are themselves built from atoms. Thus, the search for basic physical realities leads us in circles; each atom turns out to be nothing but potentialities in the behavior pattern of others. What we find, therefore, are not elementary space-time realities, but rather a web of relationships in which no part can stand alone; every part derives its meaning and existence only from its place within the whole (Stapp, 1971). This holistic character of the world, as seen in the light of quantum theory, is rendered even more complete, and incompatible with classical ideas by the interconnectedness mediated by the faster-than-light influences that seem to be required if one wishes to have any adequate conceptualization of the physical world beyond the computational rules of present-day quantum theory.

The ontology most in harmony with the structure of quantum theory is the ontology described by Heisenberg. It is similar to the ontology of Whitehead (1978), with one very important difference. Whitehead, citing developments in science, mutilated the natural organic unity of his ontology by introducing "contemporary events," which stood in a relationship of causal disjunction; no one of them could influence any other. The cited development in science was the theory of relativity, which, within the deterministic framework of classical physics, involves the nonexistence of faster-than-light influences and hence the causal disjunction of events in spacelike separated regions. On the other hand, the basic postulates of relativity theory demand only the nonexistence of faster-than-light *signals,* not the nonexistence of faster-than-light influences.

In a nondeterministic context, such as quantum theory or Whitehead's ontology, it is possible to have faster-than-light influences that cannot be faster-than-light signals. The EPR nonlocality property of quantum theory appears to suggest that any ontology compatible with quantum theory must involve faster-than-light influences. Heisenberg's ontology fulfills this requirement, whereas Whitehead's ontology, if adulterated by "contemporary events," does not, at least if spacelike separated events are contemporary events, as is indicated by Whitehead.

Metaphysics would be of little worth if it were only a game for philosophers and had no practical consequences. Although the present forum is not the proper place for a discussion of technical applications in the realm of physics, let me just mention that reasons have been given elsewhere (Stapp, 1985a) for believing that recent technological developments will require an extension of the scope of quantum theory. To move forward from the present-day computational rules, which cover only a special limiting case, to a comprehensive general physical theory will probably be possible only with the aid of a metaphysical perspective. In this connection the metaphysical ideas discussed above suggest the need for building up, by the quantum process itself, the space-time structure that underlies present-day quantum theory. Work is currently in progress on this program, which holds some promise for extracting something useful in physics from the endeavor to obtain a comprehensive understanding of nature.

More appropriate to this forum is a discussion of the impact on human values of the penetration into general human awareness of the

quantum mechanical conception of nature. The importance of developments in this area can hardly be overstated. For human values control
human decisions, and human decisions control the future of all life on
this planet.

What a person values depends largely on his or her perceived connection to his or her perceived environment. This perceived environment
can be family, community, nation, and more abstract constructs. The
rise of classical physics had a profound impact on human values through
its impact on perceived connection to perceived environment. People
were educated to see the world as a giant machine, in which each person
was nothing but a local mechanical cog, whose whole history and future
were preordained at the beginning of time. The gods upon which prior
value systems were based were reduced to total impotence, once the initial creative instant had passed. As for man himself, this reduction to
impotence was complete. Moreover, all but the most mundane of material links between a person and anything else was banished.

This classical view of man and nature is still promulgated in the
name of science. Thus, science is seen as demanding a perception of man
as nothing more than a local cog in a mechanical universe, unconnected
to any creative aspect of nature. For, according to the classical picture,
every creative aspect of nature exhausted itself during the first instant.

What science will eventually uncover is not yet known. But atomic
physics, in the form of quantum theory, has already established that this
mundane classical view is *fundamentally* incorrect; that in itself is a
tremendously important achievement, recognition of which should be
reverberating throughout our schools and faculties. Although no alternative picture of nature has gained general acceptance among quantum
scientists, the most orthodox view, and the one closest to the ideas of
most practicing quantum physicists, is undoubtedly the ontology of
Heisenberg. Its explicitly nonlocal character and present lack of detailed
explication has been a deterrent to its acceptance by practical-minded
scientists. But the first apparent deficiency, its nonlocal character, is almost certainly a necessary feature of any coherent picture of nature that
is compatible with rudimentary predictions of quantum theory. The second deficiency, its lack of explication, awaits an empirical and theoretical exploration of the boundaries of the scope of present-day quantum
theory.

In the Heisenberg ontology, the real world of classical physics is
transformed into a world of potentialities, which condition, but do not
control, the world of actual events. These events, or acts, create the

actual form of the evolving universe by deciding between the possibilities created by the evolving potentialities. These creative acts stand outside space-time and presumably create all space-time relationships. Human mental acts belong to this world of creative acts, but do not exhaust it (Stapp, 1985b).

The scientific task of explicating this general quantum-mechanical ontology is just beginning. But even the general features of the quantum ontology involve a conception of man and nature profoundly different from the picture provided by classical physics. For man appears no longer as an isolated automaton. He appears rather as an integral part of the highly nonlocal creative activity of the universe. This revision of the conception of a person, and of his perceived relation to the rest of nature, cannot help but have an immense impact on what is perceived as valuable. It must inevitably lead us away from the egocentric bias that was the rational product of the ontology of classical physics, to the values inherent in the image of self, not as a local isolated automaton but rather as a nonlocalizable integrated aspect of the creative impulse of the universe. The critical question is whether this offering of science in the realm of human values can come to fruition soon enough to avert the perils that have arisen from the power of science in other realms.

References

Bell, J. S. 1964. On the Einstein-Podolsky-Rosen Paradox. *Physics* 1: 195–200.

Bohm, D. 1952. A Suggested Interpretation of Quantum Theory in Terms of "Hidden" Variables. *Physical Review* 85: 166–93.

Bohm, D., and Aharanov, Y. 1957. Discussion of Experimental Proofs for the Paradox of Einstein, Podolsky, and Rosen. *Physical Review* 103: 1070ff.

Bohm, D., and Hiley, B. J. 1986. An Ontological Basis for the Quantum Theory. *Physics Reports* 144: 321ff.

Clausen, J., and Shimony, A. 1978. Bell's Theorem: Experimental Tests and Implications. *Rep. Prog. Physics* 41: 1881ff.

Einstein, A., Podolsky, B., and Rosen, N. 1935. Can Quantum-

Mechanical Description of Physical Reality be Considered Complete? *Physical Review* 47: 777–86.

Einstein, A. 1951. Einstein's Reply. *Albert Einstein: Philosopher-Scientist.* Ed. P. A. Schilpp. New York: Open Court.

Everett, H., III. 1957. "Relative State" Formulation of Quantum Mechanics. *Reviews of Modern Physics* 29: 454–62.

Heisenberg, W. 1930. *The Physical Principles of the Quantum Theory.* New York: Dover.

_____. 1958. *Physics and Philosophy.* New York: Harper & Row.

James, W. 1890. *The Principles of Psychology.* New York: Henry Holt.

Stapp, H. 1971. S-Matrix Interpretation of Quantum Mechanics. *Physical Review* D3: 1303–20.

_____. 1972. The Copenhagen Interpretation. *American Journal of Physics* 40: 1098–16.

_____. 1975. Bell's Theorem and World Process. *Il Nuovo Cimento* 29B: 270–76.

_____. 1982. Mind, Matter and Quantum Mechanics. *Foundations of Physics* 12: 363–99.

_____. 1985. Bell's Theorem and the Foundations of Quantum Physics. *American Journal of Physics* 53: 306–17. (a)

_____. 1985. Consciousness and Values in Quantum Universe. *Foundations of Physics* 15: 35–47. (b)

_____. Forthcoming. Are Faster-Than-Light Influences Necessary? Lawrence Berkeley Laboratory Report LBL 22107. *Quantum Mechanics versus Local Realism—The Einstein, Podolsky, and Rosen Paradox.* Ed. F. Selleri. New York: Plenum Press.

Whitehead, A. N. 1978. *Process and Reality.* Ed. D. R. Griffin and D. W. Shernburne. New York: Free Press.

Chapter 4

HOW TO KILL SCHRÖDINGER'S CAT

Jeffrey Bub

Introduction

I must confess that I find the world view of modern physics a rather daunting subject for debate, and the task of outlining an appropriate new metaphysics even more sobering. I feel a little like the elephant in one of Gary Larson's (1984) cartoons, captioned "The Elephant's Nightmare." In a large concert hall, audience hushed after the final round of coughs and throatclearings, an elephant is sitting at a piano with an alarmed expression on his face. His thoughts read: "What am I doing here? I can't play this thing! I'm a *flutist* for crying-out-loud!"

My own interest in physics has been largely confined to certain foundational problems in quantum mechanics: the problem of hidden variables or completeness, the problem of measurement or collapse of the wave function, problems of interference and locality, and so on. I want to discuss some of these problems here and to show where the tension lies between quantum theory and a common-sense metaphysics.

A good starting point is the Bohr-Einstein controversy, which began to make the headlines around the middle of 1935, after publication of the Einstein-Podolsky-Rosen (1935) article. In the Sunday issue of *The New York Times* (28 July 1935)—oddly enough, in the travel section, sandwiched between advertisements for "Gay One Day Cruises Up the Cool Hudson and a 12 day cruise to Havana for $108"—there is an article entitled "The Week in Science: Bohr and Einstein at Odds: They Begin a Controversy Concerning the Fundamental Nature of Reality."

I quote from the *Times* article:

> The Einstein-Bohr controversy has just begun this week in the current issue of *Nature,* British Scientific Publication, with a preliminary challenge by Professor Bohr to Professor Einstein and with a promise by Professor Bohr that "a fuller development of this argument will be given in an article to be published shortly in the *Physical Review.*" Undoubtedly, Professor Bohr will answer, and there is the possibility that other leading scientists will enter the arena.

What was this controversy all about? Bohr's "challenge" in *Nature* is essentially an announcement of his forthcoming reply (1935) to the Einstein-Podolsky-Rosen article, in which a quantum mechanical counterexample to the Copenhagen interpretation is proposed involving two "complementary" quantities (represented by noncommuting operators in the theory) that appear to have "simultaneous reality." If the reasoning of Einstein, Podolsky, and Rosen is correct, Bohr's complementarity thesis (which takes quantum mechanics as a complete theory and denies the simultaneous reality of complementary quantities) does not do justice to the pattern of statistical correlations between coupled systems in quantum mechanics.

Einstein was quite contemptuous of the philosophy of complementarity. In a letter to Schrödinger, he (1928/1967) remarks:

> The Heisenberg-Bohr tranquillizing philosophy—or religion?—is so delicately contrived that it provides a gentle pillow for the true believer. So let him lie there. (p. 31)

It seems to me that Einstein saw the conceptually puzzling features of quantum mechanics as a statistical theory in the apparent incompatibility of the theory with certain fundamental principles of *realism.* Formally, the problem concerns the difficulty of relating the probability assignments defined by the quantum state to distributions over determinate values of the physical magnitudes.

Einstein's position is clearly articulated by Pauli (1954/1971a) in correspondence with Max Born.

> Now from my conversations with Einstein I have seen that he takes exception to the assumption, essential to quantum mechanics, that *the state of a system is defined only by specification of an experimental arrangement. Einstein wants to know nothing of this*. . . . It seems to me that the discussion with Einstein can be reduced to this hypothesis of his, which I have called the idea (or the 'ideal') of the 'detached observer.' (p. 218)

In a subsequent letter (1954/1971b), Pauli adds:

> In particular, Einstein does not consider the concept of 'determinism' to be as fundamental as it is frequently held to be (as he told me emphatically many times) . . . he *disputes* that he uses as criterion for the admissibility of a theory the question: 'Is it rigorously deterministic?' Einstein's point of departure is 'realistic' rather than 'deterministic,' which means that his philosophical prejudice is a different one. (p. 221)

Einstein clearly distinguishes *realism* from *determinism*. What he requires of a physical theory is that the properties of systems described by the theory are *determinate,* that is, that the values of the physical magnitudes are definite without regard to any consideration of the observational context. Whether or not the properties of a system at one time are determined by the properties of the system at an earlier time is a further issue, which Einstein (1950/1967) regards as "thoroughly nebulous":

> If one wants to consider the quantum theory as final (in principle), then one must believe that a more complete description would be useless because there would be no laws for it. If that were so then physics could only claim that the interest of shopkeepers and engineers; the whole thing would be a wretched bungle. . . . But it seems to me that the fundamentally statistical character of the theory is simply a consequence of the incompleteness of the description. This says nothing about the deterministic character of the theory; that is a thoroughly nebulous concept anyway. (pp. 39–40)

What are the difficulties in the way of completing the quantum theory *in principle*? Why can we not reconstruct the statistics on the basis of a hidden variable model? Such a theory introduces parameters labeling what might be termed "property states" and probability measures over these property states, which generate the statistics defined by the quantum mechanical "statistical states" (specified by unit vectors or statistical operators in Hilbert space).

By a *property state* I mean an assignment of values to the quantum mechanical magnitudes or "observables," that is, a list of properties of the system, or an assignment of truth values to the propositions of the system. Formally, such a state might be represented by an ultrafilter in an algebra, or the atom generating the ultrafilter. A *statistical state* is an assignment of probabilities to the properties of the system. Usually we understand such a statistical state as a probability measure in the standard sense over the atoms, or ultrafilters or phase points or lists of properties. For example, suppose the logical space of a theory (which specifies the logical relations between propositions or events) is a Boolean algebra, represented mathematically as a set of subsets of a set (as in classical mechanics, the set being the position-momentum phase space of the system). The property state can be represented by a point (which corresponds to an atom in the Boolean algebra), or collection of sets to which the point belongs (this is the ultrafilter of propositions generated by the point), or a listing of all the properties characterizing the system at a particular time. The statistical state is represented by a probability measure over the phase points.

A fundamental problem of interpretation arises for quantum mechanics because the theory provides us with a set of states that are apparently statistical states, without specifying any property states. The question is then, What do these statistical states mean? The problem of interpretation might be formulated this way: What are the property states of quantum systems, and how are the statistical states related to the property states? (One possible answer is that there is no property states for quantum systems, but something still has to be said about how to understand the statistical states.)

Two core results in contemporary foundational research are relevant here. A corollary to Gleason's (1957) theorem, proved independently by Kochen and Specker (1967), suggests that property states are only possible for spin-1/2 systems; in the case of more complex quantum systems, value assignments to the observables simply do not exist. Bell's argument (Bell, 1964) relates the nonexistence of hidden variables underlying the quantum statistics to the violation of a physically reasonable locality condition.[1] Here it is the probability measures and not the property states that are deemed impossible (on physical, not logical grounds).

Bell's Results

I would like to discuss the contents of these results here, as I see them.

Consider a spin-1 system. The magnitudes or observables of the system—spin in a certain direction in real space—all take three possible values, represented conventionally as -1, 0, $+1$. These magnitudes are represented by self-adjoint operators in a three-dimensional Hilbert space, which for the purposes of the discussion you can picture geometrically as a Euclidean space. (A finite-dimensional Hilbert space is in fact a Euclidean space of vectors with complex coefficients). As you probably know, such operators do not form a commutative algebra. But how does noncommutativity prevent the assignment of a list of values to the observables? How can there be a logical contradiction—prior to any question of assigning probabilities to the hypothetical property states—in specifying a list of values for a set (perhaps the entire set) of noncommuting observables?

Kochen and Specker (1967) consider a particular set of 117 spin magnitudes corresponding to 117 directions in real space. Each of these magnitudes has three possible values, associated with an orthogonal triple of lines in a Hilbert space of three dimensions. So picture 117 orthogonal triples of lines in Hilbert space. A list of values of these 117 spin observables—for example, 0 for observable #1, -1 for observable # 2, and so on—picks out one and only one line in each orthogonal triple. So far so good. But it turns out that the set of 117 observables is so chosen that for *any* selection of one line from each of the 117 triples, it is possible to find at least three observables, representing *orthogonal* directions of spin in real space, that involve a problem. The problem is this. Take such a set of spin observables, representing spin in three orthogonal directions. This gives us three orthogonal triples of lines in Hilbert space, or nine lines altogether. Because the three triples of lines are associated with spin in three orthogonal directions in real space, the three lines (in the nine) corresponding to the 0 spin value in each case also form an orthogonal triple in Hilbert space; that is, it turns out that the three pairs of orthogonal lines in Hilbert space are so oriented that the 0-lines form a fourth orthogonal triple.

Now this triple—formed by the 0-lines of the three orthogonal spins—does not represent a spin magnitude. It is a physical magnitude, measurable by electric fields and not magnetic fields, but not a spin magnitude. Since this magnitude, call it H, can only have one value specified by a given property state, *it follows that only one of the three orthogonal spin magnitudes can have the 0 value,* if we assume what might be termed a *meshing condition,* which means the line picked out by the property state in the H triple must also be the same line picked out by the property state in the associated spin triple (since each of the lines in H belongs to one of the orthogonal spin triples as the 0 line).

The impossibility of assigning a list of values to the 117 spin observables arises because any assignment of values will involve at least three orthogonal spins getting values inconsistent with the assignment of one and only one value to the associated H observable, on the assumption that value assignments by the property state must mesh for spin observables (J-observables) and H-observables.

So the Kochen and Specker problem—a problem in the way of defining property states—is in a sense a multiple-field problem: It involves a contradiction in assigning values to sets of observables, J-observables and H-observables, measurable by different fields (magnetic and electric). As long as we restrict ourselves to the spin observables alone, or the H-observables alone, there is no problem in assigning all these observables precise values, in a purely mathematical sense. It is only when we require a meshing of the values assigned to the spin observables with the values assigned to the nonspin observables like H that we have a consistency problem.

So suppose we assign values hypothetically to all the spin observables, for example, all the observables generated from a single spin observable, spin-in-the-direction, by the rotation group. It turns out that we run into another problem if we try to reconstruct the quantum statistics by probability measures over these value assignments. We can generate the probabilities assigned by any quantum state to all the spin observables by an appropriate choice of probability measure over the set of value assignments, but we cannot get the probabilities that quantum mechanics assigns to sequences of values of noncommuting spin observables. This is a single-field problem and applies even for a spin-$1/2$ system, where we have only two possible spin values, $+1/2$ and $-1/2$. The simplest way to see this is to derive a version of Bell's inequality for sequences of measurements of noncommuting spin observables on a single system, which quantum mechanics violates. In effect, this is simply a way of expressing quantum mechanical interference; the inequality expresses a relationship between probabilities we would expect to get if sequential probabilities were derivable via classical conditionalization, where each measurement in the sequence gives us new information that we use additively to change the probability distribution according to the usual (Bayesian) rule for revising probabilities. (See Bub, 1981, pp. 280–83 for details.)

We *can* get the correct probabilities for sequences of measurements if we assume a disturbance by the measuring instrument, which modifies the probabilities over and above the standard modification induced by the mere addition of new information. But then we run into a further difficulty, as Bell showed by an ingenious extension of the original Einstein-Podolsky-Rosen argument. It is possible to create in the laboratory pairs of correlated quantum systems that are, in a sense, mirror images of each other. Instead of considering a sequence of measurements on a single system, for example, spin-in-the-x-direction followed by spin-in-the-y-direction, we consider a pair of measurements, spin-in-the-x-direction on the first system and spin-in-the-y-direction on the second system. We get a similar inequality for the pair of measurements as for the sequence, expressing in essence the same interference effect. Only now, we cannot account for this effect on the basis of an assumption of disturbance by the measuring instrument, since the two systems can be far apart (even separated by a spacelike interval). (See Bub, 1981.)

So much then for the notion of a property state in the sense of a list of values for *all* the observables of a quantum mechanical system. Any attempt to "complete" quantum mechanics by defining property states is going to come up against some aspect of the problem of interference.

What about the possibility of defining a property state as a list of values of *some* of the observables of a quantum system? There are a variety of versions of this proposal. Jauch and Piron (1969) first proposed defining a quantum mechanical property state as an ultrafilter in the non-Boolean lattice of quantum propositions, just as a classical state is definable as an ultrafilter in the Boolean lattice of subsets of phase space. What this means is simply that, for a quantum system associated with a certain statistical state represented by a vector or one-dimensional subspace in Hilbert space, all the quantum propositions represented by subspaces above this one-dimensional subspace or line are assigned the truth value "true"; all those that are orthogonal to these are assigned the value "false," and the remaining propositions are assigned no truth value. Equivalently, all those propositions assigned probability one by the quantum statistical state are taken as true; all those propositions assigned probability zero are taken as false, and all the rest are regarded as neither true nor false.[2]

Schrödinger's Cat

Now it is precisely this proposal, or any proposal to define a quantum property state as a listing of *some* of the system's properties, that leads to the measurement problem, or the problem of Schrödinger's cat. The cat simply dramatizes the difficulty inherent in defining a property state for quantum systems as a partial list of properties, leaving the rest indeterminate—what Schrödinger (1935/1983, p. 157) referred to as a "blurred model" of reality.

Schrödinger considers a cat, initially alive, placed in a box with a device capable of killing the cat if triggered. What triggers the device is a quantum event, say the passage of a spin-1/2 particle through a Stern-Gerlach magnet with two possibilities for the result, up (or +1/2) and down (or –1/2). If the particle goes down, the device is triggered and the cat is killed; if the particle goes up, the cat remains alive. If the initial state of the quantum system is a superposition of the two spin states, with equal possibilities for spin-up and spin-down, we would predict the demise of the cat with probability 1/2. The difficulty is that, according to the theory, after the particle has passed through the magnet but before we open the box and look, the state of the entire system, particle + cat (or, more precisely, particle + apparatus + cat) is described by a linear superposition with equal coefficients for [spin-up, cat alive] and [spin down, cat dead]. If we now apply the Jauch and Piron (1969) rule, only the propositions about the composite system that are above this vector in the lattice ordering (those assigned probability one) are true, and only those that are assigned probability zero are false. Since neither the proposition "the spin of the particle is up and the cat is alive" nor the proposition "the spin of the particle is down and the cat is dead" is assigned probability one or zero, neither of these propositions is true or false.

On this proposal, therefore, prior to opening the box the cat must have made a transition from a property state of being alive to a state of limbo, neither alive nor dead. This is clearly absurd. A further transition from the indeterminate state of limbo to a final state of alive, or a final state of dead (exclusively), is required to account for what we actually find when we open the box and look—and this is not accounted for by the theory. There is no way of avoiding this conclusion on the proposal that the property state is defined by a partial list of properties, essentially because of the linearity of state transitions in the theory and the way in which the coupling between interacting systems is represented in quantum mechanics.

Therefore, taking the property state of a quantum system as represented by a list of *all* the possible properties (in the sense of a consistent yes-no assignment[3] to every range of values of every observable of the system) leads to the well-known difficulties of Kochen and Specker and of Bell, ultimately the inability to deal adequately with quantum interference. Taking the property state as represented by *some* of the possible properties leads to the measurement problem.

A Suggested Resolution

The proposal I want to consider is that we simply drop the notion of a property state for quantum systems with a finite number of degrees of freedom: *a finite quantum system has a statistical state, but no property state.* This is the significance of the "irreducibility" of the quantum statistics; there is no "list of properties" characterizing a finite quantum system at a particular time.

What do the probabilities generated by the statistical states mean if there are no property states for such systems? What are the measures defined over if not possible lists of properties? One answer to this question is provided by Bohr's complementarity interpretation. The probabilities refer to "individual phenomena appearing under conditions defined by classical physical concepts," where the term *phenomenon* is used "to refer to the observations obtained under specified circumstances, including an account of the whole experimental arrangement" (Bohr, 1949/1983, p. 46).

I want to consider a different proposal that depends on a fundamental qualitative difference in quantum mechanics between systems with a finite number of degrees of freedom and systems with an infinite number of degrees of freedom.

In the finite case, according to a theorem of von Neumann (1931), there exists exactly one irreducible Hilbert space representation of the canonical commutation relations (up to unitary equivalence). This uniqueness theorem breaks down in the infinite case: There exist many inequivalent, irreducible representations of the canonical commutation relations. (For an account see Emch, 1972, 1984; and Sewell, 1986.

Consider now a macroscopic measuring instrument as a quantum system with an infinite number of degrees of freedom. The "pointer readings" corresponding to different values of a macromagnitude are associated with inequivalent Hilbert space representations of the algebra, and the appropriate Hilbert space for the measuring instrument can be represented as a *direct sum* of these Hilbert spaces.[4] The direct sum is itself a Hilbert space with a *restricted superposition principle;* linear superpositions of vectors corresponding to different "pointer readings" are excluded. In other words, the Hilbert space of the macroinstrument incorporates a "superselection rule" for the macromagnitude associated with the "pointer readings." The important point here is that *this super-selection rule reflects the underlying possibility structure of the system* (the projection lattice of the Hilbert space representation) and is not imposed *ad hoc*.

Suppose a measuring instrument, M, characterized in this way inter-acts with a quantum system, S, with a finite number of degrees of free-dom, so as to set up a correlation between pointer readings of M and values of an S-magnitude, 0. It can be shown (Hepp, 1972; Wan, 1980) that the final statistical state of the composite system is represented by a *mixture* of tensor products of 0-eigenvectors and vectors corresponding to pointer readings of M on a direct sum of Hilbert spaces, each compo-nent of the direct sum being a product of the Hilbert space of S and one of the Hilbert spaces associated with a particular pointer reading of M.

What we have then is the following picture: A quantum system is associated with a noncommutative algebra of physical magnitudes of a non-Boolean logical space (the projection lattice of the algebra). Such systems do not possess a property state (except in the infinite limit), but they can be characterized by a statistical state. Only quantum systems with an infinite number of degrees of freedom have determinate proper-ties. The possibility of determinate properties at the macrolevel depends on the existence of superselection rules, reflecting the decomposition of the Hilbert space representation of the algebra into a direct sum of Hilbert spaces, which is a feature of the infinite case. The probabilities specified by a statistical state, say, for the spin components of an elec-tron, do not refer to measures over property states of the electron ("lists of spin component values"). Rather, the probabilities refer to measures over the determinate alternatives associated with the direct sum of Hilbert spaces characterizing the electron-instrument composite system: the electron-cum-Stern-Gerlach-apparatus.

What is objective before the measurement interaction is the possibil-ity structure of the electron and the initial statistical state of the electron, the possibility structure of the measuring instrument and the initial sta-tistical state of the measuring instrument, and the determinate macro-properties of the measuring instrument (the property state of the macroinstrument). The final position of the pointer depends on the ini-tial statistical state, the nature of the interaction, and the underlying possibility structure or logical space. The important point for the mea-surement problem is the qualitative difference between systems with a finite number of degrees of freedom and systems with an infinite number of degrees of freedom.

Let me now try to sum up the discussion. I should perhaps first clear up two loose ends. One concerns Bohr's (1935) reply to the Einstein-Podolsky-Rosen (1935) challenge. The other concerns Bell's (1964) extension of the Einstein-Podolsky-Rosen argument as a difficulty for Einstein's position. The Einstein-Podolsky-Rosen argument posed the following dilemma: Either quantum mechanics is incomplete (in a sense analogous to classical statistical mechanics relative to classical mechanics), or two complementary quantities (represented by noncommuting operators in the theory) cannot have simultaneous reality. The statistical correlations of the coupled systems in the Einstein-Podolsky-Rosen example cannot be understood, so the argument goes, without assuming that certain complementary quantities have simultaneous reality. It follows that quantum mechanics is an incomplete theory. Bohr's response to this argument defends a particular completeness thesis, while Bell's extension of the argument seems to exclude any sensible notion of incompleteness. It would seem, then, that Bohr is the ultimate victor in the debate with Einstein.

I have shown how the results of Kochen and Specker (1967) and Bell (1964) exclude taking a property state in quantum mechanics as defined by a list of values for *all* the quantum mechanical observables. The measurement problem rules out defining a property state by a list of values for *some* of the observables. The proposal that a quantum system with a finite number of degrees of freedom has no property states has some affinity with Bohr's position, but borrows also from Einstein's realism.

For Bohr, quantum systems manifest their properties under experimental conditions defined by classical concepts. Change the conditions over here, and you modify the properties of quantum systems over there, not via a "mechanical disturbance" of the system but merely in virtue of the fact that a quantum system *has no properties* except in the context of a specific (experimental) macroenvironment that is described in terms of the concepts of classical physics. This conception shatters the unity of classical physics, because we can no longer conceive of the macrosystems that are our measuring instruments as mere aggregates of microsystems, for *these* systems have no properties except in the context of a super-macro-environment. How macrosystems, considered as many-body microsystems in quantum mechanics, ever come to have (classical) properties is a mystery in the Copenhagen interpretation. Yet Einstein's realist alternative seems to be excluded by the theorems of Kochen and Specker and Bell.

I think the realist intuition is that to make sense of a quantum mechanical picture of the world we must have *determinateness* at *some* level in the theoretical description. On the view I have sketched, determinate properties emerge at the macrolevel on the basis of a purely quantum mechanical picture in which a macroscopic system is idealized as an infinite collection of particles. The trick is to notice that property states are only definable to the extent that the superposition principle (interference) breaks down. This occurs for systems with an infinite number of degrees of freedom through the failure of von Neumann's representation theorem. So superselection rules are not imposed on the theory by fiat but follow naturally from the failure of von Neumann's theorem for infinite systems.

The superposition principle characterizes the behavior of quantum systems with a finite number of degrees of freedom and is responsible for all the phenomena of interference and nonlocality. For the reasons outlined above in the analysis of the Kochen and Specker theorem, Bell's result, and Schrödinger's cat argument or the measurement problem, such systems can have statistical states but no property states. We get determinateness or definiteness of properties at the macrolevel through the emergence of macroscopic property states as a *collective* phenomenon following the breakdown of the superposition principle. And superposition fails because von Neumann's representation theorem no longer holds for systems with an infinite number of degrees of freedom.

Clearly this view requires the idealization of macrosystems as quantum mechanical systems with literally an *infinite* number of degrees of freedom. For von Neumann's representation theorem does not fail for a system with a very large but finite number of degrees of freedom, and the superposition principle still applies to such systems. The question we have to consider now is whether this idealization, which is clearly essential to the interpretation outlined, is compatible with realism in the sense we have been considering.

Realism

I think it is worthwhile to make a distinction here between two very different kinds of idealization involved in the application of a physical theory. We often employ what might be termed *pragmatic idealizations*. For example, to derive the Boyle-Charles law relating pressure, volume, and temperature for a gas, we idealize the system as a collection of point particles that interact only through perfectly elastic collisions (the intermolecular forces are assumed to be zero). A more sophisticated model yielding van der Waals' law assumes that the molecules are spheres that occupy a finite volume and interact by short-range repulsive forces and long-range attractive forces. Maxwell's theory of the electromagnetic field idealizes matter as continuous, with no atomic structure. To account for the phenomenon of dispersion—the variation of refractive index with wavelength—we use an atomic model in which the field interacts with the electrons in the atoms. Each such idealization is pragmatic in the sense that it provides a convenient theoretical description that can be improved upon, in principle, by a "more realistic" idealization. The mark of a pragmatic idealization is that it forms an element of a sequence, satisfying conditions of mutual consistency, reducibility, and convergence.

The application of a physical theory also involves *essential idealizations,* as in the classical (statistical) mechanical descriptions of thermodynamic properties such as temperature or entropy. Here we idealize a macrosystem, which we think of as composed of a very large but finite number of particles, as an infinite system in order to provide a description of collective phenomena at the macrolevel (such as phase transitions). These phenomena are relatively insensitive to the number of constituent particles and their precise motions at the microlevel and involve macroconcepts (such as "gas," "liquid," "solid," "temperature," and so on) that do not apply to single particles. For example, Boltzmann's derivation of the Maxwell velocity distribution law for a gas at equilibrium at a given temperature applies classical mechanics and statistical assumptions to a model of N particles with total kinetic energy E divided into J discrete units e with $E = Je$. A microstate of the system is defined by assigning J_1 units of energy to particle 1, J_2 units of energy to particle 2, and so forth, such that $\sum_i J_i = J$. The Maxwell distribution is obtained by taking limit $J \to \infty$, $e \to 0$, $N \to \infty$, with E/N fixed. (See Brush, 1983, p. 64 for a discussion. Brush points out that for a finite number of particles, the velocity distribution for a single particle depends on the velocities of the other particles and this velocity has a finite maximum.) The model is in effect an asymptotic idealization sanctioned by classical mechanics that yields properties characterizing the collective behavior of large ensembles of particles that are qualitatively different from the properties of individual systems in the collective. As such, the asymptotic character of the idealization is essential and cannot be dispensed with, if we want to describe the thermodynamic features of the system within the framework of classical mechanics.

It seems to me that the situation in quantum mechanics is quite analogous, with one crucial difference. In a classical world, thermodynamic properties emerge as collective phenomena in a many-body system that has determinate property states at the microlevel. In a quantum world, *the very determinateness of properties is itself a collective or cooperative phenomenon.* Schrödinger's cat is presumably composed of 10^{24} particles, give or take a few, but if we want to describe features of this many-body system that are essentially collective in nature, an asymptotic idealization is required that is essential to the description and not merely pragmatic. The determinateness of properties (via the failure of von Neumann's representation theorem) follows automatically in such a model, but this is achieved through the formal vehicle of an idealization that is not exclusive to quantum mechanics but characterizes the description of genuinely collective phenomena in both classical and quantum theories.

I conclude that if realism is a viable philosophical position for classical physics, it is no less viable for quantum physics. We can kill Schrödinger's cat if we take into account the difference between microsystems and macrosystems in quantum mechanics.

Notes

1. This is the *locus classicus* of what has now become an extensive literature. For further references see Wheeler and Zurek (1983).

2. One could also take Bohr's complementarity interpretation as a similar proposal, with the property states defined as Boolean ultrafilters in the maximal Boolean subalgebras selected from the lattice of quantum propositions by different complete specifications of the experimental conditions.

3. Consistent in the sense that if the range of values R of an observable 0 is assigned the value 'yes,' then the complement of R is assigned 'no,' and so on. Formally, a consistent yes-no assignment to every range of values of every observable is a 2-valued homomorphism on the algebra of properties defined by the ranges (each range of values of each observable corresponds to a proposition).

4. A direct sum of two Hilbert spaces is a Hilbert space generated from the set of ordered pairs of vectors, one from each of the component Hilbert spaces, with a scalar product defined by $<(u,v)|(u',v')> = <u|u'> + <v|v'>$, and vector addition and scalar multiplication defined by $(u,v) + (u',v') = (u+u', v+v')$ $c(u,v) = (cu,cv)$. It follows from the definition of the scalar product that states represented by vectors in different components of the direct sum do not show interference: $<(u,0)|(0,v)> = 0$.

References

Bell, J. S. 1964. On the Einstein-Podolsky-Rosen Paradox. *Physics* 1: 195–200. Reprinted in J. A. Wheeler and W. H. Zurek, eds. 1983. *Quantum Theory and Measurement*. Princeton: Princeton University Press.

Bohr, N. 1935. Can Quantum-Mechanical Description of Physical Reality Be Considered Complete? *Physical Review* 48: 696–702. Reprinted in J. A. Wheeler and W. H. Zurek, eds. 1983. *Quantum Theory and Measurement*. Princeton: Princeton University Press.

_____. 1949. Discussion with Einstein on Epistemological Problems in Modern Physics. *Albert Einstein: Philosopher-Scientist*. Ed. P. A. Schlip. Evanston Ill.: Open Court. Reprinted in J. A. Wheeler and W. H. Zurek, eds. 1983. *Quantum Theory and Measurement*. Princeton: Princeton University Press.

Brush, S. G. 1983. *Statistical Physics and the Atomic Theory of Matter From Boyle and Newton to Landau and Onsager*. Princeton: Princeton University Press.

Bub, J. 1976. Hidden Variables and Locality. *Foundations of Physics* 6: 511ff.

_____. 1981. Hidden Variables and Quantum Logic—a Sceptical Review. *Erkenntnis* 16: 275–93.

Einstein, A. 1967. Letter to Schrödinger. *Letters on Wave Mechanics*. Ed. K. Przibram and trans. M. J. Klein. New York: Philosophical Library. (Letter dated 31 May 1928.)

_____. 1967. Letter to E. Schrödinger. *Letters on Wave Mechanics*. Ed. K. Prizbram and trans. M. J. Klein. New York: Philosophical Library. (Letter dated 22 December 1950.)

Einstein, A., Podolsky, B., and Rosen, N. 1935. Can Quantum-Mechanical Description of Physical Reality Be Considered Complete? *Physical Review* 47: 777–86. Reprinted in J. A. Wheeler and W. H. Zurek, eds. 1983. *Quantum Theory and Measurement*. Princeton: Princeton University Press.

Emch, G. G. 1972. *Algebraic Methods in Statistical Mechanics and Quantum Field Theory*. New York: John Wiley & Sons.

Emch, G. G. 1984. *Mathematical and Conceptual Foundations of 20th Century Physics*. Amsterdam: North Holland Mathematics Series (Volume 100).

Gleason, A. M. 1957. Measures on the Closed Subspaces of a Hilbert Space. *Journal of Mathematical Mechanics* 6: 885–93.

Hepp, K. 1972. Quantum Theory of Measurement and Macroscopic Observables. *Helvetica Physical Acta* 45: 237–48.

Jauch, J. M., and Piron, C. 1969. On the Structure of Quantal Proposition Systems. *Helvetica Physica Acta* 42: 842–48.

Kochen, S., and Specker, E. P. 1967. The Problem of Hidden Variables in Quantum Mechanics. *Journal of Mathematical Mechanics* 17: 59–87.

Larson, Gary. 1984. *The Far Side Gallery*. New York: Andrews, McMeel, and Parker.

Neumann, J. von. 1931. Die Eindeudigkeit der Schrödingerschen Operatoren. *Mathematischen Annalen* 104: 570–78.

Pauli, W. 1971. Letter to M. Born. *The Born-Einstein Letters*. Ed. M. Born. New York: Walker & Co. (Letter dated 3 March 1954.) (a)

_____. 1971. Letter to M. Born. *The Born-Einstein Letters*. Ed. M. Born. New York: Walker & Co. (Letter dated 31 March 1954.) (b)

Schrödinger, E. 1935. Die Gegenwärtige Situation in der Quantenmechanik. *Naturwissenschaften* 33: 807–12, 823–28, 844–49. J. Trimmer, trans. "The Present Situation in Quantum Mechanics: A Translation of Schrödinger's 'Cat Paradox' Paper," in J. A. Wheeler and W. H. Zurek, eds. 1983. *Quantum Theory and Measurement*. Princeton: Princeton University Press.

Sewell, G. L. 1986. *Quantum Theory of Collective Phenomena*. Oxford: Clarendon Press.

Wan, K. K. 1980. Superselection Rules, Quantum Measurement and the Schrödinger's Cat. *Canadian Journal of Physics* 58: 976–82.

Wheeler, J. A., and Zurek, W. H., eds. 1983. *Quantum Theory and Measurement*. Princeton: Princeton University Press.

Chapter 5

THE UNIVERSAL QUANTUM*

David Finkelstein

The Great Rift

I wish I could address the subject of "The World View of Contemporary Physics," but I cannot because I have none, or there are too many, which comes to the same thing. The closest I can come to the topic is to tell where my simple-minded quest for this fabled treasure has brought me, and to share with you a conjecture about a good direction for the future search.

The main obstacle to a world view, most of us believe today, is the rift between gravity theory and quantum theory that has existed, as Dirac (1948) points out, since their respective origins in astronomy and

*This work is supported by National Science Foundation Grant PHY-8410463. I thank C. F. von Weizsäcker for a conversation that stimulated this work and W. Unruh for the hospitality of the Summer Institute, "The Early Universe," during which most of this work was done.

spectroscopy. The astronomer courteously refrains from disturbing our stars, and therefore need not replace them with new ones for each new observation. However, even the most virtuous spectroscopist may excite atoms, stimulate their decay, and discard them for fresh ones. The astronomer is a remote observer while the spectroscopist is an involved experimenter. Thus, prequantum theories have an air of absoluteness and maintain an aloof gods-eye viewpoint, often never even mentioning a physicist or an experiment, and are appropriately called classical; a quantum theory, however, starts from a partition of the universe into (I shall say) a relatively small *endosystem* (the atom of the spectroscopist) and a relatively large *exosystem* (the spectroscopist and everything but the atom) and describes the endosystem relative to the exosystem. This is the most critical difference between these two world views.

Early in this century we bridged two lesser fissures in the world of physics: the prerelativistic one between mechanics and optics and the prequantum one between particles and waves. To traverse these we had to cache some of our baggage, specifically, two axioms we had carried so long that we were hardly aware of them: the pre-Einstein axiom to the effect that all physicists use one universal clock; and the pre-Heisenberg axiom that all physicists do one universal experiment, the determination of all the variables of the system. I believe that the trip before us requires us to find and lay down yet another implicit axiom, and again one that need only to be stated to be doubted.

To explicate this covert axiom, it is helpful to reexamine the transformation theories of gravity and quanta. The two work on different levels, in the sense that I discuss here. From this analysis flows a natural proposal for a postquantum transformation theory that operates on all levels, including that of ontology itself.

Present Transformation Theories

Ontology is the theory of the nature of existence, and ontography is its description. Because there are many experimenters, there are more descriptions than entities, and each of us describes the system from a special point of view or *frame*. The system of such a description is a kinematics (or better ontography), and the theory of the relations among these frames is *transformation theory* or relativity theory.

Ontology depends in a reciprocal way on ontography and transformation theory. Increasing the scope of ontography and transformation theory act in opposite ways on ontology. What one theory says is a physical entity a later theory may say is an artifact. This makes changes in transformation theories more striking than other developments in physical theory.

Relativity is traditionally the transformation theory of time and space, and quantum theory is that of transformations between complementary experiments. This division within transformation theory is part of the gap we must cross. I formulate next the divided prequantum and quantum transformation theories (ontologies) that a postquantum one must bridge.

Prequantum Transformation Theory. In a prequantum kinematics, each entity X has a unique sample space S(X), customarily also called phase space or configuration space according to context. Here X stands for some proper name, for example, X = Mars, and each point of the sample space is a complete description of X. A frame is a labeling of the points of the sample space.

Each property (or predicate, or class—I take all of these as substantially synonymous) of X is represented by some subset of the sample space, and conversely, as part of the ontography of prequantum physics. This correspondence builds in important tautologies about classes. Different observers give different labels to the same points of the sample space: I say "there" and you say "here." Our frames are related by permutations of the sample space.

Quantum Transformation Theory. A quantum kinematics, in the form I use here, has, instead of a sample space, a collection of all the processes that may be carried out on the entity X by any experimenter. These processes form a kind of algebra in which the product of two processes means: do first one and then the other.

The most basic process is sometimes called *creation* (standing for processes of production, emission, polarization, and so on) and is often designated by a symbol ψ, here called a creation operator or (abbreviated) *creator*. The prototype of all ψ's is an arrow drawn on a polarizing filter to show its orientation.

For every creator ψ there is also a *destructor* designated by ψ^*, read *psi star*, representing a process such as absorption, registration, analysis, and detection of a quantum. More general processes are represented by products of creators and destructors. Such a representative is called an *operator*. Each creator or destructor describes a determination of maximum information, before or after the fact respectively. Such quantum processes of maximal information, and by extension the quanta they produce, are call~d *pure* or *coherent*.

The star symbol * may also be applied to the most general operator, when it converts creators into destructors of the same quanta and reverses the chronological order of the constituent processes. It is thus a kind of time-reversal, although not the one usually designated by T, which turns each creator into a creator of a quantum with reversed motion.

The simplest experiment consists of a creator ψ followed by a destructor ϕ^* and is called a transition. An operator of the form $\psi\psi^*$ corresponds to the prequantum notion of a predicate, specifically one of maximal information (also called pure).

The quantum algebra not only describes experiments but also prognosticates their outcomes. It tells us which transitions are forbidden, which are compulsory, and which are neither (the vast majority). For this purpose it assigns to each operator a number called its amplitude.

When the amplitude is zero, the process is forbidden. This means that no quantum ever reaches the final destructor to be counted. When the amplitude assumes a certain maximum possible value, the process is compulsory. This means that a quantum is counted every time we do the experiment.

The amplitude usually assumes an intermediate value. The quantum does not become fuzzy or split in two then. The theory still tells us what the possibilities are and that one of them will happen, but it does not tell us which one will happen. It says, "Try it and see." For example, when a photon from a vertically oriented polarizer strikes a rotated one, the usual quantum theory tells us whether or not the photon goes through, rather than, for example, splitting, but does not say which. Instead, it tells us that the result is not predictable. In the sense that it fails to answer such well-posed questions, quantum theory is incomplete, but then, as Gödel proved, so is arithmetic itself (if it is consistent).

The probability of a transition—which becomes more meaningful when the experiment is repeated many times—is proportional to the square of the amplitude, which is, therefore, also called the *probability amplitude*. Born presents this probability formula as a separate postulate, but it is now recognized as a consequence of the law of large numbers.

Any prequantum ontology can be cast in the algebraic language of creators and destructors. Each point p of the sample space may be considered a creator, with corresponding destructor designated by p*. The product pp* represents a predicate, and the transition p*q is forbidden when p and q are distinct points, and compulsory when p = q. That leaves no processes indeterminate, to be sure. But we have not yet seen why there is indeterminacy in the quantum theory either.

The evolutionary leap from the prequantum to the quantum is the *principle of superposition:* If two operators describe possible processes, then they have a sum that does so as well. The superposition of a forbidden transition and a compulsory one is neither. Superposition forces indeterminacy. This has no parallel in prequantum physics, though the mathematical structure is familiar from projective geometry. The superposition principle has the consequence that operators representing predicates all *commute* in prequantum theories—this means that the order of their execution does not matter—and fail to commute in quantum theories, and that logical "and" and "or" distribute in prequantum theories but not in quantum theories. It makes quantum ontology seem bizarre to the prequantum world view. Is this algebraic language indeed an ontology?

From the prequantum point of view, the quantum algebra of creators and destructors is "merely" a language for the description of experiments, not of nature (where nature means the thing in itself, independent of observation). From the quantum point of view, however, experiment is an access to nature, and the prequantum languages "merely" support illusions of direct perception.

These two attitudes to quantum theory represent stages in an educational process akin to a shift in perception, or a conversion. For a familiar example of this process, put a penny and a pencil on the table, close your eyes, pick up the pencil, at first quite loosely; try to find the penny using the pencil. At first you perceive the pencil with your finger tips. Then, if you tighten your grip on the pencil, you perceive the penny with the pencil. Similarly, a blind person, instead of feeling his fingers around the handle of a cane, feels the ground with the end of his cane.

A quantum theory is also a cane. At first we perceive only its handle, the ψ's, but after we grasp it more firmly, we perceive only the system beyond it. The existence of this perceptual shift makes it likely that arguments about the true nature of quantum reality, between those who perceive the ground and those who feel the cane, will go on forever.

The three most widely accepted schools of quantum theory are those of Heisenberg and Bohr (who form the Copenhagen school), Von Neumann, and a pseudo-Copenhagen one. These schools are often called interpretations, but this suggests something used to interpret cryptic writing on a wall in an unknown language. These three schools all use quantum theory in the same way, but differ in how they express it and their attitudes toward it.

In the form of the Copenhagen formulation I prefer, a ψ *describes,* for example, a polarization process, which emits a photon (the quantum of light), which actuates a detection process, which in turn is described by φ*, some destructor. Thus, ψ describes what we do at the beginning of the experiment and φ what we do at the end, and one does not evolve into the other. Any ψ* stands for a creation process performed on endosystem by exosystem, and thus irreducibly involves the entire system. The Copenhagen formulation is a holistic one.

For Von Neumann (1932/1955), a ψ describes an ensemble of such photons. This ensemble interpretation may be considered a special case of the Copenhagen holistic formulation, where the exosystem includes a population of similar entities, and the creation process is random selection, a lottery. It fails to describe the numerous cases where the exosystem is *not* a population, such as a light bulb that is broken after it emits one photon (although quantum theory makes certain valid prognoses for one photon as well).

In the pseudo-Copenhagen interpretation, the experiment is not described by, but physically *emits,* a ψ, which collapses unpredictably to a φ at the detector, faster than light. The concept of "collapse" has no counterpart in the Copenhagen formulation and is the telltale sign of the pseudo-Copenhagen formulation. Many who use this formulation call it the Copenhagen interpretation. This is nonstandard language for the same experiences and practices as the Copenhagen formulation. It puts a description of the system into the endosystem: as if I told you that a gun emits the command "Fire!" and that this collapses into the cry "Ouch!" if it hits a target. This is not a hypothetical philosophical position, like solipsism, but has become the prevalent one, even among physicists. Its ψ wave is something like cotton candy. At first it looks as if it will fill our need for a completely described reality, but then it collapses unpredictably and superluminally, so that it is not real at all. All "nonlocal" features of quantum theory are artifacts of this formulation (except for the Aharanov-Bohm effect.)[1]

The Copenhagen formulation speaks of no anomalous "collapse" and renounces a completely describable reality at the start. I believe it is rejected—if it is heard at all—by so many of us because it calls on us to renounce our early aspirations to universal law and offers us no replacement. Later in this essay I will propose a new goal compatible with quantum theory.

A quantum frame is a collection of creators that are mutually exclusive in the sense that no transitions between any two of them are allowed, like the points of a prequantum sample space. The transformation from one experimenter to another is defined by the transition amplitudes from the creations of one frame to the other. Thus, a transformation of quantum theory is like a bilingual dictionary that provides many alternative possibilities in the language of one experimenter for each word in the language of the other and gives the probability of each possibility. Such a transformation is evidently closer to natural language and human experience than the mechanical process of prequantum theory.

Quantum theory suggests a process ontology, since its basic symbols stand for holistic processes. I use the word *real (thing-like)* for the prequantum objects, and call the new quantum entities *actual (act-like)*, like A. N. Whitehead (1978). But at present, underlying every quantum theory are still objects of the prequantum kind, such as the points of time space. Attempts at a purer quantum theory are being made, but I do not discuss them here. This tension between prequantum objects and quantum entities is part of that between gravity theory and quantum theory.

The Breakdown of the Quantum Ontology

Let us look for symptoms of our unconscious axiom in the present quantum theory. First, one may wonder whether quantum ψ's can be the correct medium of expression for a basic theory. After all, they represent processes of determination, and when we turn our attention to such a process, it proves to be highly composite on the side of the experimenter. Often the process can be factored into processes of interaction and memory. The interaction establishes a correlation between properties of endosystem and exosystem; the memory process establishes a permanent record of the actual result. The interaction is reversible and may be quite elementary, but the memory process is always complicated, and it is this complexity that makes it effectively irreversible. How can we take such a complexity to be elementary?

The answer is that we do not. What we build on is not the cane but the ground it taps, not the creators ψ but the incompletely described quanta they create. This is not where the axiom is buried.

One source of persistent symptoms is cosmology, due to the split between astronomy and spectroscopy already described. Cosmologists insist on speaking of the universe, but the universe is a difficult topic for quantum physics, not because it is so big but because it is so universal. There is a certain wild implausibility about taking the entire universe for the endosystem. Even Archimedes needed a fulcrum. As Bohr puts it, *There is no such thing as "the quantum universe."* (For more contemporary skepticism on quantum cosmology, see Weizsäcker, 1985.)

Clearly we do carry out experiments on the universe in some sense. When you determine some property of an atom, you determine something about the universe, too, namely, its atom-part. Ordinarily, however, this is not a *pure* or coherent quantum determination of the entire universe. It does not provide maximal information about the universe but only about the atom.

Here we deal with uncertain questions of self-knowledge and in particular of maximal self-knowledge. Possibly one can prove formally from the entropy law that no entity can create a pure universe. Determinations increase the purity of the endosystem only at the expense of the exosystem, and the vastness of the exosystem compared to the endosystem prevents its impurification from being disastrous. Even the maximal determination of an endosystem assumed in present quantum theory is possible only as an ideal limit, in which the exosystem is so large that it can absorb the entropy of the endosystem without disruption. When we take the universe as endosystem, leaving no exosystem at all, we are as far from this limit as we can get. Ultimately the background microwave radiation around us is the garbage dump for the entropy taken from the endosystem. If there is no exosystem, there is no place to dump garbage.

Such a proof would not be restricted to quantum theory. It shows that prequantum physicists could not determine the universe completely either. This, however, would not cause them to doubt their theory. Quantum theory claims higher standards of meaningfulness than prequantum theory.

What use to students of the universe is a theory that declares that it does not apply to the universe? This is surely a sign of trouble. There are at least two ways to go for a useful quantum cosmology, which I will now discuss.

The Cosmic Psi

One way to deal with the problem of quantum cosmology is to imagine a Cosmic Experimenter outside the universe, who creates it in a way described by some Cosmic Creator ψ. For example, Hawking (1982) proposes a unique cosmic ψ, which might describe the creation of the universe in the cosmological sense. This relaxes our standards of operationality back towards what was commonplace in prequantum physics. A Cosmic ψ, being humanly unperformable, falls outside the

Copenhagen interpretation. It describes coherently the very quantum universe that Bohr says does not exist.

This in itself does not mean that a Cosmic ψ is entirely meaningless. While we cannot carry out such a ψ, it implies correlations between us and other parts of the universe, and we can test for these. To relate human measurements to cosmic ones, we should also imagine Cosmic Destructors ϕ^* at the end of the Cosmic Experiment, able to verify our instrument readings over our shoulder. If ψ predicts enough of our experimental results, we will gratefully accept it as true.

But a Cosmic ψ seems to pay too little attention to what we actually do, just as the ψ describing our production of an atom ignores the inner processes of the atom. For any ψ and any quantum partition of the universe, there are variables of the endosystem and of the exosystem that are forever correlated by ψ. This seems to contradict ordinary quantum theory and practice, which allows us to break such a correlation by determining some complementary variable. The Cosmic ψ puts us in the position of Schrödinger's Cat and Wigner's Friend, ignorant and impotent subjects of a greater Physicist.

Our Cosmic ψ is strikingly similar to Newton's Absolute Time t. Like Newton, we invoke a God whose determinations of the universe curiously resemble those we make in our laboratories. When we reify our constructs we inevitably deify ourselves.

Nevertheless, theology aside, a Cosmic ψ suggests two valid ways to extend present-day quantum theory: First, a Cosmic ψ may represent a process carried out by the universe on itself. Surely the existence of such processes is indubitable. When I polarize a photon, we may say that the universe polarizes itself. Second, the Cosmic ψ dispenses with a certain duplication that has seemed essential until now. A quantum ψ acts on both sides of the quantum partition. On the endosystem, ψ acts as a creation process. On the exosystem, ψ includes an act of memory, a representation (or anticipation) of the process. When we dispense with the exosystem we lose this representation. Yet the physical existence of such unrepresented processes also seems indubitable. To insist that all processes must center on people would seem anthropocentric and pre-Copernican and would forestall a comprehensive quantum ontology. I shall not do this.

The Relative Psi

Newton's Absolute t and our Cosmic ψ are products of classical thought, and I cannot take them seriously. I turn now to an alternate way to a comprehensive theory, one that is romantic, at least in the literary sense: post-classical and expressed in the vernacular. To eliminate the anthropocentric tendency of quantum theory, and also to deal with the problem of quantum cosmology, I propose not to eliminate but to generalize the experimenter, to make the quantum partition of the universe freely movable instead of ignoring it, freezing it, or erasing it. Even if no experimenter can create a pure universe, we may still cover the universe in a quantum theory if we do so piece by piece, with an atlas of charts rather than a single map.

The Atlas Method. The atlas method is already basic to general relativity, which has faced the problem of the universe, and is significantly lacking from the quantum theory, which has not. If we make a flat map of a closed universe, we omit points, as Mercator omits the North and South Poles, and we badly distort nearby regions, as Mercator does Greenland. To avoid such poles in general relativity we cover the universe with overlapping charts and provide transformations from one chart to another at the overlaps. Likewise, in a quantum theory we may think of the universe as composed of experimenters who may experience—"create" and "destroy"—each other or parts of each other.

This calls for an extension of quantum theory with movable partitions between endosystem and exosystem and for a further, "third," level of transformation theory.

A transformation theory specifies all the transformations relating one physicist to another and how physical properties transform under these transformations. Since it tells us how to get to any physicist starting from one as a benchmark, a transformation theory is also a theory of physicists. For example, Einstein (in special relativity) characterizes a physicist with ten parameters (four for date and place, three for velocity, and three for orientation); Einstein (in general relativity) does it with an infinity of parameters, comprising four smooth functions of the time-space variables, representing the transformation to new time-space variables; Dirac, in his transformation theory of quantum mechanics, requires the still greater infinity of transition amplitudes from one experimenter's ψ's to another's.

This sequence of relativities recognizes progressively the physicist's complexity and differentiation. To seek a next term in the sequence is to seek differences among physicists that we presently repress in quantum theory. Perhaps another axiom is hiding there.

The confrontation between cosmology and quantum theory exposes one repressed differentiation and a corresponding axiom. Experimenters actually partition the universe differently, yet all experimenters (described within one quantum theory) are assumed to share the same partition and to experience the same endosystem.

Indeed, to state this assumption is to doubt it. Actually, one physicist studies a solid and another a nucleus, each with its own quantum theory. Sometimes, as lip service to unity, we claim that it is merely for practical convenience that we carve out all these different systems from one overarching system, the universe. If there is no quantum universe, this rationalization fails in quantum theory. We must admit that actually and as a matter of principle (not convenience) different physicists experience different systems.

In cosmology especially, they must *in principle* experience different endosystems, if only because in seeking to describe the entire universe, they must inevitably experience each other. Two experimenters who are so great that they can maximally determine the universe around them will not elude each other's notice.

Post-Quantum Transformation Theory

To clarify the proposed evolution, let us order our transformation theories hierarchically. In an absolute, nonrelativistic science, all experimenters would agree on (1) the data, (2) the experiments, and (3) the system. This would be naive realism, or solipsism. I propose the following terminology: A transformation of the *first level* transforms (1), one of the *second level* transforms (2), and one of the *third level* transforms (3). Transforming one of these levels *a fortiori* implies transforming the higher-level ones. If you and I work on different systems, we cannot be doing the very same experiment.

The next three paragraphs illustrate this ordering of transformation theories, which has evolved from c, cq, and q theories in Finkelstein (1972).

First-level Transformations. On this level, physicists all do the same experiment to the same system and use the same sample space, but permute its points. The transformations relating two such observers is like a primitive bilingual dictionary, with a one-word definition for each word. The relativity theories of Galileo, Newton, and Einstein all are of this level. Noncommutativity (the dependence of a product on the order of its factors) on this level produces the twin effect of special relativity and the time-space curvature of general relativity.

Second-level Transformations. Here we recognize that we know nature through experiment and that actual experiments interfere; for example, one experiment determines momentum, another position. Physicists cannot all do the same experiment or some will not get done. Different physicists have different repertoires of creations, described by different collections of ψ's, called frames. Interframe transformations are not causal; a position determination fixes momentum in quantum theory no more than in prequantum theory. Instead, interframe transformations are defined by transition amplitudes. Thus, a quantum transformation is like a bilingual dictionary that offers many possible definitions for each word and gives each possibility a numerical probability. This evidently comes one step closer to natural language and human experience than the prequantum transformation concept. Noncommutativity on this level produces complementarity.

Third-level Transformations. Here we recognize that each experiment reveals only a part of nature and that different experimenters work with different parts. Their frames are, therefore, related by transformations that change the structure and content of the endosystem. Here experimenters may experience each other for the first time.

A third-level transformation is like a bilingual dictionary in which some words in each language lack any translation in the other.

Transformations of the three levels act differently on the frames of experimenters. Those of the first level merely permute creators; those of the second level superpose creators, and those of the third may create creators, or destroy them.

Following are several examples of third-level transformations that have already been studied.

Dirac. In his quantum electrodynamics, Dirac (1967) introduces photon creators and destructors that change the constitution of the endosystem and are thus transformations of the third level. They have analogues in all subsequent quantum field theories. They are usually not considered as invariance transformations, for they do not respect important properties of the endosystem (namely, the Hamiltonian and the Hilbert space metric). By the same token, I infer that these important properties are not absolute but relative in a third-level transformation theory.

Von Neumann. Von Neumann (1932/1955) discusses measurement by comparing two ways of associating a tripartite system (I, II, III). One way we may call I → (II → III), the arrow representing the quantum partition. In this analysis, the exosystem I acts on the composite endosystem II → III. In the other analysis, (I → II) → II. Since the partition has been shifted, this is a first-level transformation. Von Neumann proves the general principles and the experimental predictions of quantum theory to be invariant under this transformation. This result is an invariance principle of the first level.

Cantor. Prequantum logic, specifically the set theory of Peano and Cantor, uses transformations that may be regarded as first-level. For example, if p is any predicate (and also the class that is the extension of that predicate), then [p], the class whose sole element is p, which Peano actually designated by ιp, may be regarded as a predicate of predicates, namely, that predicate that holds for the p predicate only. Similarly, in the quantum theory, if p is a predicate about some endosystem, defined by some apparatus in the endosystem, [p] may be used to represent an assertion about that apparatus: namely, that it determines exactly the predicate p. Thus, [. . .] has shifted the partition. If we assume that the same laws of logic hold for [p] as for p, this assumption is an invariance principle of the first level. The levels of transformation theory are, therefore, related to the orders of the predicate algebra.

Kron. The most developed first-level transformation theory we have in physics seems to be Kron's tensor analysis of electric networks and machines. Kron (1939) notes that the (third-level) topological transformations describing the interconnection of his endosystems (the hookup of power distribution networks, for example) are linear transformations, much like the (second-level) changes of variable (from branch currents to loop currents, for example). He is led by this similarity and difference to his second and third generalization postulates (his first is a relativity principle of the first level):

> All the networks in the world are components of one generalized network. All physical systems are aspects of one universal physical system.[2]

Kron gives the dynamics of each actual network in terms of the universal network and the topological transformation relating the two. For physics, his program seems to require a topological physics, in that the structure of any system may be described purely topologically, by specifying how invariable modules are interconnected. Exactly because the dynamical law is not an invariant of his transformation theory, he may give a law of laws determining it. While he leaves out gravity and quanta, Kron's concept of universality may survive our renunciation of the universe.

Hermes Trismegistus. One of several ancient first-level invariance principles that come to mind is the Hermetic doctrine, "As above, so below." But the main theme of this work is the converse of this principle.

From Universe to Universal

In summation: A transformation theory is a theory of physicists. The increasing richness of our transformation theories expresses our growing awareness of the physicist's complexity. But physicists are not only more complex than any of our present theories admits, they have *kinds* of complexity not yet depicted in present day transformation theory: their hierarchic modular construction, their quantum structure, and the differences that must exist in principle between our endosystems.

A transformation theory of these structures may take from quantum theory the concept of the partition of the system into endosystem and exosystem and from relativity theory the equivalence of all experimenters; however, it will act on a deeper level than the present theories of quanta and of gravity and will express a unity of all systems as well as all experimenters. It will thus give up the axiom of the universe and provide not absolute ψ's or dynamical laws for the universe but relative ones, relative to our partitions of the system of the universe into exosystem and endosystem. But it may provide a universal quantum system, of which all individual ones are aspects. Because topology and dynamics are not invariants of this theory, it may provide laws for their determination. If there is no quantum universe, perhaps the universal quantum will fill this void in our world view.

Notes

1. This brings to mind an irreverent comic strip: (1) Heisenberg comes down the mountain bringing to the assembled populace a tablet proscribing the worship of symbols. (2) He finds us worshipping a golden calf. (3) He drops the tablet to demolish our icon, and (4) Behind his back we transfer our worship to the tablet.

2. Where I write "universal" Kron first wrote "primitive" and then "orthogonal."

References

Dirac, P. A. M. 1967. *Principles of Quantum Mechanics.* 4th ed. rev. Cambridge: Cambridge University Press.

Finkelstein, D. 1972. Space-time code. II. *Physical Review* D5: 320–28.

Hawking, S. W. 1982. H. A. Brück, G. V. Coyne, and M. S. Longair, eds. *Astrophysical Cosmology: Proceedings of the Study Week on Cosmology and Fundamental Physics*. Vatican: Pontificiae Academiae Scientiarum Scripta Varia.

Kron, G. 1939. *Tensor Analysis of Networks*. New York: John Wiley & Sons.

Neumann, J. von. 1932. *Mathematische Grundlagen der Quantenmechanik*. Berlin: Springer. R. T. Beyer, trans. 1955. *Mathematical Foundations of Quantum Mechanics*. Princeton: Princeton University Press.

Weizsäcker, C. F. von. 1985. *Aufbau der Physik*. Munich: Hanser.

Whitehead, A. N. 1978. *Process and Reality* (corrected ed. D. Griffin and D. Sherburne). New York: Free Press.

Chapter 6

DO THE NEW CONCEPTS OF SPACE AND TIME REQUIRE A NEW METAPHYSICS?

Milič Čapek

Introduction

The central question of this symposium, "Does contemporary physics need a new metaphysics?," requires some preliminary clarification. First, what do we mean by *metaphysics?* When we characterize it as mere speculation, more or less independent of the empirical content of science, it appears naturally suspect not only to rank-and-file scientists, but also to the philosophers of science as well. If, on the other hand, we regard it as a search for the reality underlying the totality of our experience, including the empirical material of the physical sciences, then the term *metaphysics* (or as I would prefer to call it *ontology*) acquires a different meaning, one entirely compatible with science and, in a sense, complementary to it. I am going to use the term *metaphysics* in the latter sense; as William James (1890/1950, p. 145) correctly stated almost a century ago, "Metaphysics means nothing but an unusually obstinate effort to think clearly."

The second question is equally important: it is obvious that the term *new metaphysics* or *new ontology* is meaningful only if it stands in contrast to *the old metaphysics,* which allegedly prevailed before the coming of modern physics. But was there any such thing as the "old metaphysics"? A mere glance at the great variety of metaphysical systems in the nineteenth century suggests there was not. Still, the situation was more complex than it appears: While there were sharply conflicting views about "the ultimate reality," there was no disagreement concerning the structure of the physical world. They all—or nearly all—accepted the Newtonian model of the physical world; Hegel was the only one, as far as I know, who ridiculed it to the great embarrassment even of his faithful followers. The only difference between the idealists (neo-Kantians and neo-Hegelians) and materialists was whether the Newtonian world was the only one; it was such for the materialists, while the idealists differentiated it from "the noumenal world" of which the Newtonian world of matter and motion was an appearance, structured and organized by the *a priori* apparatus of our minds. Although it may sound paradoxical, the phenomenal world of Kant and neo-Kantians was as mechanistic and as rigorously deterministic as the world of Moleschott, Vogt, and Büchner or other epistemologically innocent materialists. What is even more significant is that even those who, like the neo-Kantians and positivists, repeatedly stressed that physics deals with phenomena only were unconsciously committed to a certain metaphysics that was lurking behind their phenomenalistic declarations; and their metaphysics was tinged by the accepted Newtonian framework. No one stressed more emphatically the unknowable character of "Ultimate Reality" than Herbert Spencer, yet his alleged "Unknowable" was really nothing but the classical nineteenth-century concept of energy thinly disguised by agnostic and positivistic terminology.

This leads us finally to our most important question: In what sense and to what extent do the radical changes of the classical conceptual framework in contemporary physics threaten the metaphysical assumptions—whether explicit or implicit—of the last century and thus call for a new kind of ontology? More specifically, how may the revolutionary revision of the classical concepts of space and time influence the development of twentieth-century metaphysics?

The Classical Concept of Space

Consider first the concept of space. According to classical physics, it was *homogeneous* and *Euclidean;* in other words, it was infinite, infinitely divisible, absolute (that is, independent of its changing physical content), and immutable, "always similar and immovable" in Newton's words (that is, unchanging through time). All these features were implied by its homogeneity and Euclidean character; the latter was not explicitly mentioned by Newton, so obvious and self-evident did it appear in his time.

But not only in Newton's time. A century later Kant regarded Euclidean space as a necessary condition of our experience, as a part of the unchanging *a priori* structure of our minds. In other words, no matter what our future experience will be, it will always exhibit the same geometrical structure; no future empirical discovery will ever violate the validity of Euclidean geometry. When Gerolamo Saccheri, an older contemporary of Kant, unwittingly discovered non-Euclidean geometry, he completely misunderstood the significance of his own discovery in believing that he succeeded in demonstrating indirectly the fifth postulate of Euclid. By drawing certain consequences from its denial, he obtained propositions that appeared to him so strangely different from Euclidean geometry that he viewed them as absurd; except for that, they were as free of contradiction as the propositions of Euclid. The misunderstanding of his own discovery is reflected in the proud title of his work *Euclides ab omni neavo vindicatus*. When Gauss, a younger contemporary of Kant, corresponded with Taurinus about the possibility of non-Euclidean geometry, he cautioned his correspondent not to disclose it to anyone; such a characteristic shyness of the great mathematician showed the enormous prestige traditional geometry then had. But even when it was established that non-Euclidean geometries are as free of contradiction as the classical geometry of Euclid, the latter was still preferred by both philosophers and physicists.

In 1897 the young Bertrand Russell, in his *Essay on the Foundations of Geometry* (1897/1956), while conceding the noncontradictory character of non-Euclidean geometries, nevertheless viewed the geometry of Euclid as empirically valid. On this point he agreed with Henri Poincaré, who claimed that every allegedly observed deviation from Euclidean geometry must be only apparent, as it can be explained by some auxiliary physical hypothesis. Thus, for example, if it were observed that rays of light are not propagated in the void along straight lines, it would be always simpler, that is, more economical, to assume that space itself was not completely empty and that the curvature of rays was due to the presence of some subtle refracting medium, not due to the curvature of space itself. Today we know that Poincaré was wrong. Louis Couturat, one of the founders of symbolic logic, held against Russell that the homogeneity of space requires not only "the axiom of free mobility," which allows a displacement of figures without changing their shape and size (which is possible not only in Euclidean space but in all spaces of constant curvature), but also the possibility of constructing similar geometrical figures on any scale; this is possible *in Euclidean space only*, and this is why Euclidean geometry is preferable. This possibility of constructing models on any scale was one of the *essential assumptions of classical physics* to which I shall return later.

The Relativistic Concept of Space-Time

Of all the features of the concept of space listed above, its independence from time was challenged first by the special theory of relativity that proposed a union of space with time. Since such a union of space and time equally affected the latter, I shall deal with it in discussing the meaning of relativistic space-time or, as I prefer to call it, time-space. What is less known, or at least less emphasized, is the fact that the same theory challenged the Euclidean character of space as well. Most often it is the general theory of relativity that is credited with a negation of Euclidean space; the special theory allegedly retained it. Stated in such a way, it is a misleading half-truth. What remains Euclidean in the special theory is its *instantaneous* space, that is, a space at a certain instant, but such space is nothing but an ideal fiction to which no concrete physical reality corresponds. As we shall see later, it is a mere artificial, instantaneous cross section of the four-dimensional world or, to speak more appropriately, of the *four-dimensional history* of the world. But is it not true that the geometry—or rather *chronogeometry*—of this four-dimensional continuum remains Euclidean? Is not the formula for the constancy of the world-interval separating two events a mere generalization of Pythagoras' theorem? This is true in a purely formal way under the condition that the fourth dimension is made imaginary, as is clear from the formula:

$$(x_2-x_1)^2 + (y_2-y_1)^2 + (z_2-z_1)^2 + [ic(t_2-t_1)]^2 = \text{const.}$$

Even the mathematical symbolism expresses the heterogeneous character of the temporal dimension. But nothing discloses better the non-Euclidean character of space-time in the special relativity than its kinematics. Thus, no Euclidean diagram can elucidate the paradoxical character of the relativistic theorem for the addition of velocities, nor of the particular case: c + v = c. Long ago G. N. Lewis established the identity of relativistic kinematics with the geometry of asymptotic rotation. Such a geometry is sometimes (and more correctly) called *semi-Euclidean;* it is obtained by the negation of the third postulate of Euclid, according to which a circle may be described with *any* center and with *any* radius. Again, only instantaneous space in the special theory remains Euclidean, but in it neither a genuine motion nor any kinematics is possible; they both are possible only in space-time. The only "velocity" that instantaneous space admits is an *infinite velocity,* which was in principle admitted by Newtonian mechanics (for instance, the velocity of gravitation was assumed to be infinite), but is excluded by the special relativity.

Relativistic kinematics implies another consequence that is rarely, if ever, mentioned: a denial of *the physical inertness of space,* more accurately, of space-time. In the classical concept of space-time—which was very different from its relativistic counterpart—both components of it were physically *inefficacious* because of their homogeneity, because of the absence of any interaction between them and their concrete physical content. This followed from Russell's axiom of free mobility, referred to above, according to which a mere displacement of a geometrical body will not affect either its size or shape; this apparently guaranteed the very concept of solid body and the possibility of measurement. Although there are no rigorously solid macroscopic bodies, it was generally believed that the minute microbodies of which they consist are such; this constituted the very essence of atomism from the time of Democritus to that of Newton and even that of Lorenz. This guaranteed not only the principle of constancy of mass, anticipated long before its empirical verification in the eighteenth century, but was welcomed as a justification of the principle of induction; the results of experiments were independent of its place and time precisely because of the causal inefficacy of both space and time. Any physical change (according to classical physics) must be due to some *physical* cause *in* space and *in* time and not to the action *of* space and time themselves. The appealing neatness of the classical Euclidean-Newtonian view was based on the assumed homogeneity of space and time that implied both an independence of physical content and a causal inefficacy.

These assumptions were radically modified by the new kinematics and dynamics of relativity. Bertrand Russell still held (as late as 1897) that any form of an "impassable barrier" in space "cannot, in philosophy, be permitted for a moment, since it destroys that most fundamental of all axioms, the homogeneity of space" (1897/1956, p. 9). Yet only a few years later such an "impassable barrier" was found in the velocity of light that cannot be attained by any physical body (contrary to Newtonian mechanics, according to which space was *indifferent* to any increase in velocity). Within the Newtonian framework it was indeed inconceivable that a physical body moving with a velocity near that of light could not eventually attain or even surpass it; any upper limit for the velocity would have appeared not only as an arbitrary stipulation but also as a violation of the principle of causality. For how could a body with a velocity approaching the velocity of light possibly "ignore" a steady physical force that would accelerate it beyond *any* finite limit? How could a certain physical force remain without physical effect? But such an objection holds only within the classical mechanics, not in relativity; even the principle of causality is not violated if we assume that the growing resistance to acceleration that manifests itself in an increase of the inertial mass comes from the *very structure* of time-space itself. But this definitely implies that time-space itself *ceases to be causally inert.* In other words, the classical distinction between the homogeneous and inert spatio-temporal container and its heterogeneous and changing physical content is given up.

The Crisis of the Concept of Particle

This merging of space-time with its physical content is much more pronounced in the general theory of relativity. In it the Euclidean character of space-time was more explicitly denied as the gravitational field itself was reduced to a local irregularity in Riemannian space-time. Consequently, the very concepts of matter and motion were profoundly transformed. In classical mechanics, motion was viewed as a displacement of the unchanging particles (with a constant mass and volume) in static absolute space. In relativity it is viewed in a Cliffordian fashion as a disappearance of a local curvature in one region and its reappearance in a neighboring region; this creates for our senses an illusion of a displacement of a passive material in an equally inert space.

This means that the distinction between "the full" and "the empty" that was the very basis of the classical concept of particle loses its traditional sharpness. This has far reaching epistemological and even metaphysical consequences. The very concept of material substance is now at stake and, as Hans Reichenbach (1951) observed, "with corporeal substance goes the two valued character of our language, and even the fundamentals of logic are shown to be the product of an adaptation to the simple environment in which human beings are born" (pp. 189–90). This view is fairly close to Bergson's view (even though Reichenbach was not aware of it) that our logic (to wit: traditional two-valued logic) is a *logic of solid bodies,* which itself is a result of the adjustment of *homo faber* to the macroscopic region of the middle dimensions. Jean Piaget's (1950) researches, establishing that the logical and mathematical operations result from an "internalization" of the operations executed originally with solid bodies, point in the same direction. Professor David Finkelstein (1969), in his interesting paper "Matter, Space and Logic," pointed out that after the profound revision of the foundations of mechanics and geometry, it is now time to broaden logic itself, which would not be possible without recognizing its empirical, that is, *non a priori,* character.

The revision of the distinction between "the full" and "the empty" implies also a revision of the concept of an isolated particle. This inspired A. N. Whitehead to make his famous criticism of "the fallacy of simple location," which he viewed as a special case of the fallacy of "misplaced concreteness." He was not the first one to criticize it; Michael Faraday more than a century ago pointed out that the atom, because of its inseparability from its own field that spreads in all directions without limits, is virtually present in the whole universe. James Clerk Maxwell reached a similar conclusion when, after analyzing the third Newtonian law, he pointed out that the concept of a single solitary particle is physically meaningless as the same law requires an interaction of at least two particles. This led J. B. Stallo to conclude that every physical body is nothing apart from the network of relations, of dynamical links, that connect it with the whole universe, thus anticipating Mach's view that in the principle of inertia a reference is made to the rest of the universe. Does this mean that every physical individuality is, so to speak, resorbed in the cosmic whole, in what William James called "the bloc universe"? The extreme monists would be delighted; did not Spinoza write to Oldenburg in 1661 that an annihilation of one part of matter would imply the destruction of the whole universe? Unfortunately—or rather fortunately—it is not so; neither the atom nor any other elementary particle can be "omnipresent" because the field of which it is a source is spreading with a *finite* velocity into the rest of the universe. Relativity definitely excludes infinite velocities, that is, instantaneous connections. The duality of the field and of its source is still preserved; it is, of course, a duality of an altogether different kind than the traditional static duality of "the full" and "the empty."

On this point there is apparently still some ambiguity: Is matter (or, more accurately, *mass*) reduced to a local curvature of space-time as Eddington and Meyerson suggested, or is a local curvature *caused* by the presence of matter? The latter alternative would apparently retain a certain dualism between the physical content and its chronogeometrical container, even though it would admit—unlike classical physics—their causal interaction. The textbooks of relativity and sometimes even Einstein himself used a *causal* language: matter *causes* a local warping of space, a gravitational field. Yet what remains of matter if in a thought-experiment we take away from it its gravitational field? What remains of an electric charge without its electrostatic field? Nothing but a mere word.

But not all physicists reach the same conclusion. Thus, Hermann Weyl, following in this respect Bernard Riemann, regarded matter as "the field-exciting agency" (*das Feld erregende Agens*) coming from the outside of space; the electron according to him was a tiny opening or a *hole* in space, which is a source of its field. In such a view, space becomes "a multiply connected continuum" (*das mehrfach zussammenhängende Kontinum*) and loses its original intuitive continuity. Not much was heard about this theory for sixty years, although a similar concept ("black hole") reappeared in a different context in cosmology. On this point some ambiguity apparently still prevails, even though it is rarely mentioned. I find one exception in the following passage of Professor Whitrow, who is clearly aware of the problem:

> Space-time is curved in the neighborhood of material masses, but it is not clear whether the presence of matter gives rise to the curvature of space-time or whether this curvature itself is responsible for the existence of matter. Indeed, in developing the theory this ambiguity continually arises. The expressions for the energy and momentum of a given material system depend on certain numbers characterizing the structure of space-time, but these numbers in turn depend on the distribution of matter contemplated. (1959, p. 96)

Thus, the dilemma of unity or duality of the field and its source is apparently still open. A complete geometrization of matter was Descartes's old dream, but he could not succeed in his time since the only space he knew was a Euclidean one whose homogeneity and immutability prevented its fusion with its changing and diversified content. Modern physics is in a better position to create the concept of space-time, admitting space-curvature, which is *variable both locally and in time.* Thus, the fusion of such a spatio-temporal container with its diverse and changing content is, in principle at least, possible. But the task becomes enormously complex when a geometrization should be extended to other forces besides gravitation—electromagnetic and nuclear. In any case, a return to the Newtonian and sharp dualism of homogeneous and static container and its heterogeneous and changing physical content is, to put it mildly, extremely improbable.

The further development of the concept of particle in contemporary physics made its difference from its classical counterpart even more striking. Its intrinsic vibratory character, discovered by wave mechanics, cannot be interpreted in a visual, intuitive way (as a sort of rotation, for instance); it very probably reflects the quantized or, as I would prefer to call it, *pulsational* character of time-space itself, another illustration of the merging of time-space with its physical content. Evidently this would mean giving up the homogeneity of time and its infinite divisibility, which is implied by it; this is a very difficult intellectual step to take as it runs contrary to the habits that, since the discovery of infinitesimal calculus, dominate the mind of theoretical physicists. None of them, so far as I know, dared to challenge the dogma of infinite divisibility of time prior to Poincaré, who was the first physicist to use the term *atom of time.* He was followed eight years later by A. N. Whitehead who mentioned the possibility of the existence of a *quantum of time.* After that, under the impact of quantum theory and, in particular, of wave mechanics, the hypothesis of *chronon* cropped up time and again in scientific periodicals. It was natural that physicists in general were not aware that at the end of the nineteenth century some French neo-criticists and Bergson expressed doubts about the infinite divisibility of time and advocated a rather daring view, according to which the ultimate elements of matter are events, not particles. Since they also questioned the applicability of strict determinism to the basic physical events—an unheard of heresy at that time—their views have been largely ignored and only recently (Čapek, 1971; Jammer, 1966) have they received some credit for their anticipatory insights.

The Inadequacy of the Visual Models of the Microphysical and Megaphysical Scale

Philosophically, the most significant feature of the development of the concept of particle is its radical difference from the substantial microentities of Democritus and of classical physics. It is obvious that such evanescent entities are far more appropriately called "events" than "particles" or "corpuscles." To call an entity that "lasts" only a trillionth of a second a "particle" is nothing but a concession to the inertia of our macroscopic, object-oriented language. There can hardly be a sharper contrast than that between the allegedly everlasting atoms of classical physics and the vanishing "particles" of modern physics. Here we perceive the inadequacy of one of the most fundamental ideas of classical physics: the alleged similarity of the microphysical world and the world of our daily experience. It was generally accepted that molecules, atoms, and electrons did not differ basically from the bodies of our experience. It is true that since the time of Galileo, they were stripped of their "secondary qualities" (colors, sounds, and so on), but *geometrically* they differ only by their dimensions. The microcosmos was thus viewed as a miniature of the macrocosmos; this was the leading idea of Descartes and Huygens up to William Thomson and Lorenz. The failure of all such mechanistic pictorial explanations is one of the most conspicuous features of contemporary physics.

But the mechanistic and the visual models proved to be equally inadequate on the megacosmic scale. Before the coming of relativity and wave mechanics, the same logic was applied in constructing the models of the megacosmos as that of the microcosmos. Since the space of classical space was Euclidean, similar geometrical figures existed at different scales of magnitude; consequently, it was believed that the only difference between the atomic and the celestial realm was that of dimension. Thus, the difference between an electron, a billiard ball and a star was, geometrically speaking, that of a radius.

Today the situation is very different. The finite, non-Euclidean, expanding space, though mathematically conceivable, resists our spontaneous Euclidean imagination, conditioned by its contact with the region of middle-sized dimensions as much as a junction of the "corpuscular" and "undulatory" properties of microphysical events. (Incidentally, it is incorrect to say that the microphysical entities are both corpuscular and undulatory, since they are *neither*. It is more correct to say that by some of their properties they *remind us* of the behavior of particles, while other features *remind us* of the behavior of waves.)

In a resumé of this kind, only the most essential features of relativistic time-space can be outlined. The very essence of special relativity is an elimination of *absolute simultaneity*. There is no universal cosmic present, no *world-wide instant,* to use Eddington's term; in other words, no *Everywhere-Now* in the sense of an instantaneous cross section in the four-dimensional world history. It is important to realize that the relativity of simultaneity is not merely relativized but simply *denied,* as Einstein (1951, p. 61) explicitly stated in his *Autobiographical Notes.* The reason for it, he wrote, is that there is no such thing as immediate, instantaneous action at a distance; in other words, there is no such thing as a purely geometrical, instantaneous distance. As Whitehead observed as early as 1919, "the spatial relations must stretch across time" (p. 6).

On Some Static Misinterpretations of Time-Space

Yet the union of space with time was quite often interpreted—and not only in popular and semi-popular treatises—as a *spatialization of time,* as a creation of a sort of hyperspace in which time represented an additional fourth dimension, intrinsically as static as the other three dimensions. On this point we can see how powerful the influence of traditional metaphysics could be, especially on those who are not aware of it because of their limited interest in the history of ideas. There is no question that Minkowski's static interpretation is the last instance of the general tendency of the traditional intellect, from Parmenides and Zeno to Laplace, to eliminate time. This persistent tendency was systematically criticized by Bergson and, in an especially documented way, by Emile Meyerson (also by Hans Reichenbach, at least in some of his writings, by Eddington and, more recently, by Karl Popper, and Ilya Prigogine).

The most plausible argument for the static interpretation of the world of Minkowski was the absence of the universal cosmic "Now," which would separate the past from the future. The truth is that in the time-space of Minkowski the past and the future are separated *even more effectively* than in the classical space-time; instead of being divided by a single universal "Now-line," it is the whole four-dimensional region of "causal independence" or "causal contemporaries" that separates them. Through this region, called by Eddington "Elsewhere" (it could also be called "Elsewhen"), different observers will draw different fictitious "Now-lines", fictitious because no concrete physical connections correspond to them because of their *instantaneous* character. None of these "Now-lines" can *ex definitione* intersect my own causal part or future, nor can my own causal future be included in the causal past of any of my contemporaries. In addition, no causal future of *any* of my contemporaries can ever be perceived by me (that is, be observable in my present "Here-Now"). All such impossibilities follow from the limit-character of the velocity of light and/or from Minkowski's formula for the constancy of the world-interval, which prevents the possibility of observing the causally related events in an *inverse chronological order* in *any* frame of reference. Thus, while there is no omnipresent absolute "Now," there is *the absolute future,* not only for any particular "Here-Now" but for *all* the contemporaries of a "Here-Now."

The paradoxical character of the denial of simultaneity of distant events ceases to be unintelligible when we realize that there are no instantaneous actions; it was precisely a network of such instantaneous "actions" (or geometrical links) that in classical physics was a substratum of absolute simultaneity. The fact that the time-space of Minkowski does not yield to instantaneous three-dimensional cuts is entirely compatible with its dynamic nature; in truth, it is *implied* by it.

We only use different words when we express the same fact by saying that the category of *object* or *substance* is inapplicable not only on the microphysical level (as we have seen) but also on the megacosmic scale. The universe is simply not a *megabody* or *megaobject* differing from the solid bodies of our experience only by its dimensions. Yet this was the idea that was common to the former physics, Newtonian as well as pre-Copernican. In ancient philosophy the universe was regarded either as a sphere or as an infinite aggregate of minute microsubstances. In medieval cosmology, the universe was a huge sphere whose boundaries were still retained by Copernicus and Tycho Brahe; Newton, following in this respect Bruno and Gassendi, negated its boundaries, but retained its thing-like, substantial character. His philosophical contemporaries, Cartesians and Spinoza, still called it *res extensa* or *substancia extensa; sensorium Dei* was simply a theological term for it. This concept seemed to be so obvious and clear that Kant regarded it as a part of our *a priori* mental equipment. Its most obvious feature is that it implied *the simultaneous coexistence of its parts.* The very meaning of the statement "the whole consists of its parts" or "the whole contains its own parts" is based on the assumed simultaneity of different parts of the object. This is especially clear in the case of geometrical figures and solid objects. But today we know that the category of object or substance is *not* an *a priori* property of the mind. David Hume previously pointed out its empirical origin, a mere name for the complex of *simultaneous* sensations. Moreover, Jean Piaget (1950) showed that the concept of permanent object is absent from the child's mind in the first eighteen months. The "category" of object, therefore, is a result of our limited macroscopic experience, illicitly applied outside the realm of the middle dimension. Piaget (1950, pp. 212–13) also pointed out that when we continue to speak of the universe as a megaobject, we fail to realize that we are illegitimately transferring our category of object (which is a diaphanous replica of the macroscopic solid body) beyond the realm of its applicability. He could have used a powerful argument from relativity: Because of the nonexistence of the universal cosmic "Now," it is meaningless to treat the universe at large as an aggregate of *simultaneously* coexisting parts. The concept of the expanding universe in which relativistic "dislocation of simultaneities" is far larger because of enormous mutual velocities of the galaxies is an additional blow to the traditional concept of cosmic megaobject, whose parts rigidly cohere by instantaneous links, whether physical or geometrical. The world cannot be properly designated by a grammatical singular; it is more appropriately called "multiverse" rather than "universe," or, in a more technical language, a dynamical network of the asymmetrical and irreversible causal links ("world-lines") that, while interacting, encloses the regions of "contemporary independence" preventing us from regarding them as a single, rigidly cohering "block universe."

We encounter the impossibility of instantaneous cuts also on *the microphysical level*. This is expressed in the second form of Heisenberg's principle, according to which the product of the uncertainty of energy and that of time cannot be smaller than Planck's constant of action. Like other forms of Heisenberg's principle, it follows from the indivisibility of the quantum of action (Louis de Broglie). The dispute over whether these uncertainties are real indeterminacies in an ontological sense or mere uncertainties of measurement will certainly go on, at least for some time. I think that the circumstantial evidence against a recovery of classical determinism on the subquantum level is rather strong. The opposite view is based on the hope, inspired largely by traditional conviction, that strict causal necessity is the only alternative to the irrational, "chaotic," "miraculous" universe. Here we again see how powerful the pressures of some traditional metaphysics can be even on the greatest minds. Einstein was open-minded enough to recognize it; more specifically, he admitted the decisive influence of Spinoza on his thought, even though (according to the testimony of Rudolph Carnap and Karl Popper) he had moments of hesitation in the last years of his life. In a number of my writings (Čapek, 1965; 1969, chap. XVII; 1975; 1976, especially the introduction and pp. 501–24; 1983; 1985), I stated the reasons why I prefer "the open universe" (or rather "multiverse") of Karl Popper, Prigogine,

Bergson, and Whitehead to the static "bloc universe" of classical physics and traditional metaphysics.

References

Čapek, M. 1965. The Myth of Frozen Passage: Status of Becoming in the Physical World. *Boston Studies in the Philosophy of Science* 2: 441–63. New York: Humanities Press.

_____. 1969. *The Philosophical Impact of Contemporary Physics.* 2d ed. Princeton: D. Van Nostrand.

_____. 1971. *Bergson and Modern Physics. Boston Studies in the Philosophy of Science* 7. Dordrecht: D. Reidel.

_____. 1975. Relativity and the Status of Becoming. *Foundations of Physics* 5: 607–16.

_____. ed. 1976. *The Concepts of Space and Time: their Structure and their Development. Boston Studies in the Philosophy of Science* 23. Dordrecht: D. Reidel.

_____. 1983. Time-Space Rather than Space-Time. *Diogenes* 123: 30–49. Paris: UNESCO.

_____. 1985. The Unreality and Indeterminacy of the Future in Light of Contemporary Physics. *Physics and the Ultimate Significance of Time.* Ed. D. R. Griffin. Albany: S.U.N.Y. Press.

Einstein, A. 1951. Autobiographical Notes. Ed. P. Schilpp. *Albert Einstein, Philosopher-Scientist.* Library of Living Philosophers 7. Evanston, Ill.: Open Court.

Finkelstein, D. 1969. Matter, Space and Logic. Ed. R. Cohen and M. Wartofsky. *Boston Studies in the Philosophy of Science* 5: 199–215. Dordrecht: D. Reidel.

James, W. 1950. *The Principles of Psychology.* 2 vols. New York: Dover. (Original work published in 1890.)

Jammer, M. 1966. *The Conceptual Development of Quantum Mechanics.* New York: McGraw-Hill.

Piaget, J. 1950. *Introduction à l'épistémologie génétique 2. La pensée physique.* Paris: Presses Universitaires de France.

Reichenbach, H. 1951. *The Rise of Scientific Philosophy.* Berkeley: University of California Press.

Russell, B. 1956. *An Essay on The Foundations of Geometry.* New York: Dover. (Original work published in 1897.)

Whitehead, A. N. 1919. *An Enquiry Concerning the Principles of Natural Knowledge.* Cambridge: Cambridge University Press.

Whitrow, G. J. 1959. *The Structure and Evolution of the Universe.* New York: Harper & Row.

Chapter 7

SPACE-TIME AND PROBABILITY: CLASSICAL AND QUANTAL

Olivier Costa de Beauregard

Introduction

I intend to emphasize the great explanatory power of the paradigm of an extended time, including all-at-once past, present and future ("all-at-once" meaning, of course, not "at the same time"). This paradigm displayed its power as early as 1626 and 1744, in the so-called stationary principles from which Fermat and Maupertuis, respectively, deduced the laws of motion of light and of a particle of matter. But it is within the scheme of a four-dimensional geometry, using the space-time metric discovered by Poincaré in 1905 and used largely by Minkowski in 1908, that the paradigm of an extended time displayed the full range of its explanatory power. Not only time-extendedness, but also time-reversibility, or past-future symmetry, is present in the two classical stationary principles and in space-time geometry, where its correct interpretation requires additional comments to be presented in due time.

That the paradigm of an actually extended time ("actually" meaning here, of course, not the same thing as "presently") fits wonderfully well with the concept of probability and with a calculus of probabilities may seem at first sight quite surprising. This is proven, however, by the Feynman (1949a, 1949b) graphs and the computational techniques that are used with great success in relativistic quantum mechanics. So, contrary to a long held belief, a space-time description of physical evolution is definitely not committed to a deterministic metaphysics. However, a few explanations need to be added concerning the way in which probability should be understood and used in relation to a space-time description of physical evolution.

Behind Feynman's scheme there is an algebra: the algebra of a brand new, wavelike calculus of transition probabilities, proposed by Born (1926), and developed that same year by Jordan (1926), being the one appropriate in quantum mechanics. The "new quantum mechanics" had appeared just prior, through the works of Heisenberg, Louis de Broglie, Schroedinger and Dirac (1947). It was also termed "wave mechanics," as it included the wave-particle dualism invented in 1905 and 1913 by Einstein (Einstein's light quantum or photon) and in 1924 by de Broglie (matter-wave).

Wave-particle dualism may appear as a mismatched marriage of the continuous and the discrete; it is quite usual in such cases for the probability concept to act as mediator, but in this case the classical calculus of probabilities, for reasons to be explained, was not adequate, and so a new, wavelike calculus of probability had to be invented. This was achieved by Born and by Jordan. Later this calculus was cast by Dirac (1947) in the form of a very efficient symbolic calculus using "bras" $<|$ and "kets" $|>$.

It has occurred to me over the last few months, while studying the presently much discussed Einstein-Podolsky-Rosen (1935) correlations, either proper or reversed, and also Wheeler's (Miller & Wheeler, 1984) smoky dragon metaphor, that the classical, 1774, Laplace (1891) algebra of conditional probabilities can easily be recast in a form strictly paralleling the Born-Jordan-Dirac algebra of transition amplitudes, with Laplace's *conditional probabilities* "corresponding," in a Bohrian sense, to Dirac's *transition amplitudes*. It turns out that the two epithets, *conditional* and *transitional* are strictly equivalent to each other and that, therefore, either can be used depending on the context.

Time reversibility of a probability algebra obviously needs clarifying comments. Such loose statements as "physical irreversibility is easily explained on a probabilistic basis" are completely misleading, as they tacitly and unduly equate "probabilistic reasoning" with "predictive probabilistic reasoning," which is something much more restrictive; Thus, they beg the question.

In fact both Laplace in the years following 1774, and independently Boltzmann (1898/1964) in 1898, having devoted second thoughts on the whole matter, resolved it in depth; they both proposed exactly the same solution, the one in terms of the calculus of probabilities per se, the other in the more restricted context of statistical mechanics. The point is that, intrinsically speaking, statistical prediction and retrodiction are exactly symmetric to each other, displayed in this one fundamental aspect of the time-reversibility of the probability calculus. "Factlike asymmetry" between the two (in Mehlberg's [1961] wording), if any, rests *entirely* on a numerical inequality between the prior probabilities of the initial and the final states—as explained by both Laplace and Boltzmann.

If there is a need to persuade anyone that "blind statistical retrodiction" (in Watanabe's [1955] wording) may be operational in physics, a very convincing example can be given: Heisenberg's microscope thought experiment. In this little parable, Heisenberg imagines that, in the "object plane" of a microscope an electron scatters a photon that, going through the microscope, is captured in a photographic plate in the "image plane," where it makes a pointlike impact P. From this one retrodicts, the best one can, the place where the electron was when it scattered the photon. One imagines the light going backwards through the microscope from a pointlike light source at P. Thus, a diffraction pattern is produced in the object plane, and, considering also the angular aperture of the microscope, Heisenberg deduces his famous uncertainty relation as the "moral" of the fable. The point for us is that the argument in the fable is "blind statistical retrodiction."

The Classical and the Wavelike Probability Formalisms

Tables 1 and 2 display in parallel fashion the classical Laplace algebra of conditional probabilities and the Born-Jordan-Dirac algebra of transition amplitudes. The "corresponding" equations are numbered the same way, making a direct comparison immediately possible. The reader is warned that, by its very essence, an algebra is timeless, and so a timeless concept of probability, to be explained later, is thus employed; in this, a new aspect of the basic time-reversibility of the transition or conditional probabilities is implicit.

Olivier Costa de Beauregard

Table 1:

Reformalization and Reconceptualization of Laplace's Algebra

Definitions and notations

Joint probability	$\|A)\bullet(B\|$
Intrinsic conditional probability	$(A\|B)$
Extrinsic conditional probabilities	$\|A\|B),(A\|B\|$
Prior probabilities	$\|A),(B\|$
Background probabilities	$\|E), (E'\|$

Formulas

$$(A|B) = (B|A) \tag{1}$$
$$|A) \equiv (A|, \ (B| \equiv |B), \ |A|B) \equiv (B|A| \tag{2}$$
$$|A|B) \equiv |A) (A|B), \ (A|B| \equiv (A|B) (B| \tag{3}$$
$$|A)\bullet(B| \equiv |A) (A|B) (B| = |A|B) (B| = |A) (A|B| \tag{4}$$
$$\Rightarrow |A)\bullet(A| \equiv |A) (A|A) (A| \tag{4'a}$$
$$\Rightarrow (A|A) = 1, \ |A|A) = |A), \ |A)\bullet(A| \ \text{projector} \tag{4'b}$$
$$\text{Orthonormalization: } (A|A') = \delta(A,A') \tag{5}$$

Laplace's and Boltzmann's theory of fact-like irreversibility:
$$|A|B) \neq |B|A) \ \text{iff} \ |B) \neq |A) \tag{6}$$
Maximal irreversibility if all B's equal.
$$(A|C) = \Sigma(A|B) (B|C) \tag{7}$$
Markov chains:
$$|A) (L| = \Sigma\Sigma. \ . \ . \ . \ |A) (A|B) (B \ . \ . \ . \ K) (K|L) (L| \tag{8}$$
End prior probabilities ~ background probabilities:
$$|A) \sim (E|A), \ (L| \sim (L|E') \tag{9}$$

Table 1, summarizing the Laplace algebra of conditional probabilities, begins with a list of new concepts and corresponding notations, which I have developed to produce an automatically going symbolic calculus, which turns out to be strictly "corresponding," in Bohr's sense, to Dirac's symbolic calculus of transition amplitudes. *Intrinsic conditional probability* is a concept that Laplace formulated in 1774, in the first of his series of papers devoted to this subject. Shortly thereafter he dropped this concept in favor of what I call the *two converse extrinsic conditional probabilities* that have been used almost exclusively since then. I believe that much clarity is gained by reintroducing the intrinsic conditional probability concept. *Prior probabilities* of the two occurrences entering a conditional probability need no special comment. Background probabilities are a familiar concept in the Bayesian approach, and it will turn out that they combine with the prior probabilities to form conditional probabilities, which are thus finally the only fundamental concept left.

Now we go to the formulas. Formula (1), expressing reversibility of an intrinsic conditional probability in the mathematical form called matrix transposition, is Laplace's fundamental 1774 assumption. It reads, "intrinsic conditional probability of A if B equals intrinsic conditional probability of B if A." Formulas (2) are no more than computational rules. Formulas (3) define the two converse extrinsic conditional probabilities as products of the intrinsic conditional probability by one of the two prior probabilities. This is why I call them "extrinsic." Formula (4) defines the *joint probability* of two occurrences A and B as the product of three independent probabilities: what I propose to call the intrinsic conditional probability and two prior probabilities. The dot is inserted in analogy with an ordinary scalar product, as (A|B) truly is a cosine. Two alternative expressions follow that have been commonly used since Laplace's days: "Joint probability of A and B equals extrinsic conditional probability of A if B times prior probability of B," and the converse. Setting B = A in formula (4) one gets formula (4′a), which teaches us three things (4′b): namely, "intrinsic conditional probability of A if A is unity; extrinsic conditional probability of A if A equals prior probability of A; joint probability of A and A is the sort of operator known as a projector." Knowing that (A|A) = 1 allows us to define "orthonormalized sets" of exclusive occurrences, according to formula (5), with δ = 1 if A = A′ and δ = 0 if A ≠ A′. Formula (6) is the basis of Laplace's and Boltzmann's identical theories of "fact-like irreversibility." It says that the necessary and sufficient condition for equality of the two converse extrinsic conditional probabilities is equality of the two prior probabilities. *Maximal irreversibility* corresponds to the case where, for example, all (B|'s are equal among themselves, so that one need not mention them. Formula (7) is the generating formula of the so-called Markov chains, implying a summation over an orthonormalized set of "intermediate states." *Intermediate* is understood in the algebraic sense displayed by the formula: *nothing more*. Formula (8) is a "Markov chain." Finally, formula (9) says that prior probabilities are merely shorthand notations for conditional probabilities linking the system to its environment—a well-known Bayesian concept. The two symbols, E and

E′, are used to allow pictures of the environment (for example, an x or a k picture). (It should be mentioned that "conditional probability" is synonymous with "transition probability" between two, orthonormalized, "representations of a system," this being a timeless definition.)

Table 2, summarizing the Born-Jordan-Dirac algebra of transition amplitudes, exactly parallels Table 1. In this algebra the intrinsic transition amplitude is the basic familiar concept, while the two converse

Table 2:

The Born-Jordan-Dirac Algebra Completed

Definitions and notations

Joint Amplitude	$\|A> \bullet <B\|$
Intrinsic conditional amplitude	$<A\|B>$
Extrinsic conditional amplitudes	$\|A\|B>, <A\|B\|$
Prior amplitudes	$\|A>, <B\|$
Background amplitudes	$\|E>, <E'\|$

Formulas

$$<A|B> \ = \ <B|A>^* \text{ (Hermite)} \tag{1}$$

$$|A> \ \equiv \ <A|^*, \ <B| \ \equiv \ |B>^*, \ |A|B> \ \equiv \ <B|A|^* \tag{2}$$

$$|A|B> \ \equiv \ |A><A|B>, \ <A|B| \ \equiv \ <A|B><B| \tag{3}$$

$$|A> \bullet <B| \ \equiv \ |A><A|B><B| \ = \ |A|B><B| \ = \ |A><A|B \tag{4}$$

$$\Rightarrow |A> \bullet <A| \ \equiv \ |A><A|A><A| \tag{4'a}$$

$$\Rightarrow <A|A> \ = \ 1, \ |A|A> \ = \ |A>, \ |A> \bullet <A| \text{ projector} \tag{4'b}$$

Orthonormalization: $<A|A'> \ = \ \delta(A,A')$ $\tag{5}$

Formalization of fact-like irreversibility:

$$|A|B> \sim |B|A>^* \text{ iff } |B> \sim |A>^* \tag{6}$$

$$<A|C> \ = \ \Sigma<A|B> \ <B|C> \tag{7}$$

Landé chains:

$$|A><L| \ = \ \Sigma\Sigma \ldots |A><A|B><B \ldots K><K|L><L| \tag{8}$$

Generalized as Feynman graphs.

End prior amplitudes ∼ background amplitudes:

$$|A> \sim <E|A>, \ <L| \sim <L|E'| \tag{9}$$

Dirac's interpretation of state vectors as transition amplitudes:

$$\psi_a(x) \sim <a|x>, \ \theta_a(k) \sim <a|k> \tag{10}$$

Born-Jordan (1926) formula

$$(A|B) \ = \ |<A|B>|^2 \tag{ω}$$

extrinsic transition amplitudes have not been used, as far as I know. Formula (1) expresses reversibility of the intrinsic transition amplitude in the form of Hermitean conjugation of a (complex) matrix. This is routine in quantum mechanics. Formulas (2) are merely computational rules. Formulas (3) are built as similar to those in Table 1, but I do not know if they have been used. Formula (4) expresses the joint amplitude of two occurrences as the product of three independent amplitudes: the intrinsic joint amplitude and the two prior amplitudes. Setting A = A in formula (4) one gets formula (4′ a), showing (4′ b) that the intrinsic transition amplitude between A and A itself is unity and that the joint amplitude of A and A is a projector. Orthonormalization of a "representation" is then allowed according to formula (5). Fact-like irreversibility could be discussed on the basis of formulas (6). Formula (7) is the generating formula of Landé (1965, pp. 76–89) chains, implying a summation over (orthonormalized) intermediate states B. Formula (8) displays a Landé chain. An important generalization of Landé chains consists of Feynman graphs, where more than two links such as $<A|B>$ can be attached to any vertex A. Formula (9) says that end prior amplitudes are shorthand notations for transition amplitudes connecting the system to its environment. This Bayesian-like concept has been used by Dirac and Landé (independently) in their interpretation of a set of state vectors $\psi_a(x)$ or $\theta_a(k)$ as transition amplitudes between two representations, namely, $<a|x>$ or $<a|k>$. Thus, one can dispense with the state vector concept, including its so-called collapse, thus avoiding much trouble with relativistic invariance.

Last but not least comes formula (ω). It is Born's link between a transition probability and a transition amplitude, entailing that the two strictly parallel Laplace and Dirac algebras are *not* superposable as far as interpretation is concerned. While the classical Laplacean algebra uses addition of partial *probabilities* and multiplication of independent *probabilities,* the wavelike, Dirac algebra does the same with *amplitudes.* The two coincide only when the representation used is such as to suppress the off-diagonal terms in formula (ω). But such a suppression merely is a sort of perspective effect in the Hilbert space, somewhat like a parallelepiped looks like a mere rectangle when viewed in one out of three peculiar directions. These off-diagonal terms are wavelike *interference* terms, whence the "nonseparability" concept, to be explained shortly, comes in.

Born's (1926) original "statistical interpretation of wave mechanics" proceeds from the very natural assumption that the probability that the particle is manifested at some point-instant is proportional to the classical intensity of the wave. But, as is well known from classical acoustics and optics, in "pure" phenomena where there is phase coherence (sound as opposed to noise, for example), the amplitudes not the intensities are added to each other. Therefore, the necessity of a "scientific revolution": the invention of a "wavelike probability calculus." While the intermediate states B that are summed up in a Markov chain could be thought of as "real but hidden," this is no more so in a Landé chain or a Feynman graph because of the off-diagonal terms in formula (ω). These entail interference style effects, that is nonseparability. From this stem the thousand and one quantal paradoxes, all very well substantiated experientially, all expressing "quantal nonseparability" when thought of in algebraic terms, or "quantal nonlocality" when thought of in (four-dimensional) geometrical terms. Finally, Dirac's "transition amplitudes" can be equivalently termed "conditional amplitudes," as is quite obvious when the end prior amplitudes $|A>$ or $<L|$ refer to partial preparations or measurements performed upon an evolving system.

So, when a space-time connotation is attached to the chance occurrences A,B,C, . . . quantal nonseparability shows up as quantal nonlocality. Also, the transition amplitudes $<A|B>$ . . . are then termed propagators (Feynman propagators). Therefore, in the quantal, wavelike calculus of probabilities, the two intrinsic symmetries between retarded and advanced waves and between increasing and decreasing probabilities go hand in hand, as explained by Fock (1948), as do the two aspects of fact-like irreversibility, macroscopic wave retardation and probability or entropy increase. I recall in this respect a famous Ritz-Einstein (1909) controversy, in which both opponents were using *reciprocal* rather than *contradictory* assumptions. I also recall that in Planck's thinking both aspects of fact-like irreversibility were present, and finally synthesized in the form of the definition of the entropy of a light beam, involving an entropy increase even in phase coherent scattering of light.

Due to the Laplacean or Hermitean symmetries expressed by formulas (1), a Markov or a Landé chain can zigzag arbitrarily throughout space-time or the momentum-energy space, completely disregarding the macroscopic time or energy arrow. This is the "topological invariance" of Markov or Landé chains, and also of Feynman graphs.

Discussion of a Few Examples

Example Displaying a Timeless Use of the Probability Concept. The number of male U.S. citizens having a height H and a weight W is the "joint number of chances of H and W" in this context. In the absence of prior probabilities of H and W, it is also the (unnormalized) "intrinsic conditional probability" of "H if W" or of "W if H." Now restricting our inquiry to, for example, the subclasses of weightlifters or basketball players, we must introduce the prior numbers of chance of H and of W, and the joint number of chances is reduced accordingly. Basketball players are usually tall and light. Therefore, in this subclass, the prior probability of a high value of H is high and that of high value of W is low. Then the extrinsic, Laplacean, conditional probability |H|W) is much larger than |W|H) is—a *logical irreversibility* where no timing is implied. We have thus discussed the "height representation" and the "weight representation" of a U.S. citizen.

Example Displaying Topological Invariance of a Markov Chain. In a U.S. national park we may be interested in the joint probability of finding at M the male and at F the female of a couple of bears, the MF vector being either spacelike, or future timelike, or past timelike. *Coupling* implies *interaction*. For example the two bears may meet at some "real hidden place" P. Summation over the possible P's is necessary, and so we use formula (7). Topological invariance means that the MPF zigzag can have, in space-time, either a V or Λ or C shape, this making absolutely no logical difference. The hidden states P are termed "intermediate" in a *purely topological* sense, completely disregarding the macroscopic time arrow. Thus, we have discussed the "male representation" and the "female representation" of a couple of bears.

Second Example Displaying Topological Invariance of a Markov Chain. The "collision probability" (strictly speaking, the number of chances of a collision) for two spherical molecules is the product of three independent (unnormalized) probabilities: their "mutual cross section" (A|C), and the initial occupation numbers |A) and (C| of their initial states A and C. This is for prediction, the ABC zigzag, with B denoting the collision, then being Λ shaped. The same formula holds in retrodiction, with |A) and (C| then denoting the final occupation numbers of the final states. Then the ABC zigzag is V-shaped. What then of a C-shaped zigzag? Again the same formula holds, with |A) denoting the initial occupation number of the initial state and (C| the final occupation number of the final state.

At this point we must pause for an evaluation. While both Boltzmann, and Laplace in similar cases, multiplied (A|C) by |A), neither of them multiplied (A|C) by (C|. This was, as I have said, their (common) way of expressing *fact-like maximal irreversibility.* However, this strategy was "intrinsically illogical" for the following reason: Multiplication by |A) does imply statistical indistinguishability inside a given sort of molecule, and, if this is so, there are (C| ways in which a colliding molecule can reach the final state C. Therefore, multiplication by (C| is a corollary to multiplication by |A). Experimentation vindicates this. "Indistinguishable particles" are either "bosons" such that |A), (C| = 0,1,2, . . . or "fermions" such that |A), (C| = 0,1. Symmetric presence of *both* the initial and final occupation numbers is well known in quantal statistics, which, in the present perspective, has a "time-symmetric sort of logic" that should not be obliterated. In the expression of (A|C) = Σ(A|B)(B|C), the intermediate summation is over the states of the two spherical molecules while in contact, as characterized by, for example, the line of their centers, that is, that one normal to their reflecting plane. Topological invariance of the formula is obvious.

A Three-Fold Example Displaying Topological Invariance of Landé Chains. In the wavelike probability calculus, a V-shaped ABC zigzag illustrates an EPR correlation proper, a Λ shaped ABC zigzag illustrates a reversed EPR correlation, and a C-shaped ABC zigzag illustrates Wheeler's smoky dragon metaphor. In all three cases, the intermediate summation at B is over "virtual," not "real hidden" states. An EPR correlation proper is between two distant measurements A and C issuing from a common preparation B. The state in B should be said to be "virtual" in terms of the two Hilbert spaces of A and C. However, in the product Hilbert space A ⊗ C, the B state is a pure state, for example, a spin-zero state in the now famous cascade experiments. A reversed EPR correlation is between two distant preparations A and C merging into a common measurement B. The comment of it mirrors in time the preceding one.

Wheeler's smoky dragon is a quantal system |B> evolving between its preparation as |A> and its measurement as |C>. As it is actually transiting from |A> to |C>, it is neither in the retarded state emitted from |A> nor in the advanced state absorbed into |C>, but in a superposition of states of the Hilbert spaces of |A> and |C>. However, in the product Hilbert space A ⊗ C, it is in a pure state, namely, the state of the virtual particle that, coupling with the system between A and C, would induce the transition from |A to |C>. Therefore, the evolving system is *not in* a state. The very concept of an evolving state vector is as misleading and as obsolete as was the late "luminiferous ether." Only the transition amplitude makes sense. The evolving system is not "down inside our world"; it is a "smoky dragon" of which only the "tail" held as |A> and the "mouth" biting as |C> are down inside our world. So, on the whole, we have three "smoky dragons": Wheeler's (of course), the one in the source of an EPR correlation, and the one in the sink of a reversed EPR correlation.

Conditional Probability or Amplitude, and Causality

In the wavelike transition amplitude, what counts is the setting of the preparing and measuring devices while the particles go through them. What they are before or after is irrelevant. The expression of the transition amplitude holds *if, and only if,* each and every partial preparation and each and every partial measurement *as written down in the formula* is performed. Therefore, the transition amplitude exactly is a *conditional amplitude.* The concept of the conditional amplitude is tightly tied with the concept of causality. If causality has any operational meaning, the implication is that something can be arbitrarily adjusted where the "cause" exists. In the EPR correlations, either proper or reversed, and in the Wheeler dragon metaphor adjustable parameters exist at A and C, not at B. It belongs to physics, not to metaphysics, to make clear where the effects do show up.

In a reversed EPR experiment where an atomic "anti-cascade" is triggered at B by absorption of two linearly polarized photons, it is easily accepted that the linear polarizers present at A and C can be rotated after the photons have gone through them without affecting the experimental result. This is because one thinks of the photons as retaining, until their absorption at B, the polarizations imprinted upon them at A and at C. In other words, one thinks in terms of "retarded causality."

In the EPR correlation experiment proper, however, it has been found quite shocking that the polarizers at A and C can be set after the two photons have left their sources—although this is what both the formula and the measurement do say. In other words, an EPR correlation proper displays an advanced aspect of causality.

Wheeler's smoky dragon is well illustrated by the C shape of the linear polarization experiments. We can have a low-intensity light beam traversing in succession two linear polarizers, and insert in-between them a birefringent crystal, the length of which is such that a zero phase shift exists between the two "rays" it transmits. Its presence does not change the transition amplitude, and even it can be arbitrarily rotated. As there is no means to "know upon which of the two beams an individual photon is travelling," this traveling photon truly is a "smoky dragon."

So, on the whole, *at the quantal level causality is time reversible, that is, arrowless*. This, of course, already was the implicit lesson of Loschmidt's (1876) fable or "parable." But the moral of the fable is much more dramatic with the wavelike probability calculus.

The connection between the two concepts of *physical causality* and *classical conditional probability* or *quantal conditional amplitude* is indeed so tight that I submit that the two should be merely identified. This is very much, I believe, in line with Laplace's thinking (as the title of his 1774 paper [Laplace, 1891] "memoire on the probability of causes" indicates), and also in line with the so-called S-matrix quantal approach. Now I come to something philosophically quite important.

Important Philosophical Implications

If picturable in space-time, a probability calculus cannot rest upon a "statistical frequency" philosophy, because there is only one world history. Thus, it is inevitable that a "space-time probability calculus" rests upon the original subjective philosophy upheld by its proponents, Bernouilli and Laplace and advocated today by E. T. Jaynes (1983).

The crucial point here is evaluation of the end prior probabilities or amplitudes, as in formula (8). This, as I will show, is a matter not only of *cognitive information* but also of *organizing information,* which opens radically new vistas. But before I go into this I need to emphasize that not only the probability or the information concept but also the space-time concept should be said to be neither objective nor subjective, because they are indivisibly both. That at the quantal level the space-time concept certainly looses the objectivity it was supposed to have at the macrolevel follows from the fact that Heisenberg's uncertainty relations oblige us to choose between a space-time *or* a momentum-energy description.

Intrinsic time symmetry of conditional amplitudes (expressed as going to the complex conjugate if exchanging a preparation and a measurement) implies reversibility of the

$$\text{negentropy} \rightleftharpoons \text{information}$$

transition, that is, intrinsic equivalence between information as gain in knowledge and information as organizing power. Therefore, down in what Popper and Eccles (1977) call "World 1," the world of "things out there," there are not only negentropy sinks (pointed to by Sadi Carnot and Clausius) but also negentropy sources that were ruled out by the much too radical irreversibility statement due to these two, and also formalized by Laplace and Boltzmann. In quantum mechanics the negentropy sinks are called *measurements* and the negentropy sources *preparations*.

The point is that *physical irreversibility does not mean suppression but strong repression of the negentropy sources*. Therefore, symmetric to the phenomenon of gain in knowledge, there *should* exist the phenomenon of *direct* conversion of information into negentropy: *psychokinesis*. This is exactly the conclusion Wigner (1962, pp. 171–84) reached at the end of a discussion about various symmetries and the statement that "to every action there corresponds a reaction." Therefore, to the direct action of matter upon mind—generation of knowledge—there should correspond a *direct* action of mind upon matter.

Do we have experimental evidence of psychokinesis? In an article by the famous neurophysiologist, Sir John Eccles (1986), entitled "Do Mental Events Cause Neural Events Analogously to the Probability Fields of Quantum Mechanics," he claims he has proven experimentally that at the origin of a human voluntary act there is a biasing of the "blind predictive probabilities," that is, a loosening of the much too radical Laplace and Boltzmann prescription: equating all the $(B|$'s to each other. Also in their article, Robert Jahn (dean of the faculty of engineering at Princeton University) and J. Dunne (1986) described successful experiments in psychokinesis. All this should surprise no one who has given thought to the temporal reversibility of conditional probabilities.

In the quantal jargon, the initial and final prior probabilities are termed "occupation numbers" (or, more generally, the expectation values of these). These must be thought of as "being there," either in space-time *or* the momentum-energy space. A comparison of the well-known style relating a relativistic evolution and a classical steady state regime will help clarify the matter.

The traffic on one of the telephone lines connecting booths two by two is the product of three numbers: the channel capacity and the occupation rates of the two booths considered. These "occupation numbers" are thought of as "being there," in ordinary space. Above this, in the quantal probability calculus, we have the wavelike nonlocality tied by direct, long range, arrowless correlations. This, together with the neo-Bayesian approach I have explained, builds up a world view where intersubjectivity rather than objectivity is the right concept—a Maya type of world, the ultimate nonsolidity of which is proven by the (happily rare) occurrences of "paranormal phenomena."

Appendix 1: CPT-Invariance

Classical, 1905, relativistic invariance consists of invariance of physical laws under (hyperbolic) rotations of the Poincaré-Minkowski tetrapod. These are past-future preserving and right-left hand preserving operations. It is only natural to assume that fundamental or "elementary" physical laws should also be invariant under reflections of the Poincaré-Minkowski tetrapod.

This has been discussed by Lüders (1952). *Strong reflection* $\Pi\Theta$ of the tetrapod has two effects: reversing motions (the network of particles' collisions) in the manner of Loschmidt, which can be termed "covariant motion reversal" and denoted as PT; and reversing the arrows of four-vectors, that is, according to the Dirac-Stuckelberg-Feynman description of antiparticles, exchanging particles and antiparticles, an operation denoted as C. So, on the whole,

$$\Pi\Theta = CPT = 1$$

This is "active strong reflection," reversing not the naming of the axes but keeping the axes, and reversing the physical evolutions.

Two CPT associated Feynman graphs should be thought of as framed pictures, because, due to factlike irreversibility of *both* motion reversal *and* particle-anti-particle exchange, we (fortunately) cannot CPT reverse the environment. So here we have a new aspect of the reversibility of conditional amplitudes, and one, as we have seen when discussing the EPR correlation, that is very relevant with respect to the understanding of nonlocality.

U (denoting the unitary evolution operator between a preparation $|\phi>$ and a measurement $|\psi>$), the Tomonaga-Schwinger transition amplitude $<\psi|U\phi> = <\psi U|\phi> = <\psi|U|\phi>$, displays, in this order, the mutually equivalent concepts of wave "collapse," projecting the retarded preparation onto the measurement; "retrocollapse," projecting the advanced measurement onto the preparation; and symmetric "collapse and retrocollapse." This is a concise formalization of Fock's (1948) remark. It is worth remarking that the prediction-retrodiction symmetry thus displayed is a corollary to CPT-invariance.

Appendix 2: On Advanced Causality

I must discard here a disastrous, but very frequent, misunderstanding concerning advanced causality. Many people think that advanced causality would imply the possibility of *reshaping* the past—for example, killing one's own grandfather in his cradle. This is sheer nonsense. The world history is one, and cannot be rewritten. Advanced causality does not mean reshaping, but it does mean *shaping* the past from the future. It is what Aristotle termed "final causes" and is appropriately expressed by Lamarck's aphorism, "The function creates the organ."

Let me borrow a comparison from classical hydrodynamics. If the tap and the sink of a bathtub are both open, the water level may remain unchanged; this is a "permanent regime" situation. Then the whole field of the velocity vectors, that is also the shape of the current lines, is determined *jointly* by the pressure from the tap and the suction from the sink. Similarly, in space-time we have sources and sinks of negentropy and negentropy current lines.

Appendix 3: What is a Wave, and What is a Particle?

The nonthings we try to speak of, down at the quantal level, are best grasped through the mathematical symbols that express them very effectively, and it is through these symbols, not through our macroscopic prejudices, that we should try to grasp them. Algebraically speaking, a wave is a transition amplitude $<A|B>$ connecting two occurrences A and B; geometrically speaking, it is an arrowless, CPT-invariant, Feynman propagator connecting two preparations and/or measurements. That this "ghost of a conditional probability" does have a sine wavelike structure has a flavor of mystery and should not be degraded by being drawn towards the image we have of the various macroscopic waves. In fact, it is easily shown to follow necessarily from the algebra *and* from translational invariance in space-time. Algebraically speaking, a particle is *nothing more* than a purely arithmetical entity, an integer occupation number of a prepared or measured state, and the value attributed to a conditional probability linking the evolving system to its macroscopic environment. So wave and particle are the continuous and the discrete aspects inherent in the concept of probability, as they are here specified in the Born-Jordan wavelike probability calculus.

Appendix 4: Repeatable Experiments and Statistical Frequencies

The very concept of a repeatable experiment implies a severance between the phenomenon studied and the environment. It is assumed that the parameters not listed in the protocol of the so-called "repeatable experiment" are negligible. In other words, *neglected* is taken as synonymous with *negligible*. Under this approximation the concept of a statistical frequency does make sense and, indeed, is the criterion used for testing the probabilities. This, of course, does not contradict the statement made in the main text, that, because there is only one world history, the statistical frequency concept of probability cannot, *strictly speaking,* be used in a relativistic context.

Appendix 5: On Paradox and Paradigm

In most dictionaries the first meaning given for *paradox* is tantamount to "A surprising but perhaps true statement." As an example one may find Copernicus' heliocentrism. A paradox of this sort finally turns into a new paradigm, or way of looking at things. As Proust puts it, "Today's paradoxes are tomorrow's prejudices." The transition from surprise to general acceptance is what Kuhn calls a "scientific revolution."

Appendix 6: Descartes on Voluntary Motion

In Descartes correspondence there are two letters (1971, p. 663; 1974, p. 219) in which he briefly discusses the nature of voluntary action, that is, "the way in which our mind moves our body." In a letter in Latin to Arnauld, dated, 29 July 1648, he writes, "That our mind, which is incorporated, can set the body in motion is shown to us not by some ratiocination or comparison drawn from something else, but by the most certain and evident everyday experience." This is the same argument as in the cogito, but applied to willing rather than to cognitive awareness. In a later letter to Elisabeth, he makes the following point: "The main cause of our errors consists of our willingness to use notions for explaining things to which they are not appropriate, as when we want to conceive how the soul moves the body in the same way that a body moves another body." Very near the time when Pascal and Fermat were clarifying the calculus of probabilities, Descartes did not think of bringing the two matters together. This said, however, it is quite clear that Descartes is advocating the existence of an internal "psychokinesis," as Sir John Eccles is doing today.

Appendix 7: The Zigzagging Causality Interpretation of the EPR Correlations

The interpretation of the EPR Correlation presented in this paper is an updated version of the one I have been defending since 1953 in a series of articles (1953, 1977, 1983, 1984, 1985, 1986 forthcoming). Other authors (Cramer, 1980, 1986; Davidon, 1976; Pegg, 1980; Rayski, 1979; Rietdijk, 1981; Stapp, 1975; Sutherland, 1983, 1985) have independently come to more or less similar conclusions, one of whom (Sutherland, 1985) has since changed his mind, and another of whom (Cramer, 1986) somewhat misunderstood my work.

References

Boltzmann, L. 1964. *Lectures on Gas Theory.* Trans. S. G. Brush. Berkeley: University of California Press. (Original work published in 1898.)

Born, M. 1926. Quantenmechanik der Stossvorgänge. *Zeitschrift für Physik* 38: 803–27.

Costa de Beauregard, O. 1953. Une Réponse à l'argument dirigé par Einstein, Podolsky et Rosen contre l'interprétation bohrienne de la mécanique quantique. *Comptes Rendus de l'Académie des Sciences* 1932: 1632–34.

_____. 1977. Time Symmetry and the Einstein-Podolsky-Rosen Paradox. *Il Nuovo Cimento* 42B: 41–64; 51B: 267–79.

_____. 1983. Lorentz and CPT-Invariances and the Einstein-Podolsky-Rosen Correlations. *Physical Review Letters* 50: 867–69.

_____. 1984. Lorentz and CPT-Invariances and the Einstein-Podolsky-Rosen Correlations. *Foundations of Quantum Mechanics in the Light of New Technology.* Ed. S. Kamefuchi et al. Tokyo: Physical Society of Japan.

_____. 1985. On Some Frequent but Controversial Statements Concerning the Einstein-Podolsky-Rosen Correlations. *Foundations of Physics* 15: 871–87.

_____. 1986. Causality as Identified with Conditional Probability and the Quantal Nonseparability. *Microphysical Reality and Quantum Formalism.* Ed. G. Tarozzi and A. van der Merve. Dordrecht: D. Reidel.

_____. Forthcoming. Causality as Identified with Conditional Probability and the Quantal Nonseparability. *New Techniques and Ideas in*

Quantum Measurement Theory. Ed. D. Greenberger. 480: 317–25. New York: Annals of the New York Academy of Science.

Cramer, J. G. 1980. Generalized Absorber Theory and the Einstein-Podolsky-Rosen Paradox. *The Physical Review* D22: 362–76.

_____. 1986. The Transactional Interpretation of Quantum Mechanics. *Reviews of Modern Physics* 58: 647–87.

Davidon, W. C. 1976. Quantum Physics of Single Systems. *Il Nuovo Cimento* 36B: 34–40.

Descartes, R. 1971. Correspondence. C. Adam and P. Tannery, eds. *Oeuvres Completes* 3. New edition. Paris: Vrin.

_____. 1974. Correspondence. C. Adam and P. Tannery, eds. *Oeuvres Completes* 5. New edition. Paris: Vrin.

Dirac, P. A. M. 1947. *The Principles of Quantum Mechanics.* 3d ed. Oxford: Clarendon Press.

Eccles, J. C. 1986. Do Mental Events Cause Neural Events Analogously to the Probability Fields of Quantum Mechanics? *Proceedings of the Royal Society of London* 22: 411–28.

Einstein, A., Podolsky, B., and N. Rosen. 1935. Can Quantum Mechanical Description of Physical Reality Be Considered Complete? *Physical Review* 47: 7–10.

Feynman, R. P. 1949a. The Theory of Positrons. *Physical Review* 76: 749–59.

_____. 1949b. Space-Time Approach to Quantum Electrodynamics. *The Physical Review* 76: 769–89.

Fock, V. 1948. On the Interpretation of the Wave Function Directed Towards the Past. *Doklady Akademia Nauk SSSR* 60: 1157–59.

Heisenberg, W. 1927. Über der Anschaulichen Inhalt der Quantentheoretischen Kinematik und Mechanik. *Zeitschrift für Physik* 43: 172–98.

Jahn, R. G., and B. J. Dunne. 1986. On the Quantum Mechanics of Consciousness with Application to Anomalous Phenomena. *Foundations of Physics* 16: 721–72.

Jaynes, E. T. 1983. Where do we Stand on Maximum Entropy? *Papers on Probability, Statistics and Statistical Physics*. Ed. R. D. Rosenkrantz. Dordrecht: D. Reidel.

Jordan, P. 1926. Über eine neue Begründung der Quantenmechanik. *Zeitschrift für Physik* 40: 809–38.

Landé, A. 1965. *New Foundations of Quantum Mechanics*. Cambridge: Cambridge University Press.

Laplace, P. S. de. 1891. Memoire sur les Probabilités des Causes. In *Oeuvres Completes* 8: 27–65. Paris: Gauthier-Villars.

Loschmidt, J. 1976. Über des Zustand das Warmegleichgewichtes eines Systems von Körpern mit Rücksicht auf die Schwerkraft. *Sitzungsberichte der Akademie der Wissenschaft Wien* 73: 139–47.

Lüders, J. 1952. Zum Bewegungsumkehr in quantisierten Feldtheorien. *Zeitschrift für Physik* 133: 325–39.

Mehlberg, H. 1961. Physical Laws and Time's Arrow. *Current Issues in the Philosophy of Science*. Ed. H. Feigl and G. Maxwell (pp. 105–138). New York: Holt, Rinehart & Winston.

Miller, W. A., and J. A. Wheeler. 1984. Delayed Choice Experiments and Bohr's Elementary Quantum Phenomenon. *Foundation of Quantum Mechanics in the Light of New Technology*. Ed. S. Kamefuchi. Tokyo: Physical Society of Japan.

Minkowski, H. 1908. Raum und Zeit. *Physikalische Zeitschrift* 20: 104–11.

Pegg, D. T. 1980. Objective Reality, Causality and the Aspect Experiment. *Physics Letters* 78A: 233–34.

Poincaré, H. 1906. Sur la Dynamique de l'Electron. *Rendiconti de Circolo Matematico di Palermo* 21: 129–75.

Popper, K. R., and J. C. Eccles. 1977. *The Self and the Brain*. New York: Springer.

Rayski, J. 1979. Controversial Problem of Measurement Within Quantum Mechanics. *Foundations of Physics* 9: 217–36.

Rietdijk, C. W. 1981. Another Proof that the Future can Influence the Past. *Foundations of Physics* 11: 783–90.

Ritz, W. & Einstein, A. 1909. Zum Gegenwärtigen Stand des Strahlung-sproblems. *Physikalische Zeitschrift* 10: 323–24.

Stapp, H. P. 1975. Bell's Theorem and World Process. *Il Nuovo Cimento* 29B: 270–76.

Sutherland, R. I. 1983. Bell's Theorem and Backwards-in-Time Causality. *International Journal of Theoretical Physics* 22: 377–84.

Sutherland, R. I. 1985. A Corollary to Bell's Theorem. *Il Nuovo Cimento* 88B: 114–18.

Watanabe, S. 1955. Symmetry of Physical Laws. *Reviews of Modern Physics* 27: 26–39, 40–70, 179–86.

Wigner, E. P. 1967. *Symmetries and Reflections.* Cambridge: M.I.T. Press.

Chapter 8

THE REDISCOVERY OF TIME

Ilya Prigogine

Introduction

I would like first to congratulate the organizers of this conference. The relationship between physics and philosophy is indeed a very timely subject. Professor Ivor Leclerc has often emphasized that it is a pity, both for philosophy and the physical sciences, that there exists such a deep divorce between their respective fields of interest.

This state of affairs may eventually be harmful even for the scientific activity of physics itself. The greatest scientists who have shaped our world view, people such as Leibniz and Newton, were as much interested in general conceptions about the world as in physical questions proper. One of the most heated debates in the history of science was that between Leibniz and Clarke (Alexander, 1956; Gerhardt, 1890)—this latter individual speaking for Newton. As we move closer to the present, we have the famous debates on quantum mechanics—Einstein, Bohr, and so on—whose content does not have much relation to the pragmatic content of these disputed questions.

By pushing this divorce too far we may end with an "all-too-pragmatic" way of doing physics, taking away one of the most important driving forces of science: The need to connect the various aspects of human experience. For this very reason, I regret that circumstances have prevented me from participating more fully in this conference.

I would like to share with you my conviction that we are at a privileged moment in the history of science (Prigogine and Stengers, 1984). We live in a period that could be called the *Darwinian Revolution of Physics*. As you know, the classical view of physics was an atemporal view, based on deterministic and time-reversible laws. In this way, the world appeared as a kind of giant automaton. Today this view is being challenged at many levels: at the microscopic level, at the classical dynamics level, and in quantum dynamics and general relativity. As a result, another view is emerging that is closer to an evolutionary view of the universe, a view that people such as Boltzmann, Peirce, and Bergson—to name just a few—dreamed about. I would like to emphasize that such an evolutionary view of the world necessarily involves at least three aspects.

First, it has to involve *probability*. Obviously we cannot speak of "evolution" when we compute the position of the moon in the future. It is only when we have some choice, described by probabilities, that we can speak of evolution; we need what Peirce (Pape, forthcoming) called *tychism*. Moreover, yesterday and tomorrow have to be different; in other words, we need *irreversibility*. In addition, in order to have really events (new structures appearing), we need mechanisms producing *coherence*. At all levels we see that the world is made up of many units associated in coherent structures; thus, the problem for the physicist is to conceive mechanisms that would make these units cooperate and produce these structures.

Now it seems to me that these three features—probability, irreversibility, and coherence—are apparent at various levels of physics. I would like to start with the macroscopic level, since this is the field in which I work the most, but also because it is the level on which these three features are present in such an obvious way that they cannot be disputed.

The Macroscopic Level

What I find so interesting about nonequilibrium thermodynamics is that it allows us to demonstrate these three features by means of very

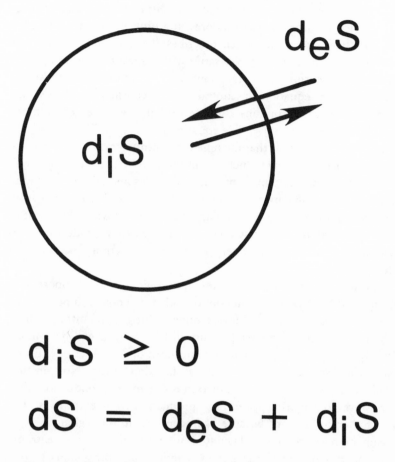

$$d_i S \geq 0$$

$$dS = d_e S + d_i S$$

Figure 1. Open system: entropy production and entropy flows.

simple experiments (there are many laboratories in the world where such experiments are performed at present). Let me first remind you of the second law of thermodynamics, even though everyone knows it.

We consider a system that exchanges matter and energy with the outside world. The change of entropy dS is equal to the entropy flow $d_e S$ with the outside world, plus the internal entropy production $d_i S$, which is produced by all irreversible processes going on inside the system. The characteristic feature of the second law is that this entropy production, due to irreversible processes, is always positive. So if the system is isolated, the entropy would grow and reach its maximum in a sufficiently long time.

The first question then is What are these irreversible processes? Irreversible processes are processes that present a broken time symmetry. If I write the "heat equation," which describes the temporal evolution of temperature, it contains a first derivative with respect to time and, therefore, has a broken time symmetry; however, if we change t to –t, we will obtain a different equation. In contrast, let us consider the wave equation in the vacuum: It contains a second derivative with respect to time, and is, therefore, a time-reversible equation.

It has often been said that the nineteenth century was the century of evolution; indeed, entropy (which was introduced by engineers and physical chemists to the amazement of mathematicians and theoretical physicists, who were unhappy with this new concept and tried to play it down), corresponds to the evolutionary approach of physics. But what is entropy production? The first idea was that entropy production was something uncontrollable, not very interesting, something like noise or waste.

Consider a system of two boxes that communicate. Suppose you heat one of the boxes while you cool the other; suppose you put a mixture of two types of molecules, for example, hydrogen and nitrogen, into the system. Because of the temperature difference, you will have more hydrogen in the warmer box and more nitrogen in the cooler one. Every physical chemist knows of this "thermal diffusion" effect. Now, in this example, one part of entropy production is due to heat conduction (this is a positive contribution to entropy production), but entropy is also related to "anti-diffusion" because hydrogen goes to the region where it is already more concentrated. Therefore, we have a positive total entropy production, yet one of the processes (conduction) corresponds to the creation of disorder, while the other corresponds to the creation of order. We see that order is created at the expense of disorder.

This is something we find in many experiments today. A very famous example is Bénard instability: You heat a liquid from below, and at some point you see beautiful convection patterns appearing. In heating it, you expend some energy but at the same time you produce patterns. In biology, one cannot produce DNA molecules from atoms; instead, one has to couple the destruction of some other molecules with the formation of DNA. We may also use the example of cities: When you build a city, pollution may result, but from this negative side-effect comes something we need and enjoy—a beautiful building, a university, and so on. I will come back to this coupling between order and disorder when discussing cosmology.

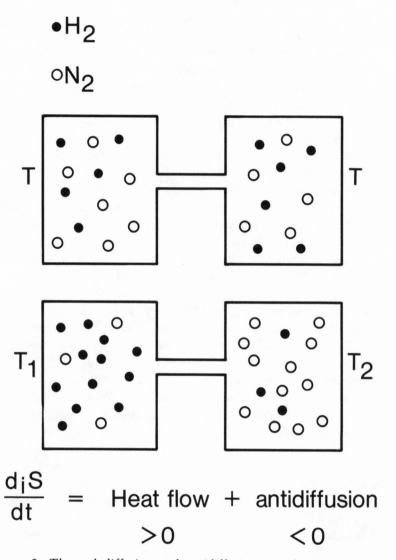

$$\frac{d_i S}{dt} = \text{Heat flow} + \text{antidiffusion}$$
$$> 0 \qquad\qquad < 0$$

Figure 2. Thermal diffusion and antidiffusion in a biatomic mixture submitted to external constraints.

Order and disorder are produced together; entropy is the price of structure. This is more obvious when we drive a system far from thermodynamic equilibrium, towards the so-called nonlinear part of nonequilibrium thermodynamics. Now why is this such an interesting range?

Because for nonequilibrium situations, we have to take into account the nonlinearity of the equations that describe the processes involved: mass transport, chemical reactions, and so on. As everybody knows, nonlinear equations have more than one solution; this multiplicity of nonequilibrium solutions in hydrodynamical or chemical systems is now studied in many laboratories. I am still amazed by the variety and the beauty of these structures.

A very simple example corresponds to chemical clocks. Everybody has heard of the Belousov-Zhabotinski reaction, in which molecules become "red," then "blue," and so on. The *Scientific American* and several other journals had this reaction on their front page. Indeed, I believe this is one of the greatest experiments of our century. A great experiment is one in which you learn something unexpected. When I look at a chemical clock, I am still amazed, because when we think about a chemical reaction, we imagine molecules traveling like dust particles in all directions, colliding at random. This would imply no coherence, no macroscopic oscillations. In fact, at equilibrium, we would have no coherence: One molecule would be red, another blue, but one would not expect to see the whole vessel becoming blue, then red. What this surprising experiment shows is that far from equilibrium, coherence may appear.

This leads to an inversion of our traditional views about order and disorder. According to the classical view, order is associated with equilibrium, and disorder with nonequilibrium. Look at a crystal; what could be more ordered than this equilibrium structure? What could be more disordered than turbulence? The present inversion runs as follows: A crystal may be described as a superposition of normal modes of waves, and these waves are incoherent at equilibrium. This is what we observe when we measure the specific heat of a solid; this is the disorder of the thermal waves. We know today, however, that turbulence is a highly ordered structure. Therefore, we are at the forefront of a complete change of paradigm in physics.

The interesting point is to analyze how nonequilibrium can give rise to structures. Some structures may be coherent in time, as chemical oscillations are, which lead to a limit cycle; others may be less coherent. Today the interest of researchers has shifted toward "dynamical chaos" arising in deterministic systems far from equilibrium. I cannot go into much detail here; let me just mention that chaos corresponds to situations where phase points describing the state of the system are attracted to regions that are formed by "many" points, in fact to point sets that have an effective dimension that may not be an integer but a fractal number. I am amazed by the large number of applications of dynamical chaos for understanding our environment. For example, very interesting papers (Nicolis and Nicolis, 1984) have been published concerning the evolution of terrestrial climate, showing that climatic equations should have this type of complexity. How would a classical physicist see the succession of Ice Ages? He may think, "This is so because the temperature on emerged continents is the outcome of many, say, 120 variables, each of them fluctuating, and thus it has to display some Gaussian distribution." Recent analysis has shown that things are not so; in fact, the (fractal) dimension of the system involved is only of the order of 3.2, which means that the climatic system could be described by four independent variables. The world around us displays an intrinsic instability, leading to a high complexity. In a paper published by some of my coworkers (Babloyantz and Destexhe, 1987; Babloyantz, Salazar and Nicolis, 1985), they show that brain waves are also characterized by such a fractal dimension, except in epileptic fits, during which the signals are described in a low-dimensional space; in other words, brain activity here becomes much more regular. I believe that in biology we encounter not only regularity (like heartbeats, or regulation of enzymatic reactions) but also instability through which very small effects may be amplified. This seems to happen with the brain, which is essentially an amplification mechanism, and for this reason requires a complex unstable dynamical structure.

As I mentioned, nonlinearity implies the possibility of many possible stationary states; transitions between those states occur at bifurcation points, in the neighborhood of which one can expect probabilistic behavior. This latter characteristic is indeed observed; we may check the outcome of experiments on bifurcations and test whether they correspond to some simple probabilistic distributions. Macroscopic physics thus illustrates the emergence of probabilistic schemes.

In conclusion, we see that the outcome of twenty years of study of nonequilibrium macroscopic physics shows very clearly that the three elements I have mentioned—probability, irreversibility, and coherence—are part of our physical environment. The question, therefore, arises, What kind of physical world gives the foundation for this behavior? In some sense, what we are trying to do in order to answer this question is somewhat similar to what Bergson and Whitehead tried in the past. First, we analyze what is going on around us. From this state of affairs we then have to infer some basic structures, which must be such that on the macroscopic level they display the behavior we observe. Of course, you can imagine many types of microscopic structures, but we have to see what kind of dynamics gives rise to the observed type of macroscopic behavior. Here again, the twentieth century is rich in unexpected developments.

The Microscopic Level

At the time of Boltzmann, it was impossible to imagine a form of dynamics that would have given rise to irreversibility. At this time, the archetype of dynamics was "integrable systems," that is, periodic systems described by angle-action variables, systems such as planetary motion around the sun, the pendulum, and other simple systems.

In the framework of the dynamics of integrable systems, nothing can change when we replace t with –t. If the world were made of only such periodic motions, there would be no chemistry, no biology; this very lecture would not have taken place. The question then is, What kind of dynamical systems do we need in order to describe the world we are living in?

We have to mention here a celebrated theorem by Poincaré. He was the first to point out that dynamical systems are in general not integrable; integrable systems correspond only to a very special case. As a consequence, action variables (which are invariants for integrable systems) do not exist in the general case. This result originates in the divergence problem due to "resonance": When different degrees of freedom interact, there may be resonance, and this leads to strong coupling, which in turn destroys the possibility of action variables. This is the main content of Poincaré's theorem, which led to a new development, still in progress now; this new theory was founded by Kolmogorov in 1954, then continued by Arnold and Moser, and therefore is called the KAM theory (see Arnold and Avez, 1968).

In systems described by this theory, most points correspond still to periodic motion (elliptic points), but we also have hyperbolic points corresponding to motion. Kolmogorov himself discovered a new class of dynamical systems in which nearly all points are points of instability. In other words, two points, which are as close as I want, will always separate, time going on. This new class was called Kolmogorov flows or K-flows.

Once we encounter such situations, we see that the concept of trajectory (which constitutes the basis of dynamics) loses its meaning (Elskens and Prigogine, 1986) because of the exponential divergence of the distance between two points marking neighboring initial conditions (this divergence is measured by the so-called "Lyapunov exponents").

Let me use an example. If I throw some dice or a coin, I will observe a probabilistic distribution. Is this a contradiction to the laws of physics? Of course not. But what then does this mean? It means that within a given range of precision I cannot prepare a trajectory corresponding to a given outcome. Therefore, I may now ask the following question: Are the laws of nature genuinely deterministic? To answer this question, I will have to increase the precision of my initial set of conditions. If for a sufficient range of precision I eventually come to a certitude for a "plus" outcome (for some set of initial conditions), then the system under study is deterministic. But if to reach this certitude infinite precision is required, if each point leading to "plus" is surrounded by points leading to "minus" and conversely, we will never reach a deterministic prediction.

This is what happens with K-flows. In other words, laws of nature become probabilistic laws. An often discussed example of dynamical system corresponding to the case of K-flows is given by the so-called "baker transformation": take a square representing some set of initial conditions and apply to it the well-known operations common to bakers: flatten, cut, fold.

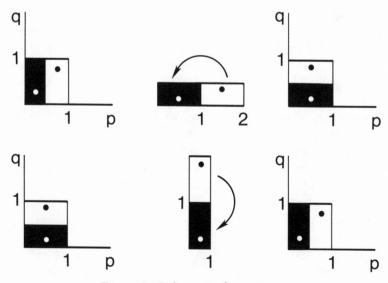

Figure 3. Baker transformation.

Any domain of initial conditions is fragmented into more and more subdivisions as time goes on. This "squashing" can be represented by a very simple, symbolic dynamical form. If we represent a point in such space by an infinite sequence of digits, then the dynamical process corresponds to "shifting" one digit to the next. There can be no simple dynamical law. Still, this dynamical law leads to a breakdown of the concept of trajectory. Suppose I do know the initial state of the system with a fifty-digit precision; after fifty shift operations, the fifty-first becomes the most important. The known number of digits is irrelevant here, since it only influences the time scale. Certainly there can be other simple dynamical processes, for example, the one in which the first digit commutes with the second and the second with the first, and so on; in this case it would be enough to consider finite information. But in K-flows, we consider infinite information; this is very important, since irreversibility results from the inevitable reduction of (postulated) infinite information to (available) finite information. Let us emphasize this conclusion. We have only a finite window open to nature around us; we never know nature with infinite precision, "point-wise." We know nature through finite regions corresponding to a nonvanishing measure; we know only regions of phase-space.

Let us come back to the baker transformation and look at the temporal evolution it induces. We may distinguish contracting (vertical) and dilating (horizontal) fibers. This is a characteristic of all K-flows. Each point occupies the intersection of a contracting and a dilating fiber; distinct initial conditions represented by points located on the same contracting fiber will converge; points located on dilating fibers will diverge.

"Finite information" means one should consider some set of points on a contracting fiber as a single "unit," because if I am unable to distinguish them now (within some given amount of precision), I will never be able to distinguish them in the future. We encounter here a principle of indistinguishability, which is propagated by dynamics. These contracting and dilating manifolds have a broken time-symmetry, which leads us to introduce an element of nonlocality for contracting fibers; we have to treat bundles of "trajectories" together that evolve towards the same future state. This has far-reaching consequences. We are indeed led from a description in terms of groups to one in terms of semi-groups: from reversibility to irreversibility.

The main point here is not that irreversibility comes from some approximation to a time-reversible description; on the contrary, reversibility is an idealization (even more so, an incorrect one), a singular

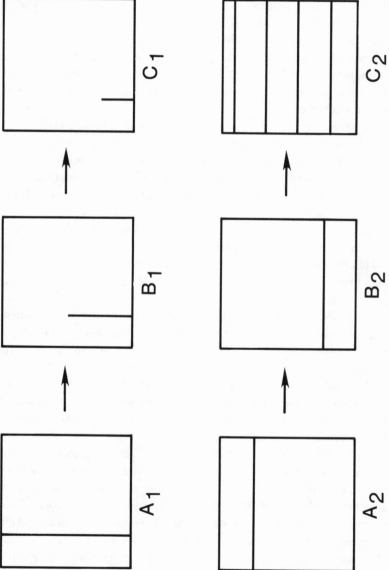

Figure 4. Contracting ($A_1B_1C_1$) and Dilating ($A_2B_2C_2$) fibers affected by the Baker transformation.

limit of irreversibility. In contrast, the classical view, which one can find in most books, is that an irreversible description is an approximation to be superimposed on exact equations of motion. However, the opposite is true: we have indeed to take into account the fact that in any physical experiment or in natural processes, interaction can only happen through a finite number of digits. The semi-group depends on the resolving power of the contracting fiber, but it remains a semi-group whatever this resolution may be. If you let this resolving power approach zero, you encounter a singular limit, and this singular limit corresponds to classical mechanics.

Of course, these considerations apply only to a limited class of dynamical systems, the class where almost each point is hyperbolic. I have shown very recently that large dynamical systems in which you have what kinetic theory calls a "collision operator" are also dynamical systems where almost all points are hyperbolic. This is because the collision operator of kinetic theory expresses the fact that there exists a continuous set of resonance (not only located at rational points like in Poincaré's theorem but at almost every point).

This has consequences also for quantum mechanics: If a quantum system presents unstable states (such as the hydrogen atom in an excited state), this unstable state is connected to the ground state through an infinite number of paths. Indeed, the atom can emit photons in all directions, the only condition being that it has the right energy. This leads then to the nonvanishing of the collision operator, which simply measures the lifetime expectancy of the unstable state.

This leads me to some recent results (even though they are not yet widely accepted). First, let us make some comments about the realm of quantum theory. One of my Parisian friends pointed out to me recently a beautiful remark by Eddington (1929, pp. 216ff) and Schrödinger (1932, p. 196).* Eddington (1929, writing in 1926) suggested that there could be some relation between the Hilbert space structure of quantum theory and time-reversibility. If you consider a wave function Ψ that propagates to the future, its complex conjugate Ψ^* goes towards the past, and thus $\Psi\Psi^*$ is time-symmetrical. Therefore, the Hilbert space description is correct if time can be resolved in two sequences, one going to the future and one going to the past. But irreversibility corresponds precisely to a situation where there is no symmetry between t and –t. Therefore, one has to expect that irreversibility would "kill" the Hilbert

---

*I owe these references to Simon Diner.

space and require a modification of quantum mechanics. Indeed, four years ago, Misra and I (Prigogine, 1980, Appendix A) proved that if there is an entropy operator in quantum theory at all, it cannot be in Hilbert space but only in the product space. The entropy operator would be nonfactorizable and would, therefore, not conserve the factorization of the wave functions in the density matrix.

More recently, we have shown that there is a classification of dynamical systems, even for quantum theory. First, let me mention some curious aspects of the history of classical and quantum mechanics. Classical mechanics started with the angle-action variables (corresponding to integrable systems), and it was only after Poincaré's theorem that people became convinced that integrability corresponds to special cases. This started a real revolution in classical dynamics: deterministic chaos, Feigenbaum sequences of cascading bifurcations, all this is the outcome of Poincaré's theorem (Lebowitz and Penrose, 1973). Now it is very amusing for a historian of science to notice that since the beginnings of quantum mechanics angle-action variables played such a dominant role. Bohr's theory started with angle-action variables; this led to Bohr-Sommerfeld quantization rule. Heisenberg's whole program was based on the analogy with angle-action variables. Because the Schrödinger equation has a discrete spectrum in a finite volume, the wave function has a behavior quite similar to that of angle-action systems. Therefore, for finite systems, there can be no problem in quantum theory. But what happens in the limit of large quantum systems? This limit is far from being uninteresting, since all of field theory deals with it. Recently, my coworker Tomio Petrosky (Prigogine and Petrosky, forthcoming) and I have developed techniques for understanding the transition from angle-action variables in this limit. We started with a quantum version of Poincaré's theorem, and the result is very simple: If continuous sets of resonance appear, the usual angle-action variable formalism cannot be implemented. More precisely, if there are unstable states with finite lifetimes, the unitary transformation leading to a diagonalization of the Hamiltonian diverges. If there are no lifetimes, but only stable states, nothing has to be changed. Of course, we know we are in a world of finite lifetimes. There was always a problem with unstable particles or states in quantum theory. An example is the conflict between exponential decay and quantum mechanics; exponential decay law is very appealing, because it is self-propagating, self-scaling, and so one. In quantum mechanics (and this is explained in all textbooks), exponential decay law cannot be correct for all times. This leads to a lot of unpleasantness; even if there is a small deviation from the exponential law, old and young mesons would be different, as their decay laws would be different. Therefore, they would not be indiscernible. Now this would bring chaos into all of physics. We should then apply Boltzmann's statistics. In fact, the question is not how small or large the deviations are; either things are discernible, or they are not.

Since the start (and this refers to what has been discussed by other people at this conference), quantum mechanics has a dual structure. As von Neumann stated, we have on one side the Schrödinger equation, and on the other the measurement process. In our interpretation, the dual structure of quantum mechanics comes from the dual structure of dynamical systems in quantum theory. In other words, for one kind of system, Schrödinger's equation is correct, but for the other type of system, we have a semi-group structure with equations close to master equations (such as the Pauli equation), including lifetimes.

Of course, then, there is no more need for the reduction of the wave packet by us or by anyone else. We have to take into account that the apparatus is part of the system; then we have a dynamical system presenting unstable states, and this requires a description in terms of semi-groups. This has still to be tested and submitted to the (it is hoped) constructive criticism of my colleagues in physics, but the existence of the dual structure of quantum mechanics from the point of view of dynamical systems is a fact that has been now established. I want to leave open (at the present time) the question if we may now disregard the measurement process in quantum theory, but I believe this is so.

Cosmology

I would now like to refer to the most spectacular field of physics—cosmology—since we cannot understand time and irreversibility without their cosmological context. (Géhéniau and Prigogine, 1986; Prigogine and Géhéniau, 1986). Conversely, the main impetus for evolutionary thinking (I would say) comes from modern cosmology, which has a dramatic history. When Einstein issued his static model of the universe in 1917, this was the realization of a geometrical universe. But then we observed the recession of galaxies, and, at the same time, Einstein's solution was shown to be unstable. Some could (and did) say, however, Do not worry about singularities; the apparent evolution of the universe is just a scaling phenomenon. I knew professor Lemaître well. He told me of his discussions with Einstein, who was the first to take singularities seriously. The idea was taken over by Gamow and my friends Herman and Alpher, and the decisive experimental confirmation was to come in 1965 with the discovery of black-body radiation, which leads to a different point of view (Weinberg, 1977).

First, the universe is made of two components, photons and baryons, the former in excess over the latter. As a result, there is no longer a purely geometric evolution, but also a thermal and a "chemical" evolution. Present cosmologies extrapolate from this radiation to initial conditions where the temperature was of the order of "Planck temperature" 10^{32}, and a high density—"Planck density." These initial conditions are difficult to understand, so we have to inquire how they came about. As would be expected, there are conflicting theories. One, the so-called "inflatory universe," has proved to be quite successful when one deals with some of the difficulties of the "standard" Big Bang theory. But it remains silent concerning the origins of matter. This is dealt with in the new approach, due to Brout, Englert, Gunzig, and Nardone (Brout, Englert, and Gunzig, 1978; Gunzig and Nardone, 1984), based on the possible instability of the Minkowski vacuum. In this latter theory, Minkowski background would become unstable with respect to production of heavy particles; this would lead to a curvature of space-time, while energy would be conserved. Our universe would then be a "free lunch," as the energy of the vacuum would be the same as the energy of the universe. (Jordan made this remark many years ago.) If you consider all the mass of particles and subtract the gravitational negative entropy, you obtain zero (as an order of magnitude). Energy does not, therefore, make the difference between "being" and "not being." Being a thermodynamicist, you would expect me to suggest that this difference resides in entropy. The price for our universe has to be expressed in the same currency as the price for Bénard instability. This is confirmed by the dual structure of our universe in which most photons are "waste products": The only thing they do is cool or heat up according to the expansion or the contraction of the universe; the "real," interesting objects are the elementary particles, such as the protons, which are nonequilibrium objects, floating in the midst of the photons ($= 10^9$ photons per baryon).

(I must say that nature has developed very clever ways of handling the problem of pollution—the ecological problem of the universe. If you would have been present at the beginning of our universe, you would have said, "What a terrible universe, full of disorder!" Today you would say, "Such an ordered universe!" And all this comes from the fact that the waste products have been very nicely taken away, simply by lowering the temperature. As the energy of the photons depends strongly on temperature, nature made them invisible by cooling the universe, through adiabatic expansion.)

The idea of the instability of the Minkowski universe is clearly connected to that of an entropy production related to the transformation of space-time into matter. First, we would have mini-black-holds, which are then transformed into a mixture of photons and protons; this corresponds to an enormous burst of entropy. In this sense, heat death is behind us and not in front of us. Most of the entropy has been around since the beginning of the universe.

In this approach, one singles out one degree of freedom of the gravitational field, which is related to the conformal factor (the "cosmological" field), and one couples it with a scalar mass field, producing heavy particles, which then decay. The irreversibility of the universe is in this way related to the evolution of the conformal factor. We obtain an irreversible "geometrical" evolution. As you know, the main element is the line element ds^2. The Minkowski line element is $dr^2 - dt^2$ and the conformal factor is what multiplies the Minkowski ds^2 and leads to ds^2.

This conformal factor determines the instability problem and the entropy production related to the transfer of gravitational energy to matter. What I find interesting in this model is that, from this point of view, time is "creating the universe": Time, in some strange way, has to precede existence. Curiously, these views combine the old "steady state" model elaborated by Hoyle, Bondi, and Gold and the "Big Bang" model (Weinberg, 1972). Indeed, in this instability model, the birth of the universe occurred as an initial phase transition, from a Minkowski space to an open Friedmann-Lemaître universe. Eventually matter would disperse according to the Hubble expansion; we would come back to a Minkowski space, and a new universe would arise.

If the initial burst, however, would give rise to a closed universe, the standard cosmology would predict a periodic universe. In our formulation, the universe would become a prisoner of the matter that has been produced. Matter would appear in higher and higher concentration as the result of the contraction. But if this process of transformation of a cosmological degree of freedom into matter is irreversible, the inverse process is impossible. It is too early to speculate on what kind of universe we are living in, but what seems certain is that irreversibility deeply affects the structure of the universe.

In this view, Einstein's equations have to be generalized. These equations relate space-time geometry and matter; in order to include entropy, they have to be generalized. Einstein himself was well aware of the phenomenological character of the matter tensor T^μ in his equation. In the case of the conformal universe, it is easy to understand how this tensor can be decomposed into a "renormalized" matter tensor plus a tensor related to entropy production. Immediately after the birth of a universe (after a Planck time), the entropy term tends to disappear, and we come back to the usual Einstein equations describing the adiabatic expansion of the universe.

Conclusion

In conclusion, I believe that we are at a very interesting moment in the history of science. The first third of the century has given rise to fundamentally new conceptual structures: quantum mechanics and relativity. But still, these revolutions were interpreted in the spirit of the preceding development of physics. The second third of this century led to unexpected discoveries.

I still remember my excitement when I was shown the first photographic emulsions proving the existence of unstable mesons. Then came the unexpected discovery of nonequilibrium structures, such as chemical clocks displaying the new type of coherence related to nonequilibrium constraints. All this seems to me to point in the same direction: the description of a universe in which time as irreversibility plays a fundamental role.

Coming back to what I stated earlier, I would say that this view integrates human history and human culture. In his introduction to my lecture, Professor Fixman was kind enough to quote my work on the kinetic theory of traffic. I happen to be very interested in that subject; indeed, I believe that the fundamental mechanisms of nature are very similar (as could be expected). Perhaps it is on the level of human society and in our environment that we can see some of these features quite clearly. When we drive a car, we "feel" a bifurcation when we go from a "dilute" traffic to a "concentrated" one (in fact, this was my first example of a nonequilibrium structure). However this may be, our views of the outside world and the "world inside us" do now converge. We thus come a step closer towards a unified view of nature, including man.

References

Alexander, H. G., ed. 1956. *The Leibniz-Clarke Correspondence.* Manchester: Manchester University Press.

Arnold, V., and Avez, A. 1968. *Ergodic Problems of Classical Mechanics*. New York: Benjamin.

Babloyantz, A., and Destexhe, A. 1987. Strange Attractors in the Human Cortex. *Temporal Disorders and Human Oscillatory Systems*. Ed. L. Rensing, W. Van der Heiden, and M. C. Mackey. Berlin: Springer.

Babloyantz, A., Salazar, J. M., and Nicolis, C. 1985. Evidence of Chaotic Dynamics of Brain Activity During the Sleep Cycle. *Physics Letters* 111A: 152–56.

Brout, R., Englert, F., and Gunzig, E. 1978. The Creation of the Universe as a Quantum Phenomenon. *Annals of Physics* 115: 78–106.

Eddington, A. S. 1929. *The Nature of the Physical World*. Cambridge: Cambridge University Press.

Elskens, Y., and Prigogine, I. 1986. From Instability to Irreversibility. *Proceedings of the National Academy of Science* 83: 5756–60.

Géhéniau, J., and Prigogine, I. 1986. The Birth of Time. *Foundations of Physics* 16: 437–43.

Gerhardt, C. J., ed. 1890. *Die philosophische Schriften von G. W. Leibniz* 7: 347–421. Berlin & Halle: Weidmann.

Gunzig, E. & Nardone, P. 1984. Scalar Trace Anomaly and Anti-Gravitational Interaction in a Perturbative Approach to Self-Consistent Cosmologies. *Physics Letters* 134B: 412–14.

Lebowitz, J., and Penrose, O. 1973. Modern Ergodic Theory. *Physics Today* 26: 23–29.

Nicolis, C., and Nicolis, G. 1984. Is there a Climatic Attractor? *Nature* 311: 529–32.

Pape, H., ed. Forthcoming. *Charles Sanders Peirce: Schriften zur Semiotik der Kosmologie*.

Prigogine, I. 1980. *From Being to Becoming*. New York: Freeman.

Prigogine, I., and Elskens, Y. 1986. Irreversibility, Stochasticity and Non-locality in Classical Dynamics. *Quantum Implications. Essays in Honour of David Bohm*. Ed. B. Hiley and D. Peat. London: Routledge & Kegan Paul.

Prigogine, I., and Géhéniau, J. 1986. Entropy, Matter and Cosmology. *Proceedings of the National Academy of Science* 83: 6245–49.

Prigogine, I., and Petrosky, T. Forthcoming. Limits to Quantum Theory? *Essays in Honor of K. Tomita.* Ed. T. Kawasaki.

Prigogine, I., and Stengers, I. 1984. *Order out of Chaos.* New York: Bantam Books.

Schrödinger, E. 1932. Une analogie entre la mécanique ondulatoire et quelques problèmes de probabilités en physique classique. *Annales de l'Institut Henri Poincaré* 2: 296–310.

Weinberg, S. 1972. *Gravitation and Cosmology.* New York: John Wiley & Sons.

Weinberg, S. 1977. *The First Three Minutes.* New York: Basic Books.

Chapter 9

THE ROLE OF PHYSICS IN THE CURRENT CHANGE OF PARADIGMS

Fritjof Capra

Crisis and Transformation in Science and Society

The dramatic change in concepts and ideas that happened in physics during the first three decades of this century has been widely discussed by physicists and philosophers for more than fifty years. It led Thomas Kuhn (1970) to the notion of a scientific paradigm, a constellation of achievements—concepts, values, techniques, and so on—shared by a scientific community and used by that community to define legitimate problems and solutions. Changes of paradigms, according to Kuhn, occur in discontinuous, revolutionary breaks called paradigm shifts.

Today, twenty-five years after Kuhn's analysis, we recognize paradigm shifts in physics as an integral part of a much larger cultural transformation (Capra, 1983). The intellectual crisis of quantum physicists in the 1920s is mirrored today by a similar but much broader cultural crises. The major problems of our time—the growing threat of nuclear war, the devastation of our natural environment, our inability to deal with poverty and starvation around the world, to name just the most urgent ones—are all different facets of one single crisis, which is essentially a crisis of perception. Like the crisis in quantum physics, it derives from the fact that most of us, and especially our large social institutions, subscribe to the concepts of an outdated world view, inadequate for dealing with the problems of our overpopulated, globally interconnected world. At the same time, researchers in several scientific disciplines, various social movements, and numerous alternative organizations and networks are developing a new vision of reality that will form the basis of our future technologies, economic systems, and social institutions.

What we are seeing today is a shift of paradigms not only within science but also in the larger social arena. To analyze that cultural transformation, I have generalized Kuhn's account of a scientific paradigm to that of a *social paradigm,* which I define as "a constellation of concepts, values, perceptions, and practices shared by a community, which form a particular vision of reality that is the basis of the way the community organizes itself" (Capra, 1986, p. 11).

The social paradigm now receding has dominated our culture for several hundred years, during which it has shaped our modern Western society and has significantly influenced the rest of the world. This paradigm consists of a number of ideas and values, among them the view of the universe as a mechanical system composed of elementary building blocks, the view of the human body as a machine, the view of life in a society as a competitive struggle for existence, the belief in unlimited material progress to be achieved through economic and technological growth and—last but not least—the belief that a society, in which the female is everywhere subsumed under the male, is one that follows from some basic law of nature. During recent decades, all of these assumptions have been found severely limited and in need of radical revision.

Indeed, such a revision is now taking place. The emerging new paradigm may be called a holistic, or an ecological, world view, using the term *ecological* here in a much broader and deeper sense than it is commonly used. Ecological awareness, in that deep sense, recognizes the fundamental interdependence of all phenomena and the embeddedness of individuals and societies in the cyclical processes of nature.

Ultimately, deep ecological awareness is spiritual or religious awareness. When the concept of the human spirit is understood as the mode of consciousness in which the individual feels connected to the cosmos as a whole, which is the root meaning of the word *religion* (from the Latin *religare* meaning "to bind strongly"), it becomes clear that ecological awareness is spiritual in its deepest essence. It is, therefore, not surprising that the emerging new vision of reality, based on deep ecological awareness, is consistent with the "perennial philosophy" of spiritual traditions, for example, that of Eastern spiritual traditions, the spirituality of Christian mystics, or with the philosophy and cosmology underlying the native American traditions (Capra, 1984).

The Systems Approach

In science, the language of systems theory, and especially the theory of living systems, seems to provide the most appropriate formulation of the new ecological paradigm (Capra, 1983, Chapter 9). Since living systems cover such a wide range of phenomena—individual organisms, social systems, and ecosystems—the theory provides a common framework and language for biology, psychology, medicine, economics, ecology, and many other sciences, a framework in which the so urgently needed ecological perspective is explicitly manifest.

The conceptual framework of contemporary physics, and especially those aspects that will be the focus of this conference, may be seen as a special case of the systems approach, dealing with nonliving systems and exploring the interface between nonliving and living systems. It is important to recognize, I believe, that in the new paradigm physics is no longer the model and source of metaphors for the other sciences. Even though the paradigm shift in physics is still of special interest, since it was the first to occur in modern science, physics has now lost its role as the science providing the most fundamental description of reality.

I would now like to specify what I mean by the systems approach. To do so, I shall identify five criteria of systems thinking that, I claim, hold for all the sciences—the natural sciences, the humanities, and the social sciences. I shall formulate each criterion in terms of the shift from the old to the new paradigm, and I will illustrate the five criteria with examples from contemporary physics. However, since the criteria hold for all the sciences, I could equally well illustrate them with examples from biology, psychology, or economics.

1. Shift from the Part to the Whole. In the old paradigm, it is believed that in any complex system the dynamics of the whole can be understood from the properties of the parts. The parts themselves cannot be analyzed any further, except by reducing them to still smaller parts. Indeed, physics has been progressing in that way, and at each step there has been a level of fundamental constituents that could not be analyzed any further.

In the new paradigm, the relationship between the parts and the whole is reversed. The properties of the parts can be understood only from the dynamics of the whole. In fact, ultimately there are no parts at all. What we call a part is merely a pattern in an inseparable web of relationships. The shift from the part to the whole was the central aspect of the conceptual revolution of quantum physics in the 1920s. Heisenberg was so impressed by this aspect that he entitled his autobiography *Der Teil und das Ganze (The Part and the Whole)* (Heisenberg, 1970/1971). More recently, the view of physical reality as a web of relationships has been emphasized by Henry Stapp (1971, 1972), who showed how this view is embodied in S-matrix theory.

2. *Shift from Structure to Process.* In the old paradigm, there are fundamental structures, and then there are forces and mechanisms through which these interact, thus giving rise to processes. In the new paradigm, every structure is seen as the manifestation of an underlying process. The entire web of relationships is intrinsically dynamic. The shift from structure to process is evident, for example, when we remember that mass in contemporary physics is no longer seen as measuring a fundamental substance but rather as a form of energy, that is, as measuring activity or processes. The shift from structure to process is also apparent in the work of Ilya Prigogine, who entitled his classic book *From Being to Becoming* (Prigogine, 1980).

3. *Shift from Objective to "Epistemic" Science.* In the old paradigm, scientific descriptions are believed to be objective, that is, independent of the human observer and the process of knowing. In the new paradigm, it is believed that epistemology—the understanding of the process of knowledge—has to be included explicitly in the description of natural phenomena. This recognition entered into physics with Heisenberg and is closely related to the view of physical reality as a web of relationships. Whenever we isolate a pattern in this network and define it as a part, or an object, we do so by cutting through some of its connections to the rest of the network, and this may be done in different ways. As Heisenberg (1971, p. 58) put it, "What we observe is not nature itself, but nature exposed to our method of questioning."

This method of questioning, in other words epistemology, inevitably becomes part of the theory. At present, there is no consensus about what is the proper epistemology, but there is an emerging consensus that epistemology will have to be an integral part of every scientific theory.

4. Shift from "Building" to "Network" as Metaphor of Knowledge.
The metaphor of knowledge as a building has been used in Western
science and philosophy for thousands of years. There are *fundamental*
laws, *fundamental* principles, basic building blocks, and so on. The
edifice of science must be built on firm foundations. During periods of
paradigm shift, it was always felt that the foundations of knowledge were
shifting, or even crumbling, and that feeling induced great anxiety. Einstein (1949), for example, wrote in his autobiography about the early
days of quantum mechanics:

> All my attempts to adapt the theoretical foundation of physics to this (new
> type) of knowledge failed completely. It was as if the ground had been
> pulled out from under one, with no firm foundation to be seen anywhere,
> upon which one could have built. (p. 45)

In the new paradigm, the metaphor of knowledge as a building is
being replaced by that of the network. Since we perceive reality as a
network of relationships, our descriptions, too, form an interconnected
network of concepts and models in which there are no foundations. For
most scientists this metaphor of knowledge as a network with no firm
foundations is extremely uncomfortable. It is explicitly expressed in
physics in Geoffrey Chew's bootstrap theory of particles (see Capra,
1985). According to Chew, nature cannot be reduced to any fundamental
entities, but has to be understood entirely through self-consistency.
There are no fundamental equations or fundamental symmetries in the
bootstrap theory. Physical reality is seen as a dynamic web of interrelated
events. Things exist by virtue of their mutually consistent relationships,
and all of physics has to follow uniquely from the requirement that its
components be consistent with one another and with themselves. This
approach is so foreign to our traditional scientific ways of thinking that
it is pursued today only by a small minority of physicists.

When the notion of scientific knowledge as a network of concepts
and models, in which no part is any more fundamental than the others,
is applied to science as a whole, it implies that physics can no longer be
seen as the most fundamental level of science. Since there are no foundations in the network, the phenomena described by physics are not any
more fundamental than those described, for example, by biology or psychology. They belong to different systems-levels, but none of those levels
is any more fundamental than the others.

5. Shift from Truth to Approximate Descriptions. The four criteria
of systems thinking presented so far are all interdependent. Nature is

seen as an interconnected, dynamic web of relationships, in which the identification of specific patterns as "objects" depends on the human observer and the process of knowledge. This web of relationships is described in terms of a corresponding network of concepts and models, none of which is any more fundamental than the others.

This new approach immediately raises an important question: If everything is connected to everything else, how can you ever hope to understand anything? Since all natural phenomena are ultimately interconnected, in order to explain any one of them we need to understand all the others, which is obviously impossible.

What makes it possible to turn the systems approach into a scientific theory is the fact that there is such a thing as approximate knowledge. This insight is crucial to all of modern science. The old paradigm is based on the Cartesian belief in the certainty of scientific knowledge. In the new paradigm, it is recognized that all scientific concepts and theories are limited and approximate. Science can never provide any complete and definitive understanding. Scientists do not deal with truth in the sense of a precise correspondence between the description and the described phenomena. They deal with limited and approximate descriptions of reality. Heisenberg often pointed out that important fact. For example, he wrote in *Physics and Philosophy,* "The often discussed lesson that has been learned from modern physics [is] that every word or concept, clear as it may seem to be, has only a limited range of applicability" (Heisenberg, 1971, p. 125).

Self-Organizing Systems

The broadest implications of the systems approach are found today in a new theory of living systems, which originated in cybernetics in the 1940s and emerged in its main outlines over the last twenty years (Capra, 1984a). As I mentioned before, living systems include individual organisms, social systems, and ecosystems, and thus the new theory can provide a common framework and language for a wide range of disciplines—biology, psychology, medicine, economics, ecology, and many others.

The central concept of the new theory is that of self-organization. A living system is defined as a self-organizing system, which means that its order is not imposed by the environment but is established by the system itself. In other words, self-organizing systems exhibit a certain degree of autonomy. This does not mean that living systems are isolated from their environment; on the contrary, they interact with it continually, but this interaction does not determine their organization.

In this essay, I can give only a brief sketch of the theory of self-organizing systems. To do so, let me distinguish three aspects of self-organization:

1. *Pattern of organization:* the totality of relationships that define the system as an integrated whole.
2. *Structure:* the physical realization of the pattern of organization in space and time.
3. *Organizing activity:* the activity involved in realizing the pattern of organization.

For self-organizing systems, the pattern of organization is characterized by a mutual dependency of the system's parts, which is necessary and sufficient to understand the parts. This is quite similar to the pattern of relationships between subatomic particles in Chew's bootstrap theory. However, the pattern of self-organization has the additional property that gives the whole system an individual identity.

The pattern of self-organization has been studied extensively and described precisely by Humberto Maturana and Francisco Varela (1980), who have called it *autopoiesis,* which means literally self-production. Sometimes it is also called operational closure.

An important aspect of the theory is the fact that the description of the pattern of self-organization does not use any physical parameters, such as energy or entropy, nor does it use the concepts of space and time. It is an abstract mathematical description of a pattern of relationships. This pattern can be realized in space and time in different physical structures, which are then described in terms of the concepts of physics and chemistry. But such a description alone will fail to capture the biological phenomenon of self-organization. In other words, physics and chemistry are not enough to understand life; we also need to understand the pattern of self-organization, which is independent of physical and chemical parameters.

The structure of self-organizing systems has been studied extensively by Ilya Prigogine (1980), who has called it a dissipative structure. The two main characteristics of a dissipative structure are (1) that it is an open system, maintaining its pattern of organization through continuous exchange of energy and matter with its environment; and (2) that it operates far from thermodynamic equilibrium and thus cannot be described in terms of classical thermodynamics. One of Prigogine's greatest contributions has been to create a new thermodynamics to describe living systems.

The organizing activity of living, self-organizing systems, finally, is cognition, or mental activity. This implies a radically new concept of mind, which was first proposed by Gregory Bateson (1979). Mental process is defined as the organizing activity of life. This means that all interactions of a living system with its environment are cognitive, or mental interactions. With this new concept of mind, life and cognition become inseparably connected. Mind, or more accurately, mental process is seen as being immanent in matter at all levels of life.

I have taken some time to outline the emerging theory of self-organizing systems because it is today the broadest scientific formulation of the ecological paradigm with the most wide-ranging implications. The world view of contemporary physics, in my view, will have to be understood within that broader framework. In particular, any speculation about human consciousness and its relation to the phenomena described by physics will have to take into account the notion of mental process as the self-organizing activity of life.

Science and Ethics

A further reason why I find the theory of self-organizing systems so important is that it seems to provide the ideal scientific framework for an ecologically oriented ethics (Capra, 1984b). Such a system of ethics is urgently needed, since most of what scientists are doing today is not life-furthering and life-preserving but life-destroying. With physicists designing nuclear weapons that threaten to wipe out all life on the planet, with chemists contaminating our environment, with biologists releasing new and unknown types of micro-organisms into the environment without really knowing what the consequences are, with psychologists and other scientists torturing animals in the name of scientific progress, with all these activities occurring, it seems that it is most urgent to introduce ethical standards into modern science.

It is generally not recognized in our culture that values are not peripheral to science and technology but constitute their very basis and driving force. During the scientific revolution in the seventeenth century, values were separated from facts, and since that time we have tended to believe that scientific facts are independent of what we do and, therefore, independent of our values. In reality, scientific facts emerge out of an entire constellation of human perceptions, values, and actions—in a word, out of a paradigm—from which they cannot be separated. Although much of the detailed research may not depend explicitly on the scientist's value system, the larger paradigm within which this research is pursued will never be value-free. Scientists, therefore, are responsible for their research not only intellectually but also morally.

One of the most important insights of the new systems theory of life is that life and cognition are inseparable. The process of knowledge is also the process of self-organization, that is, the process of life. Our conventional model of knowledge is one of a representation or an image of independently existing facts, which is the model derived from classical physics. From the new systems point of view, knowledge is part of the process of life, of a dialogue between object and subject.

Knowledge and life, then, are inseparable, and, therefore, facts are inseparable from values. Thus, the fundamental split that made it impossible to include ethical considerations in our scientific world view has now been healed. At present, nobody has yet established a system of ethics that expresses the same ecological awareness on which the systems view of life is based, but I believe that this is now possible. I also believe that it is one of the most important tasks for scientists and philosophers today.

The Central Problem in Contemporary Physics

Let me now return to physics with a few concluding remarks about what I see as the central intellectual problem in contemporary physics.*

I have come to see the understanding of space and time as the central problem in physics today. Classical Newtonian physics, as you know, is formulated in terms of solid objects moving in absolute space and absolute time. Relativity theory is formulated in terms of a four-dimensional continuum, space-time, in which all space and time measurements are relative. Quantum mechanics, on the other hand, deals with discrete, that is, discontinuous phenomena—quanta, quantum jumps, and so on—which are not embedded in space-time.

Quantum mechanics, too, has a continuous formulation, that of continuous probability functions. According to Chew (Capra, 1985), the well-known paradoxes of quantum mechanics arise because of the fact that its formalism is embedded in continuous space-time, whereas the

---

*My opinions have been greatly influenced by the ideas of Geoffrey Chew and Henry Stapp, and by the discussions within our research group at UC Berkeley, led by Chew, which also includes Jerry Finkelstein.

phenomena it describes are not. It can also be argued that the contrast between the continuous space-time formulation of relativity theory and the discontinuous nature of quantum events has so far stood in the way of unifying the two theories.

Most physicists attempt such a unification in terms of quantum field theories—again a continuous formalism—that exhibit unpleasant, arbitrary features and internal inconsistencies. A minority of physicists—David Bohm, David Finkelstein, and our group around Chew—attempt to work at a deeper level, dealing with a web of relationships that is not embedded in continuous space-time and attempt to derive both relativistic space-time and quantum mechanics from that deeper level.

Let me briefly outline Chew's approach (Capra, 1985). It is based on the notion that physical reality at the microlevel is built from discrete quantum events: particle collisions, particle decays, and so on. The Cartesian macroreality of objects embedded in continuous space-time emerges from a collection of immensely large numbers of special "gentle" quantum events. These gentle events involve the emission and absorption of photons by charged particles.

The photon is a very special particle. It is massless and may carry arbitrarily small amounts of energy; thus, the disturbance of the charged particle, when it collides with the photon, may be arbitrarily slight. Very large numbers of gentle photon events then create the illusion that the charged particle follows a continuous trajectory in space-time.

The properties of photons and of electromagnetism are also crucial to the process of observation. Every observation takes place through electromagnetic interactions, and the approximate isolation of an observer from the observed is related to the gentleness of the intervening photon connections. According to Chew, measurement will not be described as occurring within space-time but rather as generating an approximate meaning for space-time.

Chew's program, then, is to derive continuous space-time (the notion of classical objects) and a theory of measurement (which is still lacking in quantum physics) from discrete quantum events and from the special role of gentle photons.

I find it very exciting that, even at the present tentative stage, Chew's approach shows several connections with the theory of self-organizing systems. One of them is the fact that the systems of subatomic particles, like the self-organizing systems of life, are described in terms of patterns of relationships that are not embedded in space and time. The other is the pattern of mutual dependency, which is basic to the organization of subatomic particles and of living systems.

Finally, a crucial aspect of gentle photon events, which leads to the emergence of classical trajectories and classical objects, is the fact that these events represent a concerted behavior of the system as a whole. Technically, we speak of a coherent superposition of individual photons. We are dealing here with collective behavior, with an overall organization of the whole system. At present, it is not clear what kind of principle accounts for such behavior. However, the similarity with self-organizing systems is striking. As Henry Stapp (private communication, 1986) put it in a recent seminar: "I am looking for some guiding principle—maybe some kind of self-reference of the system, or some self-organization that gives the system a kind of autonomy in its environment."

All this points to a convergence between the systems approach and the leading edge of research in contemporary physics. In my view, the most exciting work in physics in the coming years will be that which explores the interface between nonliving and living systems. The evidence available today indicates that we will find that the roots of life reach deeply into the nonliving world.

References

Bateson, G. 1979. *Mind and Nature.* New York: E. P. Dutton.

Capra, F. 1983. *The Turning Point.* New York: Bantam Books.

_____.1984a. *The Tao of Physics.* 2d ed. New York: Bantam Books.

_____, ed. 1984b. Science and Ethics. Elmwood Discussion Transcript Number 1. Berkeley, Calif.: The Elmwood Institute.

_____.1985. Bootstrap Physics: A Conversation with Geoffrey Chew. *A Passion for Physics.* Ed. C. De Tar, J. Finkelstein, and Chung-I Tang. Singapore: World Scientific.

_____.1986. The Concept of Paradigm and Paradigm Shift. *ReVision, 9,* 3ff.

Einstein, A. 1949. Autobiographical Notes. *Albert Einstein: Philosopher-Scientist.* Ed. P. A. Schilpp. The Library of Living Philosophers. Evanston, Ill.: Open Court.

Heisenberg, W. 1971. *Physics and Beyond.* New York: Harper & Row. (Originally published as *Der Teil und das Ganze* in 1970.)

_____.1971. *Physics and Philosophy.* New York: Harper & Row.

Kuhn, T. 1970. *The Structure of Scientific Revolutions.* Chicago: University of Chicago Press.

Maturana, H. R., and Varela, F. J. 1980. *Autopoiesis and Cognition.* Dordrecht: D. Reidel.

Prigogine, I. 1980. *From Being to Becoming.* San Francisco: Freeman.

Stapp, H. P. 1971. S-Matrix Interpretation of Quantum Theory. *Physical Review* D3: 1303–20.

_____.1972. The Copenhagen Interpretation. *American Journal of Physics* 40: 1098–116.

Chapter 10

CONTEMPORARY PHYSICS AND DIALECTICAL HOLISM

Errol E. Harris

Philosophical Implications of Classical Physics

It should have been apparent to philosophers for the past half century that the revolution in physics required a new metaphysic, or at least an adaptation of the metaphysics of some precursors of the now prevalent ideas. As long ago as the early 1940s, Collingwood in his *Essay on Metaphysics* (1940) maintained that the discipline was the discovery and critique of the absolute presuppositions of science, and in *The Idea of Nature* (1945), Collingwood suggested that the metaphysics appropriate to contemporary science was that of A. N. Whitehead, or something like it. For the past twenty years and more, disregarded by both scientists and philosophers, I have been advocating a metaphysic founded on contemporary scientific findings, one very different from that which has become dominant in the past few decades (Harris, 1965). This essay may be considered an extension of that advocacy.

The main reason for the general failure to recognize the need for a new metaphysic has no doubt been the long prevalence of empiricism in many philosophical circles, due initially to the influence of the Vienna Circle, which, even after the recantation of some of its own members, declared metaphysics (as Hume had done long before) to be meaningless and worthless. The various forms of analytic philosophy that developed out of logical positivism and replaced it, seem to have persuaded all who came under its influence, despite cogent arguments to the contrary, that metaphysics is neither a respectable nor even a possible pursuit. But it is an historical oddity that empiricism, which was the philosophy consonant with the science of the seventeenth and eighteenth centuries, should have reasserted itself in the twentieth century, after a scientific revolution had drastically transformed the conception of the physical universe.

The so-called classical physics of the seventeenth through nineteenth centuries was materialistic and mechanistic. Its conception of matter was particulate, inspired by the Renaissance preference for Democritus over Aristotle; its fundamental laws of motion were couched in terms of forces acting between mass-points in an absolute space and time, which, in Newton's words, "flows equably without relation to anything external." Its world was a vast machine made up of bodies in presumed external relation and moved by forces dependent only on their mass and the distance between them. In such a mechanical world, no provision was made for the knowing mind—for the mind of the scientist, who was presumed to observe terrestrial and celestial phenomena, as it were, from afar, without influencing their intrinsic nature. An awkward question arose as to how ideas of external things got into the mind. And what seemed an obvious answer—through sense-perception—was taken for granted, prompting the empirical philosophy of Thomas Hobbes, John Locke, George Berkeley, and David Hume. The problem of perception led to the still more intractable question of the relation, in such a material world, of body to mind, in response to which some, like Hobbes, reduced the latter to matter and motion, and others, like Berkeley, denied the existence of matter altogether, reducing it wholly to idea. All such philosophies, however, were prompted by the scientific presuppositions of the time, and their failure to maintain themselves consistently led to the condemnation and rejection of metaphysics, first by Hume and later by Kant. This has become the heritage, out of due time, of our own age, in stubborn disregard of the twentieth-century revolution in physics.

The World View of Contemporary Physics

My own protest against the anachronism of contemporary philosophy was first made in the early 1950s; however, the alternative I offered has not been heeded, and now, at last, scientists themselves have raised their voices and are appearing on the philosophical scene demanding a new metaphysic. In some of their more daring speculations, they do not all agree, raising serious and important metaphysical questions concerning the beginning and the end of the universe, the nature of temporal passage, the need (or lack of it) to presume a supernatural creator, the question of a "beyond," or what Professor Edward Harrison (1985, Chapter 14) calls "the problem of containment." He also poses the further question of whether our present view of the universe is true of the real Universe, or is merely another ephemeral doctrine, believed, like so many of its mutually contradictory predecessors, to be the final truth, but destined, like them, to be superseded and rejected as false. If this were indeed the case, we should have to abandon ourselves to scepticism, for to seek the metaphysical implications of our modern physics would be as futile as to seek to discover the nature of the real Universe itself, which Professor Harrison tells us is unknowable and inconceivable. It is not my present purpose to pursue these matters. There is one crucial point on which the majority of contemporary physicists seem to agree, that the physical world is one unbroken, undissectable, dynamic whole. It is on this point that I shall concentrate and on this fact that I shall center my case.

In a book published in 1959, W. D. Sciama affirmed "the Unity of the Universe" (the title of the book), on the basis of evidence ranging from the solution of Olber's paradox to the dependence of terrestrial centrifugal and Coriolis forces upon the motion of the fixed stars—"that is," as he states, "relative to some suitably defined average of all the matter in the universe." Similarly, he explained (Chapters VII-IX) how Newton's gravitational constant (G) is determined by the average density of matter in the universe, in conjunction with Hubble's constant (derived from the velocity of recession of the galaxies), illustrating Eddington's (1933, p. 120) emphatic contention, occasioned by the consequences of relativity theory, concerning the widespread interconnectedness of things.

The primary effect of the revolution initiated by Einstein and Planck was unification, an effect foreshadowed earlier when Faraday and Maxwell gave precedence to the electro-magnetic field over particulate matter.

Special relativity unified space and time, energy and matter. General relativity identified field with space-time curvature, in such a way that fundamental constants, physical laws and primary physical entities all became intimately linked with one another, prompting Eddington (1933) to pronounce the radius of local curvature to be the natural unit of measurement and to declaim on "the wide interrelatedness of things" (p. 120). Similarly, E. A. Milne (1943–1944) demonstrated that "the rest of the universe" is involved in every physical measurement. Einstein, Weyl, and Schrödinger all envisaged and sought mathematical expression for a unified field theory; Heisenberg expressed the conviction that physicists would eventually discover "a fundamental law of motion for matter from which all elementary particles and their properties can be derived mathematically" (1959, p. 60; compare also 1952, p. 103).

Quantum theory has reinforced this unifying tendency. Not only has it shown the intrinsic characteristics of particles to be unisolable, with conjugate qualities, and particles and waves to be interchangeable manifestations of the same entities, it has also shown (in accordance with Pauli's Principle of Exclusion) that the behavior and interrelation of particles depends essentially on their states of motion (or quantum numbers), no two like particles with the same quantum numbers being admissible in the same energy system. In short, the system takes precedence over the particle, the whole over the part. Waves and particles being equivalent, matter cannot be dissected out of the sea of radiant energy to which it is intrinsic. Consequently, "the world," says Heisenberg (1959), ". . . appears as a complicated tissue of events, in which connections of different kinds alternate or overlap or combine and thereby determine the texture of the whole" (p. 96). And Professor Capra (1975) writes, "Quantum theory forces us to see the universe not as a collection of physical objects, but rather as a complicated web of relations between the various parts of a unified whole" (p. 150).

More recently David Bohm (1980) has maintained, by way of discovering a credible interpretation of the quantum theory, that the physical substance of the world is a dynamic totality, which he calls "the holomovement," in which a principle of order is implicated and expresses itself variously in the emergence of phenomena and entities (such as elementary particles), so that, on the analogy of the holograph, the whole is implicit in every part.

Today the most insistent proponents of the unity of the physical world are the particle physicists. S-matrix and unified gauge theories have put them on a course towards a so-called "grand unified theory";

the goal of this theory is once more the unified field, incorporating in it all the forces of nature—electro-magnetic, gravitational, strong and weak—from which a complete description of all the various elementary particles, be they quarks, leptons, or hadrons, could be derived. These theories make it no longer possible to distinguish precisely between particles and the forces through which they interact, and their direct effect is holistic. To quote Capra again:

> The basic oneness of the universe is . . . one of the most important revelations of modern physics. It becomes apparent at the atomic level and manifests itself more and more as one penetrates deeper into matter, down to the realm of subatomic particles. . . . As we study the various models of subatomic physics we shall see that they express again and again, in different ways, the same insight—that the constituents of matter and the basic phenomena involving them are all interconnected, interrelated and interdependent; that they cannot be understood as isolated entities, but only as integrated parts of the whole. (1975, p. 142)

This discovery of wholeness has progressed so far that physicists are now actually planning the construction of a super particle-accelerator, which will enable them to discover the original force, combining all others, that they calculate prevailed for the first few billionths of a second after the Big Bang—the origin of the universe—and from which the four forces now prevailing, so to speak, "froze" out.

Contemporary physics, then, is thoroughly committed to holism. If I may be permitted to quote yet another witness, Professor Paul Davies (1983) writes:

> Physicists have long since abandoned a purely reductionist approach to the physical world. This is especially true in quantum theory, where a holistic view of the act of measurement is fundamental to the meaningful interpretation of the theory. . . . However, it is only in recent years that holistic philosophy has begun to have more general impact on physical science. (p. 64)

This being so, the metaphysic appropriate to the new physics must be a holistic metaphysic. It can easily be shown, perhaps much more easily, that the other sciences—biology, psychology, and the behavioral sciences—demand a similar holistic approach, which is not, in fact, dissociated or dissociable from that of physics; therefore, holism, as I argued at length in a book that has come of age this year (Harris, 1965), is the metaphysics characteristic of the science of the age. Our task, in consequence, must be to set out the fundamental principles of holism.

Principles of Holism

A whole is always and necessarily a unity in and of differences. A merely blank unity, without content, if it is anything at all, is not a whole. Nor, properly speaking, is a mere collection of unrelated, or purely externally related, items a genuine whole; it lacks the necessary unity that requires the parts or differentiations to be mutually adapted to one another, mutually complementary so that they fit together to constitute one system. Unity and difference are thus equally necessary; this being so, every genuine whole will be governed by a principle of organization, or order, determining the nature and interrelation of its parts, to which these must conform if the unity of the system is to be maintained. This principle is obviously universal to the whole and implicit in all its constituents. But stated in its purity, it would be a mere abstraction, and it can be actualized only in its exemplifications. That is, to be real it must differentiate itself into the elements that make up the system. For the principle of order is nothing real in and by itself. It is the way the parts are organized, and not another constituent additional to those that constitute the totality.

The first corollary that follows from this account of wholeness is that all relations between the elements that constitute the system must be internal—not just in the sense that they are relations between entities internal to the whole, as opposed to relations between the whole as such and anything (if there is anything) outside it, but in the sense that the relations are internal to their terms, determining, and determined by, the characteristics of those terms. This is so because the universal principle of order is immanent in each and every one of the constituents of the whole, adjusting it to each and all of the others so that they interlock and are mutually complementary. Thus, their interrelations are dependent upon their position in the general scheme, which again is determined by that interrelation.

For example, the forces acting between the nucleus of an atom and its orbiting electrons depend upon their several electrical charges, which equally determine their several intrinsic natures as particles, and all of these decide the position and role of each subatomic constituent in the complex field of force that constitutes the atom.

For the same reason, the terms so internally related necessarily overlap, because the universal principle of order is immanent in all of them,
and each expresses it in its own perspective. Hence, terms in relation
have in common the immanent principle of structure of the system to
which they belong, while at the same time they must differ in order to be
mutually complementary. Terms in internal relation one to another,
therefore, are overlapping elements in a continuous field, in which the
homogeneous element is the principle of order implicit within the field,
and the heterogeneous elements are the specific differences that articulate
the system. The nucleus of an atom, again, provides an illustration. The
field of force binding together the nucleons is the homogeneous element,
while the diverse particles so combined are heterogeneous (protons, neu-
trons, and virtual pions).

Such internal relations are copiously exemplified in modern physics,
especially in relativity theory, which teaches that every measurement,
whether of length, time, mass, or magnetic or electrical field, is dependent on the relative velocity of the reference frame in which it is made.
And every such frame is related to every other as the rotation of axes in a
four-dimensional continuum, so that they, too, are determined by their
mutual relations. Thus, the relations between the entities concerned, be
they of motion or mass, determine the nature and properties of those
entities. Again, the presence of matter and energy determines the curvature of space, so that all these relationships are determined reciprocally
by the nature of the entities that stand in them.

The results of the quantum theory dictate the same doctrine.
Whether a quantum of energy appears as a particle or a wave will depend on the way it is observed, that is, on its relation to the apparatus
used to measure its properties. The terms of the relations overlap: particle with wave (the particle itself being a wave-packet, or superposition
of waves), field with field, atom with atom (in the sharing of electrons),
and molecule with molecule (in crystalline forms). As Heisenberg (1959)
asserts, "The world thus appears as a complicated tissue of events,
in which connections of different kinds alternate or overlap or combine
and thereby determine the texture of the whole" (p. 96).

The recognition of the internality of relations marks an abrupt departure from the current philosophical doctrine, which tolerates only
external relations between bare particulars and atomic facts (Ayer, 1956,
p. 29; Russell, 1924; Wittgenstein, 1961, propositions 1.2 and 1.21)
and for which "internal" relations mean simply those between the members of a set, as opposed to those external to the set, and between that

set and others. They are as much external to their terms as any. It is clear then that the new physics demands a new revolution in philosophy.

The second consequence of necessary differentiation in a whole, of the fact that it must always be a unity of differences, is that it will involve a dynamic principle. As any whole must be diversified, and diverse manifestations of the ordering principle cannot, in the nature of the case, all be exemplified in one point, it must be articulated, or differentiated serially; its diversity must be set out over time. The whole must, therefore, be a dynamic whole and its organizing principle must be self-differentiating, or self-specifying.

This is precisely what we find in the physical world. It is throughout and in its most elementary nature dynamic, active, a sea of energy, manifesting the implicate order in radiant and particulate forms, and differentiating itself into diverse subatomic, atomic, and combinatory entities.

In a system, the structural principle of which is immanent both in whole and part, the distinguishable elements will each carry implications of all the rest. None can be isolated from the web of relations in which it stands to the others without distortion of the system, which would distort its own character. Any attempt to isolate a single constituent leads either to a false or an inadequate description, which requires for its correction integration of the separated constituent with its neighbors. Its distinction from others depends on its difference from them, on their mutual exclusion and negation. Accordingly, each relates to its other: first, as opposite by negating and excluding it; second, as complementary, or contrary; and third as a distinct exemplification of the ordering principle governing the system to which both belong.

Yet the internal character of each depends on its relation to the others. Thus, what each is implies what it is not, and vice versa. Consequently, each is implicitly the whole; each represents the whole, as it were, from its special viewpoint and, therefore is, in itself, a whole of a sort and at the particular level at which the universal principle of order is being expressed in it.

At the same time, although every member of the whole is a whole of this sort in its own right, because of its partial and subordinate character, none is adequate to the full realization of the universal principle of order, save the entire totality. Each partial element is, therefore, in a state of tension. It seeks to maintain itself in its own right, but cannot because it is only a part; yet it implies what it excludes, and as an integral part of the structured whole, it requires supplementation by the others. By virtue of its exclusion of these others, and its own insufficiency, each will, therefore, seek its opposite and display a tendency to unite with it. By doing so it forms a new whole, more self-sufficient and expressing the universal order more fully, or in a higher degree. Consequently, the whole specifies itself through a dynamic evolutionary process in which the elements of the system relate to one another as distinct forms, mutually negating and opposed, yet also as gradations in a scale, progressively approximating to the ultimate totality.

Because each phase in the scale supersedes its predecessor and is a more complete presentation of the organizing principle of the whole, it negates and contradicts its predecessor. But because it is also the supplementation of its predecessor and the fulfillment of its potentialities and implications, it incorporates and maintains its predecessor in itself. In doing so, however, it constitutes a new and more comprehensive whole in which the predecessor, having acquired a richer context of relations, is accordingly modified and transformed. The complexity of this relationship is conveyed, if not altogether fully and satisfactorily, by the term *sublation*. Each successive phase in the scale, we say, sublates what has gone before. Therefore, every phase in the scale is, so to speak, a summation, while it is equally a transformation of the entire scale up to that point. And it follows that the ultimate phase will be at once the consummation of the scale, the absolute totality (the universe) and will incorporate the entire series of forms, or phases, through which it has developed and in which it has specified itself. Process and end consequently overlap, as they have done at every stage of the progression.

The organizing principle universal to the whole, therefore, manifests itself both in each part and in the whole scale of forms, as the law of its progression and as the structure of its product. In each successive phase, it is more fully and explicitly presented, its true character being more clearly displayed as the scale proceeds. It is the variable running through the series of degrees of its own exemplification, the matrix, so to speak, within which, and out of which, the elements it generates crystalize. As the universal immanent from the beginning, which has been the directing and governing influence throughout the series, it progressively realizes itself more completely and adequately, emerging at the end fully developed as the entire scale of systematically (internally) related phases.

A scale of forms of this kind, contrary to what many may presume, need not always be positively progressive. The conflicts between opposing differences may be such that the principle of order can only be satisfied by backtracking and making a fresh start (for example, when an electron and a positron annihilate each other). But such degenerative trends can never reduce the content to zero, because whatever is reducible depends for its very nature on the ordering principle that is specifying itself in the process and that, as a principle of wholeness, cannot be self-destructive without contradicting itself (pair annihilation results in radiant energy).

On the other hand, because the principle of organization differentiating itself in a scale, such as has been described, is one of wholeness, the scale cannot continue indefinitely. It cannot be infinite in the usual (and embarrassing) sense of that word, namely, endless. It will necessarily tend towards completeness and closure. But this does not mean that process must at some time come to a stop, because the principle is also dynamic, and its realization, while in principle it is always whole and complete, is a perpetual activity.

It follows further that the point in the scale a process has reached is the most adequate realization of the whole to date, so to speak. The most recent phase exemplifies, more adequately than any prior to it, the principle of order universal to the whole. Hence, no proper account can be given of the more rudimentary phases of the scale except in terms of the latest phase disclosed, and the current limit of our knowledge will be the best account we can give of the nature of the whole, so far. This may seem trite and obvious, but it is important because it establishes the fact that the ultimate principle of explanation lies in the outcome of the process and not at its genetic origin. Reductionism is, therefore, ruled out and explanation becomes teleological, in the legitimate sense of the word; that is, the whole explains the part and not vice versa.

This is the structure of every whole and every system (for it follows from the above that every whole must be a system). A whole differentiates itself into a graduated scale of overlapping forms mutually related as distinct exemplifications of its universal principle of order; these distinct exemplifications are both opposed to each other and yet complementary, so that they unite and progressively display the structure of the whole more adequately in successive degrees. I propose to call this a dialectical scale, and my submission is that the required metaphysic must be similarly dialectical.

From what has been said it should be obvious that, while every system is the self-specification of a universal principle of order into a scale of forms, each of which is a whole, so that the scale is a system of systems, systematicity itself is thereby deployed as a scale. The more elementary forms will be systematic only in a rudimentary degree and will express the general character of systematicity less adequately than those that follow. Thus, a mere aggregate, or collection, of similar particulars is a whole of sorts, but its constituents do not obviously display the progressive scalar relationship we have been postulating. Yet they do have this character in some degree. Each instantiates the common character by virtue of which they can be regarded as a collection or set. They can be counted only if correlated with the number sequence, which is the paradigm case of a graded series, and so arranged they form a similar series of sets. But their mutual relations are too loose and their grouping as an aggregate too arbitrary to satisfy properly the conditions of wholeness so far outlined. A spatial figure is a much better example of system, and this, in the course of construction, better exemplifies the dialectical development. More adequate still is a physical whole, like an electromagnetic field, that generates itself in successive waves and has some internal structure; so we may proceed, through forms of continuously more elaborate organization, up to forms such as the living organism, in which the dialectical character is far more apparent. Thus, systematicity itself is specified as a scale of forms, a fact always to be remembered when recalcitrant examples seem to present themselves, or when abstraction is made from higher potencies.

Physical Exemplification

The conception of the physical world engendered by the results of contemporary science is of a whole or system, like that outlined above. It is a whole, single and undivided, in fact, indivisible, yet governed by a principle of order that specifies itself in innumerable differentiations, all overlapping and interconnected, mutually determining and internally related. At the base lies space-time, itself a system of interrelated and distinguishable point-instants, but, as a whole, irrefrangible. Its physical geometry is inseparable from energy, and its curvature represents the energetic field, that again is inseparable from matter. Thus, the space-time whole is discovered to be a closed system—a four-dimensional hypersphere, self-contained and unbounded. But without physical content, space-time has no extent, as Eddington wrote (1950):

> A region outside the field of action could have no geodesics, and consequently no intervals. All the potentials would then be zero. . . . Now if all intervals vanished space-time would shrink to a point. There would be no space, no time, no inertia, no anything. Thus a cause which creates intervals and geodesics must, so to speak, extend the world. (p. 157f)

Considered in abstraction from its physical content, then, space-time is at best an abstract manifold, in which no dialectical aspect is very noticeable, though it is not altogether absent. Physically, however, it constitutes the metrical field and has in its inescapable curvature an implicit order, not merely geometrical but determinant of the gauge system and the primary physical constants.

Viewed more concretely, however, space-time is correlative to radiant energy, which is structured in undulatory forms and specifies itself into diverse forces, gravitational, electro-magnetic, and so forth; congeals the radiant energy into diverse types of particles, photons, electrons, mesons, hadrons, and their antiparticles, which, with their intermediating quarks, constitute a palpable scale of overlapping, continuous, and progressive physical wholes. Space-time and energy are contrasted, yet equivalent, as are energy and matter (wave and particle); the scale of subatomic particles displays similar relationships. These coalesce in atomic nuclei and then, bound together appropriately, form hydrogen atoms, which combine further into molecules. Suitably augmented, heavier atoms burgeon out into the Mendlejeff series of elements, capable of numerous chemical combinations in more complex molecules. So we get a progression of wholes combining in overlapping relationships into more elaborate and articulate wholes, and in a scale of forms dialectically related, as distinct things, opposites, and complementaries to specify the all-inclusive totality of the physical world.

Along with these forms we have the gravitational scale of stars, galaxies, clusters, and the expanding universe. All of them are manifestations of the universal ordering principles expressed by the relevant physical constants, which they variously instantiate as specific exemplifications.

In short, the physical world reveals itself as a dynamic, holistic system, resolving itself into a series of dialectical scales in which the ordering principles (possibly reducible to one fundamental law), inherent in space-time, the metrical field, are progressively more elaborately specified.

Beyond Physics

From the metaphysical point of view, however, the contemporary scientific account of the physical world raises difficult and serious questions to which it supplies no obvious answers. We have just observed that it involves two possible dialectical scales, deployed, as it were, in two different directions: one from radiant energy to atoms and molecules (which one might call the electro-magnetic dimension), the other from atoms and molecules to galaxies and the expanding hypersphere (which one might call the gravitational dimension). Are these really distinguishable? As yet we do not know, nor do we know how, if they are not, they are mutually continuous. The second, in particular, seems to call into question the contention made above that the explanatory principle lies in the final phase of the scale; in the physical world, the explanatory principle seems to reside in the metrical field (space-time), which is apparently the first and not the last form in the scale. Yet it is also coextensive with the hypersphere, which, in some sense, is the final phase. This difficulty will probably remain unresolved until physicists can decide the precise interrelation of the four main forces in the physical universe—gravity, strong, weak, and electro-magnetic.

Further, still more fundamental questions have been raised by some physicists. The first scale mentioned in the last paragraph continues to crystals, macromolecules (DNA, for instance) and so to viruses and living cells. Does it follow that the universe was created "in order to" produce life? And does this imply a creator outside the natural order—a conscious agent acting for a definite purpose? Or is it conceivable that the whole system arose from self-determining natural laws without supernatural intervention? The question has also been raised whether the physical universe as described and envisaged by modern scientists is anything more than a temporary conceit, doomed, like so many of its predecessors, to be superseded by others, unlike it and contradictory of it. The real universe, it has been maintained, is inaccessible to our knowledge, and our science is no more than how we conceive it. Past eras have concocted various conflicting pictures of the universe, each of which has been held as the final truth, only to be refuted, rejected as false, and superseded by another. Our own is in no better situation. If this were indeed true, it would be vain to recommend a new metaphysic, for that would be similarly tainted. To answer such questions we need to go beyond our present.

For the universe is not exhausted by the physical world. The physical basis serves, as it were, as a pediment upon which arises, continuous with it and incorporating (sublating) its elements, the living world, the biosphere; this biosphere is a universe in itself, conterminous with the physical in as much as everything in the physical world affects and is registered in the living organism. This biosphere also specifies itself in, and as, an elaborate scale, a gamut of living forms, each whole in itself, that successively manifest and express more adequately the ordering principles of life. The mounting range of living species issues in forms that are intelligent and self-conscious, sublating the preceding, preconditioning process in yet a new and more significant way to form what has been called the Noösphere, the sphere of mind (Teilhard de Chardin, 1975), bringing us to the scientific enterprise itself and beyond.

These further dialectical developments are not the subject of this paper, but the problems outlined above, which are more profoundly cosmogenic, epistemological, and metaphysical, cannot be faced without considering them in detail in their relation to the physical world, together with which they participate in the ultimate whole. For the physical, biological, and conscious orders are, again, major wholes mutually in dialectical relationship, and it is in the consummation of the last that the true principle of explanation is to be sought; that will lie in the sphere of self-consciousness and may well have theological overtones.

Meanwhile, it may be observed that even if eventually some fundamental law were discovered controlling all forces and explaining the emergence of every kind of subatomic particle, it would be, in itself, very abstract, expressible no doubt as some highly complex mathematical equation that would impart on its face very little, if any, information about specific details. Only in and through its specification into, and elaboration as, the complete scale of physical phenomena would its explanatory power become explicit. After all, the space-time metrical field is really the primordial matrix of the physical whole, and the galaxies can be regarded merely as vast complex convolutions of its curvature. So envisaged, the true dialectical scale would seem to proceed along the other line towards crystalline forms and macromolecules, leading to a whole new world of living things.

In that case, we can see that the physical world as a whole is still the most rudimentary phase in a yet more comprehensive scale and that it can, therefore, not be expected to exhibit with perfect clarity every logical feature of systematicity—hence, the difficulty we have encountered in recognizing the explanatory principle as its final phase. For this we must look beyond it. Because the final phase in the physical world, however it may be signified, is not the final phase in any ultimate sense.

Moreover, wholeness at the merely physical level is still only implicit. Although the principle of order is, indeed, immanent in every part and governs its relations to every other, as well as to the whole, this is true blindly and implicitly. It is not true for the physical whole itself but only for us who observe and reflect upon it. When we consider this fact, we realize that no whole or system can be really complete or fully explicit unless and until it becomes aware of itself as a whole and that occurs only when the natural dialectic has advanced through living forms to conscious and intelligent minds.

This is precisely what happens in the all-embracing scale that brings to consciousness the entire process actually occurring in the physical, the biological, and the psychological spheres, making them aware of themselves in our minds. We organize our experience as we react to our surrounding world, both in practice and in theory. Science itself is a late phase in this process and has been called by Bosanquet (1912), not inappropriately, "the world come to consciousness." Thus, end and process overlap, and the scientific knowledge that emerges sublates and reflects the natural process that has produced it. Its own historical advance, we may well expect to find, will be dialectical; in which case, we should not be surprised to discover that successive theories, though mutually continuous, also appear mutually contradictory. Nor should we expect the one last devised to be final or incorrigible, while we may still trust that the ultimate truth, or whole, is immanent and implicit in it as it has been in all its precursors.

This is how I should respond to Professor Edward Harrison's contention that the real universe is unknowable, and our successive world-pictures are merely masks that (presumably) obscure the reality. True, the more we learn, the more painfully aware we become of our ignorance. There is, indeed, a "cloud of unknowing" (Harrison, 1985, Chapter 16), but we may not, without self-contradiction, embrace total relativism. There must be, and is, a criterion of truth, and we do have access to it. It is comprehensive, coherent systematicity in our knowledge, in the light of which we can detect a silver lining in the cloud, capable of illuminating, however dimly, what has so far escaped from its shadow. The whole, without which there can be no being and no knowledge, must be immanent in some degree in all of its self-specifications, so that we may recognize, even in the most rudimentary way, some glimmering of the truth yet to develop out of it; a steadily growing premonition of the actual nature of the universe can be discerned in each and every projection, or model, that we succeed in making as we continually correct past errors.

Further, we have established a vantage point from which we can dispose of the tiresome dispute about realism and idealism, both of which have invariably involved philosophers in insuperable logomochies, while at the same time making room for the involvement of the observer in the phenomena observed, which both relativity and quantum theory demand. On the one hand, idealism is vindicated so far as self-consciousness does represent the whole and brings it to fruition. Because the natural world constitutes a scale of forms in which a genuine whole is progressively realizing itself, and at the stage where it becomes conscious, it actualizes the true nature of the prior phases; however, that is far from denying the existence of an external world, which, as Hegel puts it, "is the truth implicitly." So realism is also justified.

Moreover, the multifarious influences impinging upon the organism from all over the physical world are sublated in bodily feeling and are brought to cognition by the organizing activity of the mind. Perception creates its own data out of the content of primitive sentience in order to discover the outside world.* Thus, the lower preconscious phases of the evolutionary process are brought to consciousness *of themselves* in the human mind, and subject and object coincide. This is what the quantum theorists assert. Observation is the interaction between ourselves and the physical entities in which neither is independent of the other. In the whole, there can be no separation between the mind and its object.

Conclusion

The metaphysics required by the new physics should, then, be first holistic and second, as a necessary consequence, dialectical. It will seek its final explanatory principle in its outcome rather than in its beginning; although, being holistic, that principle will be implicit from the beginning and immanent throughout. It will be the guiding principle of the dialectical process, just as it is the immanent and guiding principle of the physical, biological, and intellectual processes that issue in its eventually becoming aware of itself in our minds. In other words, it will be nothing less than dialectical reason itself.

Such a metaphysic is not wholly new, for it was adumbrated in the philosophies of Spinoza and Leibniz and more explicitly in that of Hegel, not to mention Karl Marx and Frederick Engels. The last two, however, went astray by failing to notice that the "truth" of the dialectic lay in its outcome, as Hegel had insisted, that is in consciousness and mind. They accused Hegel of standing on his head, and by inverting his system, they confined the dialectic to the material world. As the physics of their day was materialistic and not holistic, the whole conception of dialectic becomes self-contradictory in their hands, and although their works remain interesting and valuable in many respects, they are apt to mislead

---

*I have developed this theory of perception more at length in Harris (1965, chapters xix and xx; 1970; 1974; 1980).

seriously their followers, especially in metaphysics. Hegel, on the other hand, is marvelously prophetic and foreshadows many modern ideas that the science of his day had not yet grasped, while at the same time his determination to remain faithful only to what in his time was considered to have been scientifically established leads him sometimes to betray his own principles. More recently, A. N. Whitehead (1929/1978) attempted to develop a process metaphysically rooted in contemporary science and, in doing so, expounded a theory that at many points converges with Hegel's. Both these philosophers recognized, as few others have, the demands of holism. And they are now being vindicated by contemporary physics, which has abandoned mechanism and materialism (pace Marx) and has revealed the essential unity of the physical world.

Addendum

Critics often express concern because of my insistence that the universal principle of order is immanent from the beginning and in every phase of the process would seem to imply a determinism eliminating all disorder, preventing any element of chance and excluding freedom. But this is not the case, especially not at the physical level.

First, the principle is holistic and dynamic; therefore, its constant and indispensable self-specification involves an unlimited proliferation of variety and differences, which, because they are severally partial and finite, necessarily generate oppositions and contradictions involving disorder, chance concurrences, and fortuitous contrapositions, particularly at lower levels. These tend to be overcome at a higher level by the operation of the same ordering principle. The only sense in which we may call it deterministic is that it is ultimately rational. But rational determination is self-determination, which is the very definition of freedom. Consequently, holism inevitably involves disorder and chance at lower levels of the scale and does not exclude freedom.

Second, I have insisted that, in the scale of forms, the highest form most adequately expresses and exemplifies the universal principle, and this to date has transpired as human thought and reason, the characteristic activity of which is judgment. Human thought cannot be anything but free, because judgment is essentially assertion that, to be genuine, must claim truth. But no truthful claim can be involved, and none can be made, by a process determined purely mechanically. (Pointer-readings are not themselves judgments, only the indicators that prompt and justify judgments on the part of observing scientists.) If then human reason, which is essentially free, is the most adequate manifestation we know of the principle immanent universally and throughout the scale, this is revealed to be the very principle of freedom itself. And instead of trying to explain human freedom (as some have done) in terms of indeterminacy at the microscopic physical level, we should rather seek to explain the latter in terms of human mentality.

References

Ayer, A. J. 1956. *The Problem of Knowledge.* Harmondsworth: Penguin Books.

Bohm, D. 1980. *Wholeness and the Implicate Order.* London: Routledge & Kegan Paul.

Bosanquet, B. 1912. *The Principle of Individuality and Value.* London: Macmillan.

Capra, F. 1975. *The Tao of Physics.* London: Fontana.

Collingwood, R. J. 1940. *An Essay on Metaphysics.* Oxford: Oxford University Press.

_____. 1945. *The Idea of Nature.* Oxford: Oxford University Press.

Davies, P. 1983. *God and the New Physics.* London: Penguin Books.

Eddington, A. 1933. *The Expanding Universe.* Cambridge: Cambridge University Press.

_____. 1950. *Space, Time and Gravitation.* Cambridge: Cambridge University Press.

Harris, E. E. (1965). *The Foundations of Metaphysics in Science.* London: Allen and Unwin.

_____. 1970. *Hypothesis and Perception.* London: Allen & Unwin.

_____. 1974. *Perceptual Assurance and the Reality of the World.* Worcester, Mass.: Clark University Press.

_____. 1980. Blanshard on Perception and Free Ideas. *The Philosophy of Brand Blanshard.* Ed. P. Schilpp. La Salle, Ill.: Open Court.

Harrison, E. 1985. *Masks of the Universe.* New York: Macmillan.

Heisenberg, W. 1952. *Philosophical Problems of Nuclear Science.* London: Faber.

Heisenberg, W. 1959. *Physics and Philosophy.* London: Faber.

Milne, E. A. 1943–1944. Fundamental Concepts of Natural Philosophy. *Proceedings of the Royal Society of Edinburgh* 62.

Russell, B. 1924. Logical Atomism. *Contemporary British Philosophy.* Ed. J. H. Muirhead. London: Allen & Unwin.

Sciama, W. D. 1959. *The Unity of the Universe.* Garden City, N.Y.: Doubleday.

Teilhard de Chardin, P. 1975. *The Phenomenon of Man.* New York: Harper & Row.

Whitehead, A. N. 1978. *Process and Reality.* New York: Free Press. (Original work published in 1929.)

Wittengenstein, L. 1961. *Tractatus Logico-Philosophicus.* London: Routledge & Kegan Paul.

CONTRIBUTORS

JEFFREY BUB, professor of philosophy at the University of Maryland, has written on the foundations of quantum physics for many years. In addition to numerous journal articles, he has written *The Interpretation of Quantum Mechanics*.

MILIČ ČAPEK, professor emeritus of philosophy at Boston University, has written several books on the philosophy of science, the most widely known of which is *The Philosophical Impact of Contemporary Physics*. In addition, he has written *Bergson and Modern Physics* and has edited a collection of essays on *The Concepts of Space and Time*.

FRITJOF CAPRA, of the Lawrence Berkeley Laboratory (Berkeley, California) is widely known for his best seller, *The Tao of Physics*. He has also written *The Turning Point: Science, Society and the Rising Culture*. In addition, he is actively involved with the Elmwood Institute at Berkeley.

OLIVIER COSTA DE BEAUREGARD, of the Laboratory of Theoretical Physics at the Henri Poincaré Institute (Paris) has written several books on philosophical and scientific problems relating to time and thermodynamics, including *Le seconde principe de la science du temps* and *La notion du temps*.

DAVID FINKELSTEIN, professor of physics at Georgia Institute of Technology, has written numerous articles on the foundations of physics, quantum logic, and the philosophy of science. He is editor of the *International Journal of Theoretical Physics*.

ERROL E. HARRIS, professor emeritus of philosophy at Northwestern University, has written on a broad range of philosophical topics.

His works relating to the present volume include: *The Foundations of Metaphysics in Science; Nature, Mind and Modern Science;* and *Hypothesis and Perception.*

RICHARD F. KITCHENER, professor of philosophy at Colorado State University, has written numerous articles in the philosophy of science. He is the author of *Piaget's Theory of Knowledge: Genetic Epistemology and Scientific Reason.*

IVOR LECLERC, professor emeritus of philosophy at Emory University, has written on the philosophy of nature for many years, including *The Nature of Physical Existence* and most recently *The Philosophy of Nature.*

ILYA PRIGOGINE, professor of physical chemistry at the University of Brussels and the University of Texas, is widely known for his seminal work in nonequilibrium thermodynamics (for which he received the Noble Prize). He has written and coauthored numerous books on science and philosophy, including *From Being to Becoming* and *Order Out of Chaos: Man's New Dialogue with Nature* (with Isabelle Stengers).

HENRY P. STAPP, of the Lawrence Berkeley Laboratory (Berkeley, California), has written extensively on the philosophical, conceptual, and theoretical problems relating to quantum mechanics. He is widely known for his work on the metaphysical implications of quantum mechanics.

INDEX

Action at a Distance, 11, 12
Aggregate, 69, 166
Aharanov, Y., 46
Aharanov-Bohm effect, 80
Alexander, Samuel, 15
Algebra
—Boolean, 62, 72n
—Born-Jordon-Dirac, 106, 107, 110–112
—Laplacean, 108–111
—predicate, 87
—quantum, 78–79, 106
Amplitude, 78, 111, 112, 115
—Conditional, 112, 115, 116, 118
—Probability, 40–45, 54, 78
—Transitional, 81, 86, 106, 107, 108, 110–112, 114, 115, 118, 119
Angle action variable, 132, 137
Aristotelian
—world view. See World View
—concept of nature, 26
Aristotle, 6, 15, 26, 27, 32, 33, 35, 37n, 119, 157
Arnold, V., 132
Aspect, Alain, 9, 13
Arrow of Time. See Time
Astronomy, 75, 81. See also Cosmology
Atlas Method, 84
Atomism, 4, 7, 14, 26, 34, 35, 54, 96. See also Mechanism; Particle
Autopoiesis, 150

Baker transformation, 133, 134
Basso, Sebastian, 26

Bateson, Gregory, 151
Becoming, 35, 139, 146. See also Being
Being, 7, 33, 35, 139. See also Metaphysics; Ontology
Bell, John, 5, 46, 52, 62–65, 66, 69, 70
Bell's Theorem, 6, 8, 9, 12–14, 62–65. See also Chapter 3
Belousov-Zhabotinski reaction, 130
Bénard instability, 128, 139
Bergson, Henri, 7, 15, 96, 98, 100, 102, 126, 131
Berkeley, George, 7, 157
Bernoulli, J., 116
Bifurcation, 131, 137, 141
Block universe, 96, 103
Big Bang Theory, 139, 140, 160
Black-body radiation, 139
Bohm, David, 7, 10, 12, 15, 40, 45, 46, 153, 159
Bohr, Niels, 6, 7–11, 12, 15, 19n, 42, 43, 45, 60, 67, 69, 72n, 79, 82, 108, 125, 137
Boltzmann, Ludwig, 71, 107, 108, 109, 113, 117, 126, 132, 133
Bootstraps Theory. See S-Matrix
Born, Max, 60, 78, 106–107, 111, 119
Bosanquet, Bernard, 170
Boyle, Robert, 7
Bradley, Francis, 15
Brahe, Tycho, 101
Bruno, Giordorno, 101
Bub, Jeffrey, 11, 12
Buechner, Ludwig, 90

CPT invariance, 118, 119
Cantor, George, 86
Čapek, Milič, 4, 8
Carnap, Rudolph, 17, 102
Carnot, Sadi, 116
Capra, Fritjof, 4, 8, 15, 159–160
Cartesian, 27, 101, 149. *See also*
  Descartes; Dualism
causality, 26, 28, 97, 100, 102, 115–
  116, 118–119
—backward, 9
—efficient, 4. *See also* Mechanism
—final. *See also* Teleology
—locality of, 12
Certainty, 11, 29, 149. *See also* Epis-
  temology; Knowledge
Chance, 9
Chaos, 9, 130, 137
—Dynamical, 130, 131
Chew, Geoffrey, 8, 148, 150, 152–
  153. *See also* S-Matrix
Chronogeometry, 93, 97
Chronon, 98
Clarke, Samuel, 125
Classical physics, 5, 38–40, 51, 55,
  69, 91–93, 95, 97, 99, 126, 136,
  137, 152, 157. *See also* Newto-
  nian Physics
Clauser, J. F., 52
Clausius, Rudolph, 117
Clifford, William, 95
Cognition, 150–151, 152. *See also*
  Consciousness; Mind; Wigner
Coherence, 9, 78, 82, 126, 130, 131
Collingwood, Robin, 80, 156
Common sense
—scientific, 4
Complementarity, 35, 60, 67, 72n,
  86 *See also* Bohr
Comte, August, 29
Conditional amplitude. *See* amplitude
Consciousness, 45, 145, 151. *See*
  also Cognition
Consistency, 148
Contextualism, 7, 15
Continuity, 35

—vs. Discontinuity, 35, 36, 95, 96,
  97, 106
Contradiction. *See* Chapter 10
Copenhagen Interpretation, 5, 7, 11,
  13, 14, 17–18, 19n, 60, 69, 79,
  80, 83. *See also* Bohr; Heisenberg;
  Orthodox Quantum Theory
—pseudo, 79–80
Copernicus, Nicolas, 101, 120
Copernican Revolution, 30
Cosmology, 7, 9, 36, 81–85, 97,
  128, 138–141, 146. *See also*
  Astronomy; Philosophy of Nature
—Quantum, 82, 84
Couturat, Louis, 92
Costa de Beauregard, Olivier, 8
Cybernetics 149. *See also* Systems
  Theory

D'Alembert, Jean, 27
Dalton, John, 34
Data
—Experimental, 6, 17, 19n, 39, 85
Darwinian Revolution in physics, 9,
  126
Davies, Paul, 160
de Broglie, Louis, 7, 102, 106
Degrees of freedom, 12, 42, 67, 68,
  70, 132
Democritus, 94, 99, 157
Descartes, René, 7, 20n, 26, 27, 30,
  32, 34, 36n, 97, 98, 120. *See also*
  Cartesianism
Determinism, 12, 39, 43, 45, 51–52,
  54–55, 61, 98, 102, 126, 130,
  133, 172
—mathematical, 39
—vs. determinate (ness), 61, 70, 72
Determination, 81–82
Dewey, John, 17
Dialectical
—scale, 165–169, 172
Differentiation, 165
Dirac, Paul, 9, 75, 86, 106–108,
  110–112
Discontinuity. *See also* Continuity

Disorder, 9, 129, 130. *See also* Chaos
Disequilibrium, 9. *See also* Equilibrium
Dissipative Structure, 9, 150. *See* Chapter 8
Double-slit experiment, 9–10
Dualism, 12, 30–32, 39, 97, 98, 105. *See also* Bohr; Cartesianism; Wave-particle dualism
Duhem, Pierre, 17
Dunne, J., 117

Eccles, Sir John, 116, 117, 120
Ecological world view. *See* World View
Eddington, Sir Arthur, 7, 16, 20n, 97, 99, 100, 136, 158, 159, 166
Einstein, Albert, 7, 8, 11, 30–32, 35, 46, 60, 61, 69, 85, 97, 100, 102, 106, 125, 138, 140, 148, 158, 159
Einstein, A.-Podolsky, B.-Rosen, N., (EPR) 9, 11, 12, 13, 30n, 47, 51, 54, 60, 65, 69
—Correlations, 114, 115, 118, 120
—paradox, 12
Electron, 10, 35, 68, 97, 107
Elementarism, 7, 19n. *See also* Atomism
Emergence, 12, 70
Empiricism, 157
—Logical, 5, 20n. *See also* Vienna Circle
Endosystem, 76, 80, 81, 82, 83, 84, 88
Engels, Friedrich, 171
Entropy, 71, 82, 112, 126, 127, 128, 129, 136, 137, 140, 150
Negentropy, 116, 117, 119
Epistemology, 5, 7, 29, 30, 32, 147–148. *See also* Certainty; Knowledge; Science
—Epistemic Criteria, 21
Equilibrium, 9, 130
—Thermodynamic, 129, 150
—Non-equilibrium, 130

Ethics, 39. *See also* Values
—and Science, 151–152
Euclid, 92
Euclidean Geometry. *See* Geometry
Euclidean Space. *See* Space
Events, 7, 8, 14, 98, 148, 153
—Actual, 35, 40, 41, 42–43, 56, 81. *See also* Heisenberg; Potentia
—"Gentle" Quantum, 153
Everett, H., 40
Evolutionary view, 126, 138, 164
Exosystem, 76, 80, 81, 82–86, 88
Experientialism, 7

Fact, 6, 18, 28, 31, 151, 152. *See also* Data; Inductive Generalization
—vs. Theory, 18
—vs. Values, 151

Fact-like asymmetry, 107
—irreversibility. *See* Irreversibility
Faraday, Michael, 96, 158
Faster than light, 12, 13, 39–40, 44–45, 54
—influences vs. signals, 13, 55. *See* Chapter
Fermat, Pierre, 105, 120
Feynman graphs, 106, 110, 111–113, 118
Field, 35, 96–97, 158, 160, 162, 167
—theory, 5, 19n, 158, 159
—Cosmological, 140
—Quantum, 86, 153
Finkelstein, David, 6, 13, 14, 19, 96, 153
Fock, V., 112, 118
Fractal, 131
Frame, 76, 81, 86, 99. *See* Chapter
Freudenthal, G., 19n

Goedel, Kurt, 8
Galileo, 7, 20n, 26, 30, 85, 99
Gamow, George, 139
Gassendi, Pierre, 101
Gauge Theory, 159, 167
Gauss, Karl, 92

General Relativity. *See* Relativity
Geometrization of nature, 7
Geometry, 94, 96, 105
—Euclidean, 91–94, 99
—non-Euclidean, 30, 92, 99
—semi-Euclidean, 94
Gestalt Theory, 19n
Gleason, A., 62
God, 27, 32, 83
Grand Unified Theory, 159
Gravity Theory, 75, 81

Harris, Errol, 4, 15
Harrison, Edward, 158, 170
Hawking, David, 82
Hegel, Georg, 15, 91, 171, 177. *See also* Chapter 10
Heidegger, Martin, 17
Heisenberg, Werner, 6, 14, 19n, 40–44, 55, 56, 79, 102, 106, 107, 116, 137, 147, 149, 159, 162
Hertz, Heinrich, 28
Hidden variables, 12, 13, 52, 59, 61, 62
Hierarchy Theory, 15
Hobbes, Thomas, 157
Holism, 7, 14–15, 54, 80, 81, 145, 160. *See also* Whole; Chapter 9 and 10
—Dialectical, 15. *See* Chapter 10
—Principles of, 161–166
—Holistic properties, 12
Holton, Gerald, 32
Hume, David, 7, 101, 157
Huygens, Christian, 98
Hypotheses, 28, 31–33
—reality of, 28

Idealism, 17, 18, 91, 170
Idealization, 70, 71, 72
—Pragmatic vs. Essential, 70–71
Induction, 36n, 94
—Inductive Generalization, 28, 31, 33
Inflationary Universe, 139
Information, 78, 116, 134
Instrumentalism, 7, 17–18

Interaction, 81, 113, 136, 151
Interference, 70
Irreversibility, 9, 106, 117, 127–128, 131, 132, 134, 136, 140, 141
—Fact-like, 109–110, 112, 113, 118, 126, 128, 132, 134, 136, 140, 141

James, William, 7, 15, 42, 90, 96
Jeans, Sir James, 7, 16
Jahn, Robert, 117
Jauch, J. M., 65, 66
Jaynes E. T., 116
Jordan, P., 106–107, 110, 119

KAM theory, 132
K-flows, 133, 134
Kant, Immanuel, 30–31, 91, 92, 100, 101, 157
Kepler, Johannes, 30
Kinematics, 93
—quantum, 77
—Relativistic, 94, 106
Kirchoff, Gustav, 28
Kitchener, Richard, 5, 20n
Knowledge, 31, 45, 117, 149, 152. *See also* Epistemology
—Approximate, 149
—Foundations of, 15
—"Building" to "Network" metaphor of, 148
—self, 82
—scientific, 20n, 29, 147, 149. *See also* Science
Kochen, S., 62, 63, 66, 69, 70
Koehler, Wolgang, 19n
Kolmogorov, A., 132
Kron, G., 87, 88n
Kuhn, Thomas, 120, 144

Lagrange, Joseph, 27
Lamarck, Jean, 119
Landé, A., 110, 111
Landé chain, 110, 111, 112, 114
Laplace, Pierre, 27, 28, 36n, 100, 106–109, 111, 113, 117
Leclerc, Ivor, 4, 8, 16, 18, 125

Leibniz, Gottfried, 125, 171
Lemaître, Georges, 138, 140
Lewis, G., 94
Locality, 12, 13, 15, 46, 51, 59, 62.
  See also Non-locality
Locke, John, 7, 157
Logic, 87, 96
Lorenz, Heindrik, 94, 99
Loschmidt, J., 116
Lueders, J., 118
Lyapunov exponents, 133

Mach, Ernst, 28, 96
Machine. *See* Mechanism
Macro-level, 12, 15, 68–72
—cosm, 8, 98–99
—scopic, 39, 43, 52, 126–132
Many-worlds interpretation, 39–41
Markov chain, 108, 109, 112, 113
Marx, Karl, 171, 172
Mass, 28, 94, 97, 147
Maturana, Humberto, 150
Materialism, 91, 157
Mathematics, nature of, 30
Matter, 8, 30, 34–35, 38, 43, 95,
  97, 140, 157. *See also* Atomism
Maupertius, Pierre-Louis, 27, 105
Maxwell, James Clerk, 20n, 29, 35,
  71, 96, 158
Measurement, 12, 13, 40–41, 43–44,
  46–48, 54, 64–65, 68–69, 86, 94,
  102, 115, 116, 117, 118, 138,
  147, 153, 160
—Problem of, 59, 65, 70
Mechanics, 26, 27–29, 30, 96
—Classical, 71, 95, 136, 137
—Newtonian. *See* Classical Mechan-
  ics; Newtonian Mechanics
—Quantum. *See* Quantum Mechanics
—Wave, 106
Mechanism, 4, 56, 145, 157
—mechanistic model, 99
—mechanistic world view. *See* World
  View
Megacosmic, 4, 8, 101
Mehlberg, Henryk, 107
Metaphysics, 5–9, 13–19, 29, 32–36,

39, 90–91, 100, 156–157, 158.
  See also Ontology; Mind
—as a science, 33
—meaning of, 6, 32–33, 90
—meaninglessness of, 20n, 157
—metholodology of, 18, 19, 33–34,
  36n, 102
—naturalistic, 20n
—rejection of, 39
—science and, 4, 16–19, 29–32. *See*
  Chapter 2
—transcendent, 5
Myerson, Emile, 97, 100
Micro-cosm, 8, 98–99,
—level, 12
—scopic, 39, 132–138
Milne, E. A., 159
Mind, 8, 28, 151, 157, 171.
—and matter, 38, 39, 42–44, 54,
  117
Minkowski, Hermann, 100, 101,
  105, 118, 140
Moleschott, Jacob, 91
Moser, J., 132
Motion, 26, 28, 36n, 95, 157
—locomotion, 30, 33

Nature, 26, 145
—Philosophy of, 25, 26, 28–29.
Negentropy. *See* entropy
Neo-Kantian, 91
Neo-Platonism, 35
Network, 8, 147, 148, 149, 153,
  159
Newton, Sir Isaac, 7, 18, 20n, 26,
  27, 28, 30, 31, 32, 34, 35, 83,
  85, 92, 94, 125, 157, 158
—Newtonian atomism, 14. *See also*
  Atomism
—Newtonian mechanics, 27, 31, 94,
  95. *See also* Atomism; Classical
  Mechanics;
—Newtonian physics, 4, 19, 31, 101,
  152. *See also* Classical Physics
—Newtonian world view. *See* World
  View
Non-equilibrium, 130, 131, 141

Non-linearity, 131, 150
Non-locality, 11, 12, 13, 14, 18, 39,
44–46, 54, 55, 57, 70, 80, 112,
118, 134. *See also* Locality
Non-separability, 12, 14, 18, 112.
See also Separability

Observables, 61–65, 69
Observation, 14, 41, 67, 76, 153,
171, 173
Ontography, 76–77
Ontology, 5, 7, 35, 39, 40–42, 44,
76, 79, 90–91. *See also* Metaphy-
sics
—Event, 7, 8
—Many worlds, 40
—Substance, 7
—Pilot wave, 40
—Process, 7, 81
—Quantum. *See* Quantum Ontology
Operator, 77–78
—Destructor, 77–80. *See also* Psi*
—Creator, 77, 98. *See also* Psi
—Entropy, 137
Order, 9, 82, 86, 128, 129, 130. *See
also* Disorder
Organismic view. *See* World View
Organization, 165
—Self. *See* Self-Organization
Orthodox quantum theory, 15, 17,
39, 42, 54. *See also* Bohr; Copen-
hagen Interpretation

Paradigm, 4, 8, 105, 106, 120, 130,
144–145, 146, 147, 148, 152. *See*
Chapter 9
—Social, 145
Parmenides, 35, 100
Particle, 35, 76, 95, 96, 98, 99, 119,
159. *See also* Atomism; Wave-
particle
Pascal, Blaise, 120
Pattern. *See* Network; Organization;
Structure
—of relationships, 146–149. *See also*
Network
Pauli, Wolfgang, 61, 159

Peano, Giuseppe, 87
Peirce, Charles, 126
Perception, 157. *See also* Observation
Person, nature of, 14, 54, 56–57. *See
also* Mind
Phenomenalism, 7, 17–18, 91
Phenomenology, 7
Phenomenon, 67, 91. *See also* Data
Philosophia naturalis. See Philosophy
of Nature
Photon, 9–10, 35, 44, 80, 107, 153
—"Gentle", 153, 154
Piaget, Jean, 70n, 96, 101
Planck, Max, 29, 35, 102, 112, 158
Pilot Wave, 40–41, 45
Piron, C., 65, 66
Plato, 35
—Platonism, 20n
Poincaré, Henri, 28, 92, 98, 105,
118, 132
Poincaré's Theorem, 132, 137
Popper, Sir Karl, 16, 100, 102, 116
Positivism, 7, 17, 18, 28–29, 91. *See
also* Empiricism
—Logical, 157. *See also* Vienna Circle
Potentia, 14, 41, 43, 44, 54, 56–57.
See also Heisenberg
Pragmatism, 7, 15, 17
Prediction, 11, 39, 41, 47, 51, 56,
87
Prigogine, Ilya, 8, 9, 16, 100, 102,
147, 150
Probability, 9, 64, 105–106, 108,
126. *See also* Chapter 7
—Amplitude. *See* Amplitude
—Bayesian, 64, 109, 111
—calculus, 8, 106, 107, 112, 114,
117
—conditional, 106, 108, 110, 113,
115, 116
—extrinsic, 108–110
—intrinsic, 108–110, 113
—distribution, 20n
—functions, continuous, 152
Process, 15, 147
—ontology. *See* Ontology
—philosophy, 15

Property state, 12, 61–64, 65, 67–70. *See* Chapter 4
Psychokinesis, 9, 117, 120
Psi, 14, 78, 79, 82–83, 84, 86, 111, 136. *See also* Probability Amplitude; Wave Function
—Cosmic, 82
—Relative, 82
—* (Psi^2), 10, 14, 20n, 78, 116, 136
Psychology, 7
Pythagoreanism, 6, 20n

Quantum Mechanics, 7, 8, 10, 12, 18, 29, 66, 106, 136, 138, 141, 152
—Relativistic, 106
—Ontology, 42–46, 81–82. *See also* Orthodox Quantum Theory
Quantum Theory, 7, 9, 13, 14, 19n, 39, 51, 75, 77, 79, 84, 153, 159, 170. *See also* Quantum Mechanics

Realism, 7, 12, 17, 60, 61, 69, 70–72, 170
—classical, 17
—critical, 7, 12
Reality, 11, 28, 40, 66, 80–81, 145
—blurred, 12, 66
—independent, 13, 17
—objective, 12, 13
—ultimate, 6, 17, 91
Reductionism, 4, 13, 160, 165
Reichenbach, Hans, 95, 96, 100
Relation, internal vs. external, 161–162
Religion, 145–146
—meaning of, 145–146
Relativity Theory, 7, 15, 16, 19n, 76, 77, 93–95, 102, 140, 152, 170
—Special Theory, 8, 31, 84, 99, 159
—General Theory, 5, 8, 84, 126, 159
Representational
—Theory of Truth, 7
—ism, 17
Riemann, Bernard, 97
Royce, Josiah, 15

Russell, Bertrand, 7, 16, 92, 93, 94
Ryle, Gilbert, 17

S-Matrix, 7, 8, 116, 147, 148, 150, 152–153, 159
Saccheri, Gerolamo, 92
Schroedinger, Erwin, 11, 66, 136, 159
—equation, 6, 20n, 40, 41, 45, 137, 138
—'s cat, 9, 11, 12, 65–67, 70, 72, 83. *See also* Chapter 4
Sciama, W. D., 158
Science
—meaning of, 27, 29, 33, 36n
—nature of, 147
—objective vs. epistemic, 147
—and ethics. *See* Ethics and science
Scientific Revolution, 3, 112, 120
Scientism, 21n
Secondary qualities, 97
—vs. Primary qualities, 7
Self-organization, 148–150, 152, 154
—Self-organizing systems, 9, 149–151
Self-production. *See* autopoiesis
Sellars, Wilfred, 16
Separability, 12, 13, 14
Shimony, Abner, 52
Simultaneity, 99
Singularity, 138
Smart, J. J. C., 16
Space, 8, 12, 35, 77, 91–93, 157
—Absolute, 4, 52, 91, 94
—Euclidean, 62, 63, 91–93, 95, 99
—Riemannian, 95
—Hilbert, 63, 65, 67–68, 72n, 86, 111, 112, 114, 136–137
Space and Time, 4, 8, 14, 77, 93, 94, 140, 152
—Absolute, 4, 152, 157
Spacelike separation, 12
Space-Time, 8, 14, 16, 46, 54, 93–95, 97, 98, 140, 152
—Absolute, 157
—Relativistic, 93–95
—Riemannian, 95

Solipsism, 85
Specker, E., 62, 63, 66, 69, 70
Spencer, Herbert, 91
Spinoza, Benedict, 15, 36n, 96, 100, 102, 171
Stallo, J. B., 96
Stapp, Henry, 8, 13–14, 147, 154
Statistical State, 12, 62, 65, 67, 68, 70. See Chapter 4
Steady-state, 140
—Equilibrium, 130
Structure, 9, 15, 126, 129–130, 147, 150, 165
—Dissipative. See Dissipative Structure
—Geometrical, 92
—Mathematical, 30–31, 79
—Semi-group, 134, 136, 138
Sublation, 164, 168.
Substance, 101
—Material, 95
Superposition, 10, 11, 40, 66, 79, 130, 162
—principle, 12, 67, 70, 79
—restricted, 67
System
—closed, 166
—open, 127, 150
—self-organizing, 9, 146–149
Systems Theory, 15, 146–149

Teleology, 165
Thermodynamic equilibrium, 129, 150
Thermodynamics, 5, 72, 127, 139, 150, 151
—Non-equilibrium, 9, 16, 98, 126, 129
Thomson, J. J., 34, 99
Time, 8–9, 25, 77, 99, 105, 126, 140
—absolute, 4, 82–83, 151, 152
—and reversibility, 8, 105–107, 116, 126, 134, 136
—arrow of, 8, 9, 20n, 113
—asymetry of, 9

—irreversibility of, 8, 20n
—fact-like vs. law-like, 8, 108
—symmetry, 105, 114, 116, 128
—broken, 128, 134
Time-Space, 100–102. See Space-time
Transformation Theory, 76–81, 84–85, 88. See Chapter 5
Transformations, 84, 86, 87
—First Level, 85
—Second level, 85–86
—Third level, 86
Transition, 14, 78, 81
Transition amplitude. See amplitude
Truth, 17, 21n, 32, 148, 171
—approximate, 15
—correspondence theory, 7, 17
—epistemic vs. ontic, 17
Tychism, 126

Uncertainty relation, 116
Unity, 161

Values, 151, 152, 154. See also Ethics
Varela, Francisco, 150
Variables, 47, 48, 52–53
—angle-action, 132, 137
—Independent, 47, 52–53
Vienna Circle, 157. See also Logical Empiricism
Vogt, Carl, 91
von Bertalanffy, Ludwig, 15
von Neumann, John, 6, 43, 70, 72, 79, 80, 86, 87, 138

wave, 20n, 76, 159
—wave function, 10, 11, 14, 59, 137
—collapse of, 10, 11, 59, 80. See also Probability Amplitude; Reduction of wave packet
—packet, 10, 14, 44
—reduction of, 45, 138. See also Probability Amplitude
—particle, 10, 34, 105, 106, 119, 159
Wavicle, 34, 35

Weierstrass, Karl, 30
Weltanschaaung, 14, 15. *See* World
  View
Weyl, Herman, 92, 159
Wheeler, John, 9, 106, 114, 115
Whitehead, A. N., 7, 15, 16, 37n,
  55, 81, 96, 98, 100, 103, 131,
  156, 172
Whitrow, G. J., 97
whole, 54, 101, 146–147, 158, 159–
  160. *See also* Holism
—differentiation of, 163, 165
Wigner, Eugene, 8, 83, 117

World View, 4, 5, 14, 75, 145, 158–
  161
—Aristotelian, 4–7, 26, 35
—ecological, 15, 145, 148. *See* Chapter 9
—mechanistic, 4. *See also* Mechanism; Newtonian World View
—Newtonian, 4, 91. *See also* Mechanistic World View
—organismic, 5, 15–16

Zeno, 100